First
CITIZEN

MARY McALEESE
AND THE IRISH PRESIDENCY

The State Reception Room, Áras
an Uachtaráin

First
CITIZEN

MARY McALEESE
AND THE IRISH PRESIDENCY

PATSY McGARRY

THE O'BRIEN PRESS
DUBLIN

First published 2008 by The O'Brien Press Ltd,
12 Terenure Road East, Rathgar, Dublin 6, Ireland.
Tel: +353 1 4923333; Fax: +353 1 4922777
E-mail: books@obrien.ie
Website: www.obrien.ie

ISBN: 978-1-84717-087-3
Copyright for text © Patsy McGarry 2008

British Library Cataloguing in Publication Data
McGarry, Patsy
First Citizen : Mary McAleese and the Irish presidency
1. McAleese, Mary 2. Women presidents - Ireland - Biography
3. Presidents - Ireland - Biography 4. Ireland - Politics and
government - 1949-
I. Title
941.5'0824'092

1 2 3 4 5 6 7 8 9 10
08 09 10 11 12

Editing, typesetting, layout and design:
The O'Brien Press Ltd

Printed by Graspo CZ. a.s., Czech Republic

Picture Credits:
Cover photographs: Gates of Áras an Uachtaráin from Axiom Images;
the President courtesy of The Irish Times
Photographs on pages 55, 79, 83, 104, 120, 121, 129, 131, 137, 156, 159,
161, 181, 189, 192, 197, 200, 202, 214, 220, 229, 246, 248, 250, 265,
281, 290, 297, 305, 309, 310, courtesy of The Irish Times
Photographs on front flap and pages 86, 142, 216, 218, 220, 233, 236,
254, 256, 277, 291, 293, 296, 303, 306, 311 courtesy of Maxwell
Photography
Photographs of previous presidents on back cover; and pages 1- 3, 8,11,
13, 15, 17, 19, 21, 23, 25, 27, 29, 31, 33, 35, 37, 39, 41, 187, 190, 310,
314-7, 319 (top) by kind permission of the Office of Public Works
Photographs on pages 5, 7, 208, 213, 225, 240, 243, 266-7, 284, 287,
297, 318, 319 (bottom), 320 by Emma Byrne
Portraits: p11, Douglas Hyde by Leo Whelan RHA; p15, Seán T Ó Ceal-
laigh by Leo Whelan RHA; p19, Eamon de Valera by Seán O'Sullivan
RHA; p23, Erskine Childers by David Hone PPRHA; p27, Cearbhall
Ó Dálaigh by Thomas Ryan PPRHA; p31, Patrick Hillery by John F Kelly
RHA; p35, Mary Robinson by Basil Blackshaw HRAA.

DEDICATION

This book is dedicated to my parents: my father
Tom ('The Haw') McGarry, who died in 1999,
and my beloved mother Teenie,
in whom I remain well pleased.

⚜ ACKNOWLEDGEMENTS ⚜

There are many people to thank for their co-operation in making this book happen. Firstly, The President, who was so generous with her time, and her husband Dr Martin McAleese who was of immense assistance. Also the President's staff, in particular Secretary General of the Office of the President, Tim O'Connor, her Private Secretary Helen Carney, her ever-helpful Communications Officer Gráinne Mooney, her Adviser Maura Grant, as well as her aides-de-camp and the catering staff at Áras an Uachtaráin, and Delia Hickey of the Office of Public Works, based at Áras an Uachtaráin — all of whom were warm, helpful and friendly. I would especially like to thank fellow Roscommon man Wally Young, the President's Media Adviser, who was my point of contact at Áras an Uachtaráin. His patience and ongoing commitment to what was essentially a team effort was of vital importance. Wally, thank you.

Publisher Michael O'Brien gave me the opportunity to write this book. It was an honour for which I am deeply appreciative. Also at The O'Brien Press there was my editor Mary Webb, designer Emma Byrne, and Íde ní Laoghaire. They are the people responsible for the beauty of the product before you.

I owe so much to my employer, *The Irish Times*, which generously facilitated me with a sabbatical last summer to work on the book. Thank you to editor Geraldine Kennedy, who approved that sabbatical, and to the Sabbatical Committee, Eoin McVey, Joe Breen, Denis Buckley and Conor Goodman who recommended I be granted it. I am also grateful to my always supportive immediate bosses, News Editor Kevin O'Sullivan and deputy News Editor Roddy O'Sullivan. Thanks, too, to Picture Editor Peter Thursfield and one of the best teams of photographers in the business for use of their photographs. I must also thank colleague Deirdre Morrissey, who transcribed some of the interviews for me. A special thank you to Maxwell Photography, Dublin for access to their excellent selection of photographs.

Research for the book could not have been completed without the co-operation of some of the busiest public figures on the island, who were very accommodating in granting me interviews. Most are named in the text and to them I express my deepest gratitude; also to those who asked — for their own reasons — that their names not be used. And, of course, there was the work of colleagues who travelled some of this terrain before and whose work was very useful to me: *Mary McAleese, The Outsider* by Justine McCarthy, published by Blackwater Press in 1999 and by the *Irish Independent* as part of its Great Biographies series in 2006; and *The Road from Ardoyne* by Ray Mac Mánais, published by Brandon Press in 2005, also published in Irish as *Máire Mhic Ghiolla Íosa, Beathaisnéis*, by Cló Iar-Chonnachta in 2003. I am indebted to reports down the years by colleagues in *The Irish Times, Irish Independent, Irish Examiner, Sunday Independent, Sunday Tribune, Sunday Business Post, Belfast News Letter, Belfast Telegraph, The Irish News* and the *Tablet* weekly, as well as to RTÉ radio and television programmes referred to in the book.

CONTENTS

The PRESIDENTS of IRELAND

1938–1945

Douglas Hyde

Douglas Hyde was born in Castlerea, County Roscommon on 17 January 1860. Instead of following his father into the Church of Ireland clergy, as his family had hoped, Hyde chose to study law at Trinity College, Dublin, graduating with an LLB in 1887 and an LLD in 1888. However, Irish language and literature were his real passions, and he never practised law. In 1893, Hyde married Lucy Cometina Kurtz, and they had two daughters, Nuala (who died of TB in 1916) and Una.

Hyde's studies and his desire to write in the Irish language led him to join the Gaelic Union (a movement dedicated to promoting the use of the Irish language) in 1880. He published under the pseudonym 'An Craoibhín Aoibhinn', partly a reflection of his desire to keep his membership of the Gaelic Union a secret, as it was regarded by many in the Ascendancy as having Fenian sentiments. In time, Hyde became a key figure in shaping the Gaelic cultural revival of the late nineteenth century. He authored many poems and plays in the Irish language and contributed to several anthologies.

In 1892, his growing status was recognised in his election as President of the new National Literary Society in Dublin. Hyde delivered a lecture to the Society that year, 'On the Necessity for De-Anglicizing Ireland', denouncing the imitation of English manners. In response to that lecture, the Gaelic League (Conradh na Gaeilge) was formed in 1893, with Hyde its first president. The success of the League attracted many politically militant nationalists, and this led to Hyde's resignation in 1915 since he saw the organisation as a cultural rather than political body.

Dubzlay de h-Ide

Although Hyde sought to avoid sectional politics (despite being avowedly nationalist), his last decades saw him drawn into the political arena. He was co-opted to serve as a senator in 1925, after the establishment of the Irish Free State. Later, when *Bunreacht na hÉireann* replaced the old Free State Constitution on 29 December 1937, the position of Governor-General was replaced with that of a directly elected President. Primary political power would rest with the Houses of the Oireachtas, and the new President of Ireland was envisaged to be above politics. After the ratification of the Constitution, De Valera and his government had a 180-day window in which to nominate, elect and inaugurate a president.

By 3 April 1938, news emerged that Hyde was going to be president. This decision was generally well received, which, in the divided politics of the 1930s, speaks volumes for the regard in which Hyde was held. It was noted that the appointment of a member of the Church of Ireland was an indication that southern Protestants need not be concerned about possible discrimination under the new constitution.

The election of the first President of Ireland was declared at 11.20am on 4 May 1938 in a simple ceremony conducted in Irish in the boardroom of the Department of Agriculture, Government Buildings. Hyde, along with his new presidential aides, began preparing not only for the inauguration but also for the new role he would have to establish.

The inauguration day, Saturday, 25 June 1938, began with a service in St Patrick's Cathedral followed by the inauguration ceremony itself in Dublin Castle. Then, following a review of the troops, the President was driven in cavalcade to the Phoenix Park and to his residence in the old vice-regal lodge, now renamed Áras an Uachtaráin. Crowds lined the route from Dublin Castle to the Áras, and the presence of many young people cheering was to be remembered fondly by the new President.

Hyde and his officials soon set up a workmanlike daily routine, which is remarkable considering that he was seventy-eight when he became President. The Presidential day would begin after breakfast with the signing of papers sent by the Government, followed by opening and replying to the voluminous amount of mail received that day. Lunch would follow with one or more invited guests and the afternoon was reserved for receiving visitors and for performing formal duties. Many evenings were dominated by formal dinners, and Eamon de Valera, as Taoiseach, would often call to the President late at night – sometimes at midnight!

An early and rare controversy from the Hyde Presidency occurred when he accepted an invitation to attend an international soccer match on 13 November 1938. Hyde was notified by the Gaelic Athletic Association (GAA) that under its rules attendance at 'foreign games' was forbidden and, for breaching this ban, Douglas Hyde, Ireland's first President, personal friend to GAA founder Michael Cusack, was to be expelled. The expulsion enraged Eamon de Valera, but Hyde himself declined to get involved in a public row.

On 12 April 1940, Hyde suffered a mild stroke, resulting in his right hand, arm and leg being paralysed. His speech, however, was unaffected, and, with grim determination, by June of that year he was able to sign his name in Irish even though he would be forever confined to a wheelchair.

Hyde's infirmity did not prevent him from dealing with important constitutional matters such as in 1944 when De Valera's government had been defeated in the passage of a Bill. Even though a general election was not regarded as good at the time for the country, Hyde advised the Taoiseach that this was the only option open to him, and the election took place.

As Hyde was now approaching eighty-five and in poor health, he decided not to seek a second term. He was given accommodation in the Phoenix Park lodge and it was there that he died peacefully on 12 July 1949. He is buried in Frenchpark churchyard in Roscommon.

1945-1959

Seán T Ó Ceallaigh

Seán Thomas O'Kelly was born in Dublin on 25 August 1882. He spent his childhood in Dublin's north inner city, one of the most poverty-stricken areas of the capital at the time, and was educated by the Christian Brothers. His first marriage in 1918 to Mary Kate Ryan ended with her death in 1934. In August 1936 he remarried, to Mary Kate's sister Phyllis, an analytical chemist.

O'Kelly was attracted to militant Irish republicanism and joined the Irish Republican Brotherhood (IRB) in 1902. He was also a member of the Gaelic League, where he was taught Irish by Sinéad Flanagan, later to become the wife of his mentor Eamon de Valera, and he worked closely with Patrick Pearse on the League's journal, *An Claidheamh Soluis* for a number of years. A founder member of Sinn Féin, O'Kelly was elected to Dublin City Council in 1906. In 1915, he was elected the National Secretary of the Gaelic League.

O'Kelly joined the Irish Volunteers in 1913 and not only negotiated between the IRB and James Connolly's Irish Citizen Army in 1914 but also was chosen to raise much-needed funds in the USA the following year, a task he performed with notable success. He played a significant part in the Easter Rising of 1916, serving under Pearse at the GPO. After release from prison in 1917, he helped establish a more militant Sinn Féin and became a member of its executive. In the 1918 general election, he won a seat for the College Green constituency in Dublin and was a member of the first Dáil. When the Dáil met in January 1919, O'Kelly's work in the establishment of this democratic parliament was recognised, and he became the first Ceann

Comhairle (Chairperson) of the House.

O'Kelly attended the Paris peace talks following the armistice, with the aim of securing recognition for the Irish Republic declared by the First Dáil. While this was unsuccessful, the attempt demonstrated the seriousness of the Irish move towards independence. He returned to Paris in 1920 as the Irish government's envoy.

The Anglo-Irish Treaty of 1921 resulted in the bitter political split within Sinn Féin that led to the Civil War. O'Kelly sided with the anti-Treaty wing led by Eamon de Valera, but his status as a political figure of importance meant that he was kept in Paris by the new pro-Treaty government led by Arthur Griffith. In February 1922, when his pronouncements in support of de Valera's position on the Treaty became too vocal, he was dismissed by the government. He was re-elected to the Dáil in the general election of 1922.

O'Kelly was arrested by Free State forces on 28 July 1922, when documents were found in his possession linking himself, Eamon de Valera and Harry Boland to a plan to import arms from the United States. He spent the remainder of the conflict in prison.

Elected again in the general election of 1923, O'Kelly was now an abstentionist member of the Dáil along with his other anti-Treaty Sinn Féin comrades. Ultimately, of course, de Valera broke with Sinn Féin in 1926 to establish Fianna Fáil, and O'Kelly ensured that American support would transfer with de Valera to the new party. He was very much second in command of the new Fianna Fáil Party, and this is reflected in his being chosen as the party's Vice-President and Editor of its newspaper, *The Nation*.

After the 1927 general election, Fianna Fáil announced that its elected members would end the policy of abstentionism and would take their seats in the Dáil. This would involve taking the Oath of Allegiance to the British monarchy, an issue which had been a root cause of the Civil War. O'Kelly declared that signing the oath would be taken as an 'empty formula', something akin to signing the visitors' book. This significant step having been taken, O'Kelly was instrumental in building Fianna Fáil into a highly organised political force.

When the party won the general election of 1932 and entered government, O'Kelly was appointed Vice-President of the Executive Council and Minister for Local Government. He oversaw a house-building programme that built 12,000 homes a year. His foreign affairs expertise was also utilised by de Valera's administration when he represented Ireland at the important Commonwealth Conference of 1932, held in Canada, and again in 1933 at the League of Nations. After the redrawing of the Constitution in 1937, he became the first Tánaiste and, in 1939, was appointed Minister for Finance.

During the Second World War, O'Kelly played a key role in economic and security planning. It came as some surprise to be considered by de Valera as a candidate for the Irish Presidency when Douglas Hyde retired in 1945, but O'Kelly accepted the Fianna Fáil nomination and stood for election.

Patrick McCartan, an Independent republican candidate and Seán Mac Eoin, a Fine Gael TD and former general in the Free State army, were the other candidates in the election. Voting in the first contested presidential election took place on Thursday, 14 June 1945 – the same day as the local elections. O'Kelly received 537,965 first-preference votes compared to 335,539 for Mac Eoin and 212,834 for McCartan. After the second count and the distribution of McCartan's votes, O'Kelly was declared President Elect with 565,165 votes compared to Mac Eoin's 453,425. He was inaugurated Ireland's second President on 25 June 1945.

In 1949, O'Kelly signed the Republic of Ireland Act which gave greater foreign recognition to the office of the Irish Presidency. His dignified nature and general popular support helped to ensure that he was nominated as an agreed candidate to continue as President in 1952, and he was re-elected for a second term without a contest.

In 1959, Seán T O'Kelly retired as President of Ireland and spent the remainder of his life in Roundwood, County Wicklow. In 1966, he took part in the fiftieth-anniversary celebrations of the 1916 Rising. This was to be his last public appearance. He died on 23 November that year and is buried in Glasnevin Cemetery, Dublin.

Eamon de Valera

Eamon de Valera was born on 14 October 1882 in New York, but his early childhood was spent in Bruree, County Limerick. He attended the Christian Brothers' secondary school in Charleville and in 1898 won a scholarship to Blackrock College in Dublin. In order to gain a teaching post with the National University of Ireland (established in 1908) it was necessary to learn Irish. De Valera fell in love with one of his teachers, Sinéad Flanagan, and they married on 8 January 1910. They would have five sons and two daughters.

Like many young nationalist men, de Valera joined the Irish Volunteers in 1913, and he took part in the Howth gun-running in 1914. During the Easter Rising in 1916, de Valera was placed in command of Boland's Mills. Following the surrender, he was court-martialled and sentenced to death, but this sentence was commuted to life imprisonment after the hostile reaction by the Irish people to earlier executions of the leaders of the Rising. Following a general amnesty for prisoners in 1917, de Valera contested the East Clare by-election of July 1917, winning by a ratio of nearly two to one.

De Valera became President of Sinn Féin in October of that year, but was imprisoned in Lincoln jail in May 1918 after the general election where Sinn Féin swept the electoral boards and became Ireland's dominant political party. In February 1919, Michael Collins mounted a successful and highly publicised escape operation, which returned de Valera to Ireland where he was elected President of the newly created Dáil Éireann and of the newly declared Irish Republic.

Eamon de Valera

During the War of Independence de Valera left for the United States, in June 1919, where he attracted much publicity and raised $6 million dollars in 'republican bonds' but ultimately failed to get the support of the US Government and, in particular, President Wilson.

When the Anglo-Irish Treaty was signed by the British Government and by the Irish plenipotentiaries on 6 December 1921, it was denounced by de Valera, who put his entire political power and reputation to ensuring that it was rejected by the Dáil and the Irish people as a whole. He failed to convince the Dáil, however, and the Treaty was carried by sixty-four votes to fifty-seven. The country quickly drifted towards civil war. De Valera became the political leader of the anti-treaty side, but spent most of the conflict in hiding and finished the civil war in prison having been arrested by Free State forces while attending an election rally in Clare in July 1923.

On release from prison, De Valera remained in the political wilderness as the new Free State government set about establishing the institutions of the state. In an attempt to return to the centre of the political stage, de Valera engineered the creation of Fianna Fáil which was formally launched as a political party on 16 May 1926. Overall, de Valera's policies were widely endorsed by the electorate, and Fianna Fáil, under his leadership, became one of the most successful political parties in western Europe, being returned to Government in the general elections of 1932, 1933, 1938, 1943, 1944, 1951, 1954, and 1957. No political leader in Ireland has ever achieved such a record of electoral victories.

The pinnacle of de Valera's political career came in 1937 when he largely wrote and then introduced a new constitution to replace the Free State Constitution. *Bunreacht na hÉireann* saw the state re-modelled to a republican form of government in all but name, and in the process replaced the position of Governor-General with a new, directly-elected President of Ireland. While there was some public disquiet that this new office could be used to form a dictatorship, de Valera had ensured in his constitution that primary political power remained in a parliamentary system dominated by the Dáil. Alongside this, the Seanad would serve as an upper house representing a more vocational form of representation. While de Valera's constitution did make a special provision for the Catholic Church's role in Irish life, it also ensured religious freedom for all the people of the country, and *Bunreacht na hÉireann*, while amended often, remains the Constitution of Ireland.

Long years of political activity took their toll, and, after being the leader of an independent Irish Government for a total of twenty-four years, the seventy-seven-year-old Taoiseach resigned and contested the Presidential election in 1959. His opponent was Seán Mac Eoin, a former Lieutenant General of the Army and a member of Fine Gael. The result was surprisingly close, with de Valera receiving 538,003 votes to Mac Eoin's 417, 536.

De Valera was inaugurated as Ireland's third President on 25 June 1959, and began the third and final phase of his career. While initially finding it difficult to adjust to his reduced political position, de Valera did carry out the role of President in the dignified, elder statesman capacity that he relished.

A significant event from de Valera's first term as President was in 1966 with the staging of celebrations to mark the fiftieth anniversary of the 1916 Rising. As President, and as the only surviving commandant from the rebellion, he played a major role in the commemorations.

The 1966 Presidential contest proved an even tougher affair than that of 1959. It was also the first occasion a sitting President had faced an election. The hotly contested campaign against Tom O'Higgins from Fine Gael resulted in the incumbent defeating the challenger by 558,861 to 548,144, a margin of just over 10,500 votes. This remains the closest electoral contest in the history of the Presidency and led to de Valera being inaugurated for his second term on 25 June 1966.

On 25 June 1973, Eamon de Valera (then aged ninety) retired from public life. His wife Sinéad died on the eve of their sixty-fifth wedding anniversary in January 1975, and Eamon de Valera died on 29 August 1975 after a brief illness. Following a State funeral, Eamon de Valera was laid to rest beside his wife in Glasnevin cemetery in Dublin.

1973–1974

Erskine H Childers

Erskine Hamilton Childers was born into an upper middle-class Protestant family in London on 11 December 1905. His father, Robert Erskine Childers, was a renowned British politician, yachtsman and author of the first modern spy thriller *The Riddle of the Sands*.

Both his parents became passionate supporters of Irish nationalism and the Childers' yacht, *The Asgard*, was used to import rifles and ammunition for the Irish Volunteers in 1914. Erskine senior was subsequently elected a member of Dáil Éireann. In November 1922 he was arrested following the discovery of a hand gun in his possession – a capital offence at the time – and was sentenced to death by firing squad.

Young Erskine, then approaching seventeen, was instructed by his father to hold no bitterness towards those who had been responsible for his death sentence. The loss of his father at such an impressionable age, and in such circumstances, was to have a large influence on the future direction of Erskine Childers, who spoke at public meetings organised by republicans during the civil war.

In September 1926, while reading for his history degree at Cambridge, he married an American woman, Ruth Ellen Dow. The marriage produced five children.

The rise of Eamon de Valera's Fianna Fáil and its newspaper, The *Irish Press*, provided the ideal opportunity for Childers to return to Ireland. In 1931 he took up the position of assistant advertising manager with the newspaper.

After a new constitution was introduced to Ireland in 1937, Erskine

Childers began his political career, albeit with an embarrassing hiccup. Put forward as a candidate for the Seanad, he was disqualified from running when it was discovered that he was ineligible because he was not formally an Irish citizen. This was rectified on 2 March 1938 when he received his Certificate of Naturalisation.

In the general election of June 1938, he was elected a TD for Longford/Westmeath, beginning an uninterrupted thirty-five-year political career. In March 1944 he was appointed by Eamon de Valera as a junior minister in the Department of Local Government and Public Health, where he earned a name for administrative efficiency and an eye for detail. He was involved in the 1947 Public Libraries Act which led to the establishment of a national library service.

His first wife having died, in 1952 he married Margaret (Rita) Dudley. Their daughter, Nessa, was born in 1954.

Appointed Minister for Posts and Telegraphs in June 1951, Childers, at the age of forty-five, became the youngest member of that cabinet. He convinced the Government to support the establishment of a broadcasting advisory council in November 1952, which began the removal of direct political control over broadcasting in Ireland. He also urged the establishment of a television service in Ireland.

Following the 1957 election, Childers became Minister for Lands, Forestry and Fisheries and became a strong advocate of reafforestation. When his political mentor, de Valera, retired in 1959, Seán Lemass became Taoiseach and Erskine Childers was made Minister for Transport and Power, a new department established under the modernising ideas of Dr T K Whitaker. This department oversaw crucial semi-state industries such as the ESB, Aer Lingus, Bord na Móna and CIE.

Childers was a long-time supporter of the political moves which led to the 1957 Treaty of Rome and the establishment of a European Economic Community. He was also an early advocate of cross-border co-operation, and, in 1963, he was the first southern Irish Minister to address the Northern Ireland Chamber of Commerce. He suggested a 'Come to Ireland' campaign under the joint control of the Bord Fáilte and the Northern Ireland Tourist Board.

After the 1969 general election Childers was the senior member of the cabinet and was appointed Tánaiste and Minister for Health. His major achievement in this ministry was the introduction of the 1970 Health Act, which transformed the operation of the public health service in Ireland.

In 1973 Erskine Childers reluctantly agreed to Taoiseach Jack Lynch's request that he run for the presidency, on the condition that the role be allowed to 'be used to greater effect'. He was announced as Fianna Fáil candidate on 6 April 1973 with the election date set for 30 May. The Fine Gael candidate, Tom O'Higgins, was favourite to win. The historical parallels were notable in that O'Higgins's uncle Kevin had been assassinated by republicans in the 1920s, while Childers's father had been executed by the Free State government. The presidential campaign was an impassioned one.

When the results were counted, Childers had secured a first preference vote of 635,867 to O'Higgins's 587,771. Erskine Childers was inaugurated as Ireland's fourth President on 25 June 1973.

Childers had promised a more vigorous style of President and at sixty-eight years of age he began a punishing routine of public engagements. By the end of his first year in office he had attended 210 functions, visited sixty-five community or social councils, as well as eighty-seven other organisations, and over 4,500 visitors had been received at Áras an Uachtaráin. He was the first Irish head of state to meet a member of the British Royal family when he and his wife met Earl Mountbatten in Sligo in 1974.

He offered to act as mediator in the Northern Troubles and suggested Áras an Uachtaráin as a venue for talks.

Immediately after speaking at a dinner in the Royal College of Physicians on 16 November 1974, President Childers collapsed, and though medical attention was at hand, he never recovered. He died early the following morning, becoming the first and only President to die in office. One of the largest state funerals ever organised was held in St Patrick's Cathedral, attended by many world leaders, including the British Prime Minister. He is buried in the grounds of Derralossary church in Roundwood, County Wicklow.

1974–1976

Cearbhall Ó Dálaigh

Born in Bray, County Wicklow on 12 February 1911, Ó Dálaigh moved to Dublin as a child and was educated at Synge Street Christian Brothers School. While studying Irish at University College Dublin under Douglas Hyde, he met his future wife, Máirín Ní Dhiarmada, and, while still students, they married in 1934.

Eamon de Valera, leader of Fianna Fáil, offered Ó Dálaigh his first job as Irish editor of the *Irish Press* in 1931. Ó Dálaigh combined this full-time work with further studies in law, the field that would dominate his future professional life. His rising reputation in legal circles saw him raised to the status of Senior Council in 1945. In April 1946, de Valera, as Taoiseach, appointed him as the government's Attorney General. At thirty-five years of age, Ó Dálaigh was to be the youngest-ever Attorney General and remained in that position until the general election of 1948. He was again appointed as Attorney General in June 1951 and served until July 1953.

Unsuccessful in electoral politics (he contested the 1948 and 1951 general elections and was also a candidate in the Seanad elections), Ó Dálaigh focused on his legal career and was made a Supreme Court judge in 1953. To be a member of the Supreme Court is the pinnacle of an Irish legal career, and it was in this role that he would make his greatest contribution. He was made Chief Justice of the Supreme Court in December 1961 and held this position until 1972.

Ó Dálaigh was appointed to the EEC Court of Justice in August 1972 and addressed his assembled fellow judges in each of the then official

languages of the organisation; through his love of languages he was fluent in French and had a working knowledge of Spanish and Italian. A long-time advocate of the benefits of membership of the EEC, in a lecture delivered in March 1971, Ó Dálaigh outlined how the personal rights and liberties of Irish citizens might be more strongly copper-fastened and extended by the European Convention on Human Rights and by numerous United Nations Conventions as they became part of Irish law.

Following the sudden death of President Erskine Childers in 1974, Cearbhall Ó Dálaigh was asked to become Ireland's fifth President. At the time, the State was struggling to contain the violence emanating from the Northern Troubles, and the Fine Gael–Labour Coalition government led by Liam Cosgrave was keen to avoid a possibly divisive presidential election. Nominated by sixteen members of the Dáil and four members of the Seanad, Ó Dálaigh was duly elected on 17 November 1974 and was inaugurated in Dublin Castle on 19 December 1974.

In 1976 the British Ambassador to Ireland, Christopher Ewart-Biggs, was murdered in Sandyford, County Dublin by an IRA bomb, which drew the Fine Gael–Labour coalition to draft an Emergency Powers Bill, introduced to the Dáil in October 1976. This granted special powers to the Government and to the Gardaí to deal with subversive violence. The controversial Bill was passed by the Dáil and, in order to become law, was sent to the President to be signed in accordance with his constitutional role.

Ó Dálaigh was the first person from a significant legal background to occupy the office, and his concerns over the constitutionality of the Bill were such that he referred it to the Council of State for advice and subsequently to the Supreme Court for their adjudication. While attending the opening of a barracks in Mullingar, however, the Minister for Defence, Paddy Donegan, made a number of disparaging remarks about the behaviour of the President and was quoted as saying: 'In my opinion he is a thundering disgrace.'

Even though Donegan apologised and offered his resignation, Taoiseach Liam Cosgrave refused to accept the resignation and, during a heated Dáil debate, refused to condemn what his Minister had said, referring instead to 'excessive verbal exuberance' on behalf of the Minister. It was on hearing news of the debate that Ó Dálaigh decided, in order to maintain the dignity and impartiality of the office of President, to resign from the position, which he did in a brief statement on 22 October 1976.

After resigning from the Presidency, Ó Dálaigh and his wife retired to the village of Sneem, in County Kerry. On 12 March 1978, at the age of sixty-seven, he suffered a fatal heart attack. He is buried at Sneem cemetery.

Patrick J Hillery

Patrick John Hillery was born on 2 May 1923 in Miltown Malbay, County Clare. He studied medicine at UCD, graduating in 1947 with first-class honours. In 1955, he married Maeve Finnegan, who was also a doctor. They had a son, John, and a daughter, Vivienne, who died in 1985, shortly before her eighteenth birthday

In 1951, Hillery was approached to stand as a Fianna Fáil candidate in the general election for the Clare constituency alongside the party's founder, Eamon de Valera. He was duly elected and was TD for Clare for twenty-one years, until his appointment as EEC Commissioner. At first, he continued to practise medicine and resisted ministerial appointment. When Seán Lemass became Taoiseach in 1959, he swept aside Hillery's objections and made the young doctor Minister for Education, where he was responsible for the establishment of comprehensive schools, the inclusion of technical subjects in the Leaving Certificate curriculum and the creation of Regional Technical Colleges.

In April 1965, Hillery replaced Jack Lynch as Minister for Industry and Commerce, although he only spent one year in the position, moving to the new Department of Labour in 1966. In 1969, Lynch, now Taoiseach, appointed Hillery as Minister for External Relations to succeed Frank Aiken. A profile compiled by the British Embassy in Dublin, released with the 1972 state papers, revealed that the British officials were impressed by the new Minister's abilities. On the whole, the British found Hillery to be, 'a powerhouse of ideas, one of the few members of Fianna Fáil who has new

policies and is eager to implement them'.

Patrick Hillery's term as Minister for Foreign Affairs was defined by Ireland's negotiations for entry into the EEC. The Treaty of Accession was signed on 22 January 1972, but entry required a constitutional amendment. Hillery played a leading role in Fianna Fáil's campaign on the referendum, held on 11 May 1972, which saw the amendment endorsed by 83 per cent of those who voted. On 1 January 1973, Ireland joined the EEC along with the United Kingdom and Denmark.

Hillery's term as Minister for Foreign Affairs also coincided with the beginning of the Troubles in the North, and he not only protested in London against the treatment of and the lack of protection for Catholics there but also addressed the Security Council of the United Nations on 19 August 1969.

The following year, on 6 July 1970, in a show of solidarity with the nationalist minority after military house-to-house searches and subsequent violence in which four people died, Hillery, without Lynch's knowledge, visited Belfast and walked down the Falls Road, much to the indignation of the British government who felt that he had breached diplomatic protocol.

Patrick Hillery became Ireland's first European Commissioner in 1973, working in Social Affairs and as vice-president of the Commission until his departure in 1976. Hillery's work on equal pay for women is his most notable achievement in Europe, and it also marked him out to be impartial and unbiased. When an application was received from the Irish government to deviate from his legislation on equal pay, Hillery dismissed the request.

At the time of Cearbhall Ó Dálaigh's resignation as president, Hillery was unsure whether the coalition government would reappoint him as EEC Commissioner: Justin Keating was being promoted by Garret FitzGerald while Dick Burke had the support of Taoiseach Liam Cosgrave. This was probably a factor in his decision to accept the position of President when he was proposed by Fianna Fáil. As Fine Gael was not in a position to offer an alternative, Hillery became the agreed choice to succeed Ó Dálaigh, negating the need for an election campaign.

Inaugurated on 3 December 1976, Hillery became Ireland's sixth President and followed in the footsteps of Sean T O'Kelly (1952) and Cearbhall Ó Dálaigh (1974) to accede to the office unopposed. The ceremony for his inauguration in December 1976 caused some controversy. A number of falsified invitations were sent to people in his home town in Clare. The misspelling of Hillery's name with an 'a' instead of an 'e' was the main indication that the invites were forged.

The government files for 1977 show that Hillery's settling-in period at the Áras was not easy and that he felt the Fine Gael-Labour coalition was hostile towards him.

Hillery travelled much during his presidency and made fifteen state visits. At the end of his first term in 1983, as there was no clear successor and as it suited both Fine Gael and Fianna Fáil for him to continue in office, Hillery nominated himself, as was his constitutional right as the incumbent, for a second term.

Overall, Hillery brought dignity and calm to the office of President. During his two terms of office, the Presidency acted, as it was envisaged under *Bunreacht na hÉireann*, as 'guardian of the Constitution'. Reflecting on his presidency in 1997, Hillery explained: 'My intention for the initial stages of my term was to bring stability to the office and to continue my predecessors' contact with the citizens of Ireland.'

Patrick Hillery died on 12 April 2008 after a short illness, one month before his eighty-fifth birthday. He is buried in St Fintan's cemetery, Sutton, County Dublin.

1990–1997

Mary Robinson

Mary Bourke was born in Ballina, County Mayo on 21 May 1944. She attended Mount Anville School in Dublin from 1954, and won a scholarship to Trinity College Dublin in 1963. She married Nick Robinson in 1970, with whom she would have three children.

Mary Bourke excelled in law, graduating with first-class honours in 1967 and winning a fellowship to Harvard University, from which she graduated the following year, again with first-class honours. In 1969 she became Reid Professor of Constitutional and Criminal Law at Trinity College, Dublin.

Her passion for law was accompanied by a passion for social change in Ireland. At twenty-five years of age, she successfully contested the 1969 Seanad elections as an independent candidate on the Dublin University panel, and introduced a number of private member bills.

In July 1976, she joined the Irish Labour Party and, in the same year, became a member of the newly formed executive of the Irish Council for Civil Liberties. She was successful in every Seanad election she contested but was not successful in winning a Dáil seat in the general elections of 1977 and 1981.

When the Anglo-Irish Agreement was negotiated between the British and Irish governments in 1985, Robinson resigned from the Labour Party in protest at what she perceived to be a lack of awareness of the rights of the unionist community. In 1989 she retired from the Seanad but continued to campaign for liberal causes in her capacity as a lawyer.

With a presidential election due in 1990, Robinson agreed to run as an

Mary Robinson

independent candidate backed by the Labour Party and began campaigning in what would turn out to be the most historically significant presidential election in the history of the State.

Fianna Fáil's candidate was the popular politician and Tánaiste Brian Lenihan, and it was widely predicted that he would defeat Fine Gael's nominee, the former northern politician Austin Currie, with Mary Robinson coming in a poor third. Robinson mounted a superb campaign, and Lenihan's campaign became mired in controversy.

Polling took place on Wednesday 7 November 1990, and, when results poured in from around the country, the first count proved dramatic. Brian Lenihan had topped the poll with 694,484 votes, but Mary Robinson (the first woman candidate for President) had polled a massive 612,265 first-preference votes. With transfers from Austin Currie's 267,902 votes still to be distributed, victory was certain. The second count confirmed this, and Mary Robinson became Ireland's seventh President with 817,830 votes to Lenihan's 731,273.

In her inauguration speech, Robinson not only made reference to the people of the island that she would be representing but to the 'fifth province — which included the seventy million people of Irish descent around the world — and often forgotten community groups.' She endeavoured to expand the role of President without breaking the constitutional 'above politics' nature of the office. Different interpretations of this role were to cause tensions from early on between 'the Park' and the government of the day.

As a highly competent constitutional lawyer, Mary Robinson was well aware of the Presidential role as guardian of the Constitution and of the reserved and dignified nature of the role compared to the cut and thrust of the other political institutions of the State. But she was also aware that her election marked a sea change in Irish life. This new energetic era of the Irish Presidency can be seen in the ninety-two interviews she gave to the media, the over 800 functions she attended, and the some 700 speeches delivered in her first year of office alone.

The relationship between the government and this evolving presidency was not always difficult, however. Charles Haughey's government approved the introduction of extra junior and executive staff, including a special adviser, as well as extra financial resources to allow the President to travel and entertain more frequently. An increased representation allowance was introduced to the Dáil for this purpose in February 1991, where the paltry £15,000 allowance set and unchanged since 1973 was raised to £100,000, allowing the President to take on far more travel and functions in the Áras than had heretofore been possible.

Representing the Irish Diaspora was another innovation of the Robinson Presidency. Mary Robinson made the symbolic gesture of placing a light in the top-floor kitchen window of the family apartments in Áras an Uachtaráin. She also made numerous visits abroad to meet Irish communities and devoted the second of her two addresses to the Joint Houses of the Oireachtas to the issue of 'Cherishing the Diaspora'. Considering that the presidential right to address the Houses of the Oireachtas has only been used on four occasions in the history of the State, this shows the importance which Robinson attached to the emigrant community.

Mary Robinson opened the Presidency and the Áras to people from the thousands of community groups on the island. This gave the office a new sense of energy and relevance to the modern society that was taking shape.

It came as a surprise that President Robinson would not be seeking a second term. She stated that she had been a fresh voice for seven years and that now was the appropriate time to move on as Ireland had been through a process of rapid change. She performed her last public duty on 12 September 1997, opening a project for the homeless, and finished her speech with the words: 'Sin é' (That's it).

Robinson's international status was such that she secured the post of United Nations High Commissioner for Human Rights, which she held until 2002. In 1998, she became the first female Chancellor of Trinity College, Dublin. Since 2002, Mary Robinson has been the Honorary President of Oxfam International as well as serving on the board of the Vaccine Fund. She lives in New York.

1997–

Mary McAleese

On 11 November, 1997 Mary McAleese was inaugurated as the eighth President of Ireland.

Before her election she set out her vision for her Presidency:

'I have a dream for the eighth presidency of Ireland which I hope you will recognise as your dream too. It is a dream for a Presidency which will embrace the future with hope and confidence.

Ours is a complex and a thoughtful democracy. A once poor young country has made of itself a confident, wealthy, modern state, a valued friend to the nations of the world. As our country has carved its unique identity, we its people have found ours and when we speak we speak with many different voices. The pace of change is too fast for some and not fast enough for others. People no longer fit into easy pigeon holes. There are many fault lines in our country, some new, some centuries old. We need to find and embrace the thing which can bridge the gaps between those who have and those who badly want to be haves; between town and country; north and south; conservative and liberal; tradition and change.

There are some things which unite some of us some of the time. Sport, politics, music, faith, family, but there are few things which unite all of us all of the time.

The Presidency offers a powerful symbol in which the many unreconciled elements of our society can find a common home. It has become the hearth of the imagination around which our large, colourful, lively family gathers. The sense of common purpose which the Presidency

Mary Mc Aleese

creates defies logic. It streams from the heart. It gives us pride in our country and in ourselves. We see ourselves in a new light and we are seen by others in a new light.

We have come to realise that the emotional reach of the Presidency is much, much greater than its modest Constitutional reach. It touches hearts thousands of miles from these shores, even hearts separated from their Irish roots by generations. Wherever the President travels he or she carries the name of Ireland. In a real way the President personifies this country.

This Presidency will ... be a bridge between the second and the third millennia. The country which will see out this last decade of the twentieth century is utterly different from the country which saw that century in. My grandfather was born in rural Ireland in the 1870s, into the hardship and aching loneliness of the post-Famine years. When electricity first made its way down his road into his small cottage he said it was the devil's own instrument and it would never catch on. Today, when I turn on the washing machine in that same home I wonder if my grandfather is spinning in his grave with indignation or smiling from heaven with pride at this brave new Ireland.

... I want to bring a Presidency of an open embrace; to be a President who can bring a cool head to protecting the Constitution and a warm heart to each person that Constitution exists to defend. A President who can show each person that he or she is utterly respected and valued.

The Presidency I want to live out is meshed into who I am and what I am. I am a Northerner who has lived through the worst of troubled times; whose roots are in Roscommon; who made her first married home in Dublin and reared her children in County Meath; who taught Law in Trinity College for many years; and who got inside the skin of every part of Ireland as a journalist with RTÉ.

My life's journey has taken me down many different paths, up and down the length and breadth of this island. Through my children I have come to understand how important is our debt to the future. My working life has kept me close to young people. I try to teach them that one life does matter. That it can make a difference.

You know what you want for Ireland. When you come to decide who you want to be President I hope you will decide that you and I can embrace our future together.'

§ § §

This book looks at the life of Mary McAleese and how she has realised that early vision in the years of her Presidency.

Belgium, 1998

On Armistice Day, 11 November 1998, President Mary McAleese opened the Island of Ireland Peace Park at Messines, in Flanders, Belgium, accompanied by Queen Elizabeth II of Britain and King Albert II of Belgium. The Park was created in memory of the 69,947 young men from both main traditions on the island of Ireland who were killed, wounded or went missing in World War I. Over 140,500 men from the island volunteered to serve in World War I. This was in addition to the 58,000 already serving. In both instances the great majority, as with the island's population, was from the Catholic, nationalist tradition.

President McAleese, also Supreme Commander of the Irish Defence Forces, said the event 'was not just another journey down a well-travelled path. For much of the past eighty years, the very idea of such a ceremony would probably have been unthinkable. Those whom we commemorate here were doubly tragic. They fell victim to a war against oppression in Europe. Their memory too fell victim to a war for independence at home in Ireland.

'In the history of conflict which has blighted my homeland for generations respect for the memory of one set of heroes was often at the expense of respect for the memory of the other … Today we are keenly aware that … we need to create mutually respectful space for differing traditions, differing loyalties, for all our heroes and heroines. The men of the 36th Ulster Division and the 16th Irish Division died here. They came from every corner of Ireland. Among them were Protestants, Catholics, Unionists and Nationalists, their differences transcended by a common commitment not to flag but to freedom. Today we seek to put their memory at the service of another common cause expressed so well by Professor Tom Kettle, an Irish nationalist and proud soldier who died at the Somme: "Used with the wisdom which is sown in tears and blood, this tragedy of Europe may be and must be the prologue to the two reconciliations of which all statesmen have dreamed, the reconciliation of Protestant Ulster with Ireland and the reconciliation of Ireland with Great Britain."'

That speech – one of the most important of her presidency, was all the more significant because it was made by an Ulster woman, born and raised in Belfast's Ardoyne.

School Photo, 1958

44

Belfast, 1951,
First World

The first child of Paddy and Claire Leneghan was born at the Royal Victoria Hospital in Belfast on 27 June 1951. Christened Mary, she would be the eldest of nine children. The Leneghans were then living in Ladbrook Drive, in north Belfast's Ardoyne, an area where many of their relations lived. But neither parent had their roots in Belfast.

Claire's parents, Cassie and John McManus, were country people, sheep farmers from the Slieve Croob area of County Down who had moved to Belfast for work. During the blitz years of World War II the children were sent back to the safety of County Down. It meant that Claire spent much of her young life with her grandmother in that county.

Paddy Leneghan was from Carroward, Croghan, near the Shannon, in north County Roscommon. The eldest of five, he went to Belfast in 1939 at the age of fourteen to where his mother's three sisters lived, all within arm's reach of each other and close to the Catholic church in Ardoyne. His aunt, Nora McDrury, had a hairdressing salon directly opposite the church steps. He stayed with Nora and got a job as an apprentice barman in the Alderman Bar on Crumlin Road.

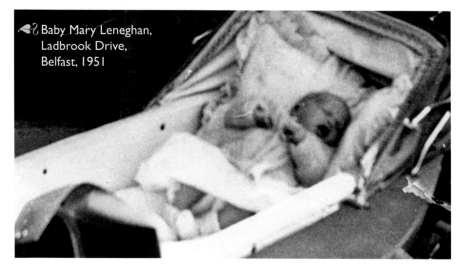

Baby Mary Leneghan, Ladbrook Drive, Belfast, 1951

Claire Leneghan, with baby Mary

John and Catherine McManus, the President's maternal grandparents, celebrate their 50th wedding anniversary

Claire McManus was training as an apprentice hairdresser with Nora when Paddy first met her. They got married on 5 June 1950 at the Holy Cross Church in Ardoyne and set up house at 60 Ladbrook Drive. Paddy was then working in Skelly's bar on the Grosvenor Road where shortly afterwards he was made manager.

That first house, a two-up two-down with a front garden and a back yard, was back-to-back with Claire's parents' home. As the Leneghan family grew and their accommodation needs became greater, they moved several times, but always to houses in the Ardoyne area. 'It was a very intimate environment in which to grow up, with numerous aunts, uncles, and cousins all within easy reach,' the President comments. Most of the addresses were in mixed Catholic and Protestant areas, predominantly Protestant.

When the family moved to 23 Mountainview Gardens, beside the fire station, they were the first Catholics to live in the area. That was a peaceful time in Northern Ireland, which meant it was safe for the Leneghans to live in a mainly Protestant part of Ardoyne. 'Historically, cycles of sectarian violence meant that in Ardoyne people tended to congregate on their own side at times of trouble and live among one another in peaceful periods,' Mary McAleese says. It also meant that most of Mary's friends as she grew up were Protestant. But her parents were unusual anyhow, in the ease with which they moved among both Catholics and Protestants. As country people they had a very limited awareness of the sectarian undercurrents which prevailed in Belfast, Paddy particularly. Neither Paddy nor Claire had any direct experience of sectarianism, even if Paddy's three aunts had come up against it soon after their arrival in Belfast in the 1920s when they lived in the Old Park Road near the home of a McMahon family, five of whom were murdered in an attack on their home.

The Leneghan children were something of a novelty when they moved to Mountainview Gardens. They were different and, apart from the occasional neighbour who wouldn't let their children play with them, the great majority of people there were welcoming. Mary attended church, chapel, and gospel halls with her Protestant peers, not two of whom went to the same church. Her best friend, Florence, introduced Mary to her minister, Rev. Sidney Callaghan, and also went to Mass on some Sundays with the Leneghans. Years later, Mary's sister, Nora, was bridesmaid at Florence's wedding to a Scottish soldier at the army barracks in Lisburn, at which Rev. Callaghan officiated. The entire Leneghan family attended.

The only time there may have been difficulty was around the 12th of July

Paddy Leneghan with Mary on Bronco the donkey at Cara Cottage, Carroward, County Roscommon

each year when tensions noticeably increased. Mary would help build 'eve of the Twelfth' bonfires, but was invariably disappointed when she wasn't allowed attend them. Her parents knew she wouldn't be welcome. One of the things she really missed from those bonfires, and which she still loves, are potatoes burnt to a frazzle. Florence, however, would come to the rescue, bringing her back a few well-burnt spuds. Their parents always took the Leneghan children to watch the Twelfth parades come up the Crumlin Road, uncomfortable as they might have felt with some of the songs. They thought it was the appropriate thing to do, to enter into the commemorative spirit. But there was undoubtedly an undercurrent of tension.

Mary's first school was on the Crumlin Road, 'a small Mercy convent which no longer exists. It was not the parish school. That was at Holy Cross, where my mother had gone. My parents wanted their eldest daughter to be educated by nuns,' the President says. The convent was wedged between the Mater Hospital and Crumlin Road Jail, with Crumlin Road courthouse directly opposite.

Bridget McDrury Leneghan (the President's paternal grandmother) at Cara Cottage

After primary school she attended St Dominic's on the Falls Road. Again it wasn't the closest secondary school. Fortwilliam, another Dominican school, was closer. Most of her friends went to Fortwilliam, but St Dominic's suited better, from her parents' point of view, as Paddy Leneghan was now working on the Falls Road. He had bought a pub there, the Long Bar. Mary worked there during

Mercy Primary School, Crumlin Road, 1961. Mary is front row, left.

the summers, at weekends, Christmas and Easter.

She would sometimes go from school to the pub for her lunch. Or to her grandaunt Mary Cassidy who lived beside St Dominic's. By then the Leneghans were living in a predominantly Protestant area called the Woodvale Road, which is almost an extension of the Shankill Road. Shankill Road travels from Belfast city centre up to a point where it becomes the Woodvale Road. It meets the Ardoyne at the Holy Cross monastery. The Leneghans' house was not too far behind the monastery's back door.

Although this was a bigger house and more suited to the growing number of children, there was no garden and the house never got sunlight. Being so close to the main road was also a drawback. But again the Leneghan children made good friends with their Protestant neighbours. Paddy's aunt Eileen also lived on that road. There was not much sectarian tension there, although Woodvale Park was the first place where Mary heard the word 'Fenian'. She remembers coming home that evening and asking her mother what a 'Fenian' was. But she also remembers how Florence and her other Protestant friends would chase those who called her names or picked on her.

In the mid-60s the family moved again, this time to 657 Crumlin Road, beside a Protestant school, now gone, called Everton School. This was a more well-to-do area. The Leneghans weren't the first Catholics there. In fact, their immediate neighbours were Catholic and there were a number of Catholic families distributed up the road. 'But again we would have been in a tiny minority and were also probably more visible because of the size of the family. But we lived there happily. It was a beautiful home, very comfortable with a big back garden,' the President remembers, 'and sunny, a contrast to the one we had come from.'

They were contented there until the Troubles began. In 1969 the divisions and inequalities of Northern Ireland society were about to cause the province to explode into violence.

Growing up in circumstances where religion and perceived political affiliation were such significant markers had an effect on the Leneghan children that continues to this day. 'We had been stretched by the experience of living in mixed, even predominantly Protestant communities but were always aware in their company that we were outsiders. We were also aware that we had no control over such matters.' It had an impact on their childhood friendships with Protestant peers, forcing them at times to take positions, attitudes and perspectives on things which carried within them a seed of conflict and division and which could very well have resulted in those relationships being either stillborn or so fractured and difficult that they could not be sustained. Mary McAleese didn't want anything similar for her own children. 'I wanted them to grow up in a world where difference was not the same thing as division,' she says.

She herself grew up very conscious that there were people who looked down on her because she was a Catholic. It wasn't a comfortable feeling. She was also aware from a young age that the story of her people was being air-brushed out of the history that she was reading and learning at school. There were two different versions of history: the one she read in the history books and the one she knew from her parents. At school, when studying the story of women in politics, they were not told that the first woman elected to Westminster was Constance Markievicz. 'I was also, and had always been, imbued with a great sense of social justice, for which I credit my parents and grandparents.'

Her father, who had one day off in a working week that often involved

Mary and Nora Leneghan, Ardoyne, Belfast, 1957

fifteen-hour days, had a voracious interest in history and local history and on a Sunday he would take the children on trips to places of interest in Northern Ireland and south of the border. He would tell them the story of those places. 'We would go to Inch Abbey, to the two Cathedrals in Armagh. He would take us to Kilmainham in Dublin, to Tara, to Downpatrick, and tell us about the history of those places. And we were expected to remember those stories.'

The Leneghan home was a very literate one, with lots of books. From a very young age, Mary had been told about Daniel O'Connell. Such was the influence of that story that on her honeymoon she and Martin McAleese went to Kerry to visit O'Connell's home place. They also visited a grandniece of O'Connell's.

By the time Mary was growing up, her grandfather, John, was an O'Connellite. But as a young man he had been in the IRA. John was ostracised by his parents and the rest of the family. His only brother, Arthur, supported the new State and became a founding member of the Garda Síochána. Arthur inherited the family farm, but John was regarded as a pariah. The President remembers John as one of the loveliest people she has ever known, and a very unusual man for his time, although as a child she didn't realise it.

He and her grandmother had eleven children, and to the day he died he loved his wife with a passion. He would tell her how wonderful she was, in front of everyone. John worked for Barney Hughes, the baker, on the Springfield Road, near the Falls, and went to work every morning wearing a three-piece suit. But her grandmother would not have Hughes's bread in the house. She made her own bread every day, because she saw it as her job to make bread. When John would come in from work her hands would be covered in flour and, every single day, he lifted her up and swung her around in their tiny two-up, two-down house. And he would say the same thing every time – that she had the walk of a queen.

The McManus grandparents lived near the Leneghans throughout their childhood. In all they had sixty grandchildren. 'I was very aware that the divisions of the Civil War were something they really wanted to put behind them. They didn't want their children to be ever drawn into violence. My grandfather had had enough of it. He had seen active service. He never spoke about it. He really was committed to peaceful means.'

John strongly supported De Valera going into government. He and his brother Arthur were eventually reconciled. Old enmities were put behind as love of family was put first. And out of it grew a real commitment to non-violence. A commitment that was passed on to the President from the day she was born, from both sides of her family. Her Roscommon grandfather Frank Leneghan used to say that violence was utterly anathema to him. He was never involved with the IRA or Sinn Féin.

Mary (age 8) wearing the medal she won in a Butlin's talent competition

Troubled Times

Mary Leneghan celebrated her eighteenth birthday on 27 June, 1969. On 14 August she was out celebrating another major milestone in her life – her acceptance to study law at Queen's University Belfast – when the heavens first threatened to fall.

She and a friend, Eileen Gilmartin, had both done well in their A levels and they had been taken to dinner to mark the occasion. Eileen had been a classmate of Mary Leneghan's at both primary and secondary school. Eileen's father was from Sligo and was a good friend of Mary's father, Paddy. Their host for the evening was Fr Honorious Kelly, a Leneghan family friend and the local parish priest.

Fr Kelly was also the uncle of actor Frank Kelly who later played the role of Fr Jack in the Channel 4 TV series 'Father Ted'. He was one of approximately forty priests at the Holy Cross monastery in Ardoyne.

Fr Kelly was proud of the two girls.

'We were part of that burgeoning generation that was taking advantage of second and third level education, which was the pride and joy of the Catholic community. They saw in us the hope of a very different future,' the President recalls.

But Fr Kelly may also have been trying to assuage feelings of guilt.

'He was the first person that I ever spoke to about my desire to become a lawyer and his instant response was to tell me I should forget about it because I suffered from two disabilities which were in his view completely unlikely to be overcome. One was that I was a woman and the other was that I had no connections in the Law,' the President remembers.

The dinner that evening was in the Woodbourne House Hotel in West Belfast, which itself later became a casualty of the IRA's bombing campaign. An RUC station was built on the site. After their meal Fr Kelly drove the girls back to Ardoyne.

Phil Coulter, his wife, Geraldine, and Frank Kelly at Áras an Uachtaráin

It was the night the notorious B-Specials came into that area of north Belfast, where they took part in the burning of Catholic homes. Fr Kelly drove up Twaddell Avenue to an intersection where they were stopped by a group of men, including Eileen Gilmartin's father. He advised the priest not to go any further because there had been an outbreak of violence. They were within about 100 yards of the Gilmartin home and about 500 yards from Mary Leneghan's house. Closer still was the hairdressing salon of Mary's aunt Una (a sister of her mother's) and nearby her grandaunt Nora's home and shop.

They got out of the car and could see the uniformed men further down the road. They seemed completely out of control, cheering and jeering as houses blazed. In an effort to stop the B-Specials from coming any further up the road, the men who had stopped Fr Kelly's car began to fire handfuls of marbles at the nearby chapel wall. They were trying to imitate the sound of gunfire.

'Fr Honorious took the scene in very quickly and ushered us back into the car, and he started a prayer and let Eileen off home and then me. I remember wondering whether he would get back safely to the chapel, because that was the locus. And then of course there was very little sleep in the house that night. There was a lot of turmoil and people arrived into the house all through the night, people who had been put out of their homes, people who were distressed, people who were fleeing,' the President remembers.

Her aunts came in looking for clothes for a family who had their home burnt to the ground. They had been out helping a pregnant woman. The younger Leneghans were all in bed, but the house was in chaos. The next morning, as she went to see her grandparents, Mary Leneghan met Fr Kelly. With typically dramatic flair he announced of their sojourn the previous evening, 'We were fiddling while Rome burnt.'

She continued on to her grandparents' house, to make sure they were all right, and then to Hooker Street where another friend, Catherine Kane, lived.

'I was very worried for her because that street was the starting point for all this. I went down, and, luckily, their house was okay. But they were nervous wrecks. They didn't know what was coming next and they didn't know whether the place was going to be safe or not. The best advice from all and sundry was to get out. So I spent the day helping them to move to a place over in the Falls Road, a rapidly set up reception centre. That was really the start of it; from then on our lives were tenuous. We were very vulnerable and very aware of our vulnerability because sectarian episodes just rained down on top of us.'

A principal reason for this was the location of their house at 657 Crumlin Road, on a corner with Hesketh Road, which runs into the Protestant Glenbryn estate. That estate would gain international notoriety in 2001 when residents from there barracked Catholic schoolchildren as they were taken to the nearby Holy Cross primary school.

'We were living in a corner house on the main road. It was an easy place to hit, regrettably, and that is where we got our first taste of very serious sectarian violence,' the President remembers.

The house was between three schools, one Catholic and two Protestant. Battles, sectarian and otherwise, between the pupils were frequent. Their teachers tried their best to avoid these conflicts by staggering the times at which the school day ended. But pupils who were allowed off early just waited until their rivals were free too. They would often hide at the back of the nearby Leneghan home. Their front wall was red brick, with cap stones and pillars, which turned into useful ammunition. And no matter how many times that wall was rebuilt by Paddy Leneghan and the cap stones replaced, they ended up as weapons in those school wars.

Mary herself was provoked into action during a more sinister incident. She had been visiting a friend, Maureen Totten, in Chatham Street nearby. 'I was in the house with Maureen's mother, just talking, and at the bottom of the street you could hear shrieks and hear the stones being thrown. When the security forces launched CS gas canisters our eyes were streaming and very sore, and with that, some guys came into the house, people that I know very well, really good, fine upstanding citizens.'

They were looking for bottles, anything they could throw at Loyalists on the other side. They had nothing else to protect themselves with, they said. At that point Mary Leneghan ran home to get bottles. There were usually a lot of milk bottles at the Leneghan house, with all its children. They were always at the front door, generally in a crate. She went to grab the crate when her father asked her what she was doing. She told him she was bringing them to the men down the road who had asked for glass to defend themselves. Paddy Leneghan said 'and his words, I will never forget, "I didn't rear a rabble".' And that was that. 'It was my only foray into the world of direct action. It was very short lived.'

In Belfast during those August days of 1969, ten people were killed and 745 seriously injured, 154 with gunshot wounds. Most of the shooting was in the Ardoyne area. As many as 1,500 Catholic homes and 300 Protestant homes were burnt out.

The Leneghans decided to get out of the city. They went to Kilmacud in Dublin for a while and then to Roscommon. They were struck by the disinterest of people in the Republic in what was happening in Northern

Dromantine Open Day, 1972. Mary and Martin with (l to r) Kevin McAleese, Damien Leneghan, Kathleen McAleese, Claire, Clement, John and Phelim Leneghan. Pat Leneghan standing.

Ireland. People were living their lives as normal, just going about their business as though nothing unusual was happening in the northern part of the country. Reflecting on this, the President says, 'I just think that the full implications hadn't entered people's consciousness fully. And they probably felt it would all be over next week, in a couple of days.'

She decided to do something about it. She was then on the National Youth Council of the St Vincent de Paul society and was good friends with the people who ran the society. She approached them and was very annoyed that they had to be prompted to do something for people in Northern Ireland and that they hadn't spontaneously organised anything up to then.

When the family moved to Roscommon, it wasn't very different. People were sympathetic but really did not understand. They'd say things such as 'isn't it terrible what is happening up there?', but without really understanding how what was happening affected the lives of people in Northern Ireland. They had no idea of how awful it was to have to leave your home and not know if or when you would go back again. Of course, refugees such as the Leneghans were also experiencing for the first time what the President has described as 'that awful vortex of disbelief and direct experience … when you are confronted with these things for the first time and you are seeing human nature at its ugliest, you really don't want to believe that it is happening. You keep wanting to believe that it will be put back to rights again and everything will be fine and you won't have to keep facing this nightmare. I think people here [in the Republic] had no real way of entering into the nightmare because it was a 100 miles away.'

Many Northern Nationalists felt desperately lonely, if not abandoned, in those early days. They knew how much help was needed but there was little evidence that it was going to be provided.

People in Ardoyne, for example, had lost their homes and had to walk away from them with one hand as long as the other. 'When we came to Dublin my father just literally threw us into the car and a heap of clothes in after us and whatever he put in the boot. And we arrived in Dublin in that state. My father went and rented a house, and paid the full commercial holiday rent for it. We were lucky we were able to do that. We knew we couldn't do it indefinitely. There was no place here for us to touch base. There was no concept of people being refugees. There was no concept of places you could go to where you could get help or support that you could plug into. We went down then to Roscommon and eventually meandered back to Belfast because life had to go on. We just had no option but to go back, like so many refugees did.'

The Leneghans had fled Belfast in terror and then returned soon afterwards, there being no alternative. They felt very vulnerable. It was not a happy time and aid came 'dropping slow'. Eventually help did come from the housing and homelessness charity, Shelter. It provided mobile homes for people, new bedding, pots and pans, knives and forks, cups. Since those days the President has had the greatest respect for that agency. 'Thank God for them,' she says.

But things were to get worse for Belfast, and for the Leneghans too.

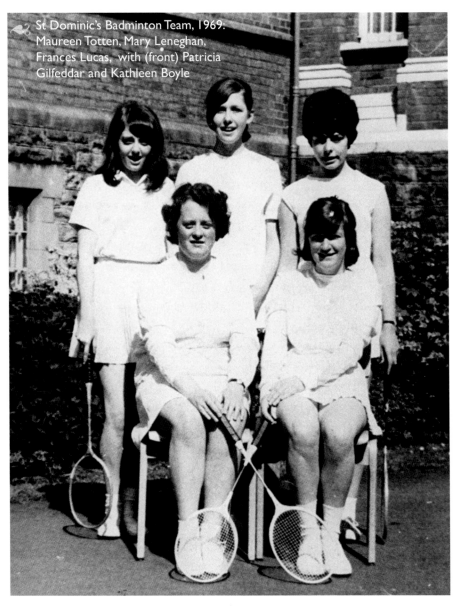

St Dominic's Badminton Team, 1969: Maureen Totten, Mary Leneghan, Frances Lucas, with (front) Patricia Gilfeddar and Kathleen Boyle

Home Sweet Home

On a damp summer's evening it takes little prompting to imagine that number 657 Crumlin Road in Belfast's Ardoyne could be a place where terror might reside. A large semi-detached two-storey house with boarded up doors and windows, it is dominated by dripping alder trees which hide under their luxuriant leaves entire universes of gloom. Its front garden is overgrown, as is the back yard with its dilapidated shed staggering to a fall against the wall. A single lush pink rose blooms at the gable end, while a fir hedge acts as boundary between the house and its neighbour, and between it and the Crumlin Road to the front. An oppressive, heavy scent from the fir defines the evening air. The adjective 'gothic' suggests itself to describe the place. But that is probably due to what is known about what happened at that house almost forty years ago.

Mary Leneghan entered the Law School at Queen's University Belfast in the autumn of 1969, not long after the family's return to Belfast following their journey as refugees in a disinterested Republic. In those days few students studied at Queen's itself. It was too dangerous to travel in Belfast in the evening or at night time. As a result, Queen's became something of a nine to five university. If she did stay late at the university library, Mary would spend the night with student colleagues, on someone's floor. But mostly she studied in her bedroom at home which she shared with three others. Sometimes she worked in the dining room when the other children were in bed.

However, and despite taking all precautions possible, the Leneghans did not escape violence. Not long after the family returned from the Republic, young Kate Leneghan was badly beaten up near their house. She was kicked on the ground by five teenage residents from a nearby loyalist estate. After

that Paddy and Claire Leneghan decided that Kate should be sent to boarding school. She went to the St Louis convent in Kilkeel, County Down. Two of the boys, Damien and Patrick, were sent as boarders to St Colman's College in Newry. That left the older girls, Mary and Nora, at home, along with the younger children.

One of the worst incidents the family suffered during that autumn of 1969 was a vicious attack on John Leneghan, who is profoundly deaf. He was sixteen at the time. As he crossed the road to his home from the bus stop opposite the house, a group of teenagers was waiting for him. An elderly man who was standing at the bus stop saw them acting strangely in a laneway across from 657. Sensing trouble, he stayed put, rather than take the bus as he had intended.

'It all happened very quickly, of course. John just simply crossed the road. These boys attacked him, broke a bottle over his head, slashed his face, slashed an artery with the broken bottle. Because John is deaf, his voice is a little bit different from your voice or mine. When he shouts or screams his voice is very strange. At first we thought it was young people coming down from St Gabriel's youth club. But then we realised that this was different and I said to Mammy, "It's John". I had very rarely heard my brother scream, but

61

I knew that it was him. We raced out. This man was coming towards our door, trying his best to carry John, who was bleeding profusely. He was really in a very, very bad way,' the President remembers.

Neighbours came around and John was brought to hospital. He was badly injured and very badly shaken. However, he had a clear recollection of his assailants, one of whom he remembered had distinctive features.

The police arrived promptly and he helped them put together a photofit. John was quite a good artist and he drew a picture of one of his assailants. Immediately he did so Eileen Gilmartin recognised the face and named the assailant and said where he lived.

Days later, John was brought in a police car to the factory where the man worked, and watched as the workers came off shift. John identified his assailant immediately. And that was that. Nothing happened. The alleged assailant was never prosecuted. The case was just let die. Years later, the Leneghans would be told by members of the RUC that attempts to bring anyone to justice for the attack on John Leneghan were actively frustrated. The case was allowed fizzle out. Mary next heard of John's assailant when she had finished her studies at Queen's and was starting to practise as a counsel at the Bar in Northern Ireland. She met the police officer who had been involved in John's case. She didn't recognise him initially. He came towards her and introduced himself. He spoke of his deep regret that charges had not been brought against John's assailant. The same young man had afterwards graduated to murder and was serving a life sentence for killing a Catholic bank manager.

The President remains certain that but for the elderly man at the bus stop that evening, her brother John would now be dead. She believes the man saved John's life. The attack on John had a deep effect on the entire Leneghan family. Awareness of John's vulnerability, of his innocence and lack of guile and of how all that made him such an easy target, meant the attack was one of the most distressing events the family experienced. It is something they remain reluctant to talk about. Still, back then when neighbours and others came to the house asking who had done it, Paddy Leneghan always refused to identify the perpetrator.

Some of those neighbours had a good idea of who was responsible. 'They would have taken the law into their hands if they had been given the opportunity, but my parents were just so overwhelmed with hurt that they didn't have any space for anger. I was angry. I remember writing at the time to the newspapers, and, God forgive me, calling for corporal punishment. It just shows you where my mind was at that time. That is something that I would despise now. I did it in anger, in distress,' the President says.

Mary Leneghan herself was almost shot dead in Belfast one night the following summer. It was Friday, 3 July 1970. She had been working as a volunteer for the Central Citizens Defence Committee, where she gave advice to people on their rights and entitlements, and was manning its office on the Falls Road that day. People were coming and going that afternoon but she was alone most of the time.

She heard the sound of pneumatic drills and went to see what was going on. Men were digging up the street. Her boyfriend, Martin McAleese, who had accompanied her to the office earlier, arrived back in a hurry. The British army had imposed a curfew on the area and was planning house-to-house searches. She and Martin began to ring around to tell people what was happening. Soon politicians such as Gerry Fitt and Paddy Devlin turned up. Journalists arrived too.

There was a lot of shooting during the night. The Army was under fire and much of the shooting took place around the CCDC offices. Mary saw a man shot dead on top of a building across from the offices. Hit several times, he fell backwards into the street. She and Martin made their way out to the high wall at the end of the backyard, intending to take a short cut out of there. ' I had popped my head over the wall … to see if there was any way I could get home, going that way, and the bullets whizzed across my head. I still remember the very English accent, telling me, in uncouth terms, what would happen if I didn't get my head down,' she recalls.

They returned to the office and spent a lot of time lying on the floor, with bullets flying past them from all directions. There were moments when they didn't believe they would make it to the morning. The curfew lasted well into the next day.

There had been a lot of unnecessary abuse and destruction as the British army searched houses in the area for arms and explosives, quantities of which were found. The army's conduct in the Falls during that curfew marked a turning point in its relationship with people in the area.

But the worst year for the Leneghan family was probably 1972. On Saturday, 7 October a bomb was placed outside Paddy Leneghan's pub in the Falls. 'Our pub, called The Long Bar, spanned two streets. It ran from Leeson Street right through to the street behind. The bomb was left in Leeson Street. My father was able to get his customers out through the back door. He then went back to make sure the place was cleared,' the President explains.

In the street a young woman was searching for her children. Paddy Leneghan ran over to get her out of the way and at that very moment the car bomb went off. Car keys hit the young woman, breaking her neck. He ran to grab her when he saw her fall. She died as Paddy Leneghan held her. He thought she had fainted. He didn't think for a moment that she was dead because she was unmarked. The young woman's name was Olive McConnell. She was twenty-three. 'She was the sister of one of my very good friends, Gerry Kavanagh,' the President says.

Years later, Mary McAleese met RTÉ cameraman Eugene McVeigh, who was one of the first on the scene that day, and they were talking about what happened when he spoke of his memories of a man holding the dead girl. It was only later that he realised that the man in question was Paddy Leneghan.

Mary's father took the incident very badly and for many years afterwards would not talk about it.

The Leneghan home was attacked a few weeks later, at Hallowe'en. A mob gathered outside the house and they smashed the latest cap stones on the wall into pieces. They also shattered paving stones. 'They broke our windows and tried to break in through the front door,' the President says. Only Claire Leneghan and the children were inside that night. Paddy was at work in the pub. The children were watching television when the windows came in around them. 'One of my younger brothers, Damien, had great presence of mind. He was twelve or thirteen. He turned off all the lights. When I asked him what he was doing, he said, "Well we know our way around the house; they don't". I was rooted to the spot. I don't remember ever in my life being so terrified.'

That night represented something of a rite of passage. The President says she has never been as terrified since. At the time, she was astonished at her own paralysis and can still see herself standing there, useless, as everyone else ran around trying to deal with the situation. Then she was spurred into action. Nora was on the phone to the police. She handed the phone to Mary and told her to talk to them, explain the situation, get help. 'It was about 10.05, and for the next four hours we waited on them and they never came until 2am in the morning, by which time we were in such a state of abject terror, we were pathetic.'

They were saved by men in a white car. Her brothers saw what happened from an upstairs window. The car came past the house. It slowed down and there was an exchange between the men in the car and the gang attacking the house. The Leneghans knew some of the attackers. They recognised them.

They knew where they came from. They were worried that the white car was part of the attack, until the mob began to scatter. It regrouped a couple of times but each time the car came back again, and the mob dispersed. The white car kept coming back and the Leneghans surmised its occupants must be plain clothes police officers. It was not so.

The RUC, of course, were targets for violence and were often lured to places with emergency calls which ended in their own deaths. But when they eventually called to 657 Crumlin Road in the early hours the next morning they didn't seem terribly anxious about what had happened. They did not endear themselves to the Leneghans. Their manner was terse, officious, disinterested. That a mother on her own with her nine children had been subjected to hours of terror did not perturb them. They went through the motions and left. The Leneghans felt even more vulnerable then. They felt they were on their own.

When the family found out in time that the men in the white car were an IRA active service unit, probably armed, they were very shocked. It was not something they had anticipated, expected or thought of. They realised how much they owed the unit, but it was with mixed feelings. The family would have preferred to have been able to rely on the forces of law, but they have had to acknowledge that without the IRA unit that night the outcome for them could have been pretty grim. That was the reality. They did not like being in that position, but they had to live with it.

After that attack, the Leneghans began to spend nights with relatives in other parts of Belfast. They would return to 657 during daylight hours. It wasn't an easy arrangement as, no matter how kind their relatives were, with six to nine (when the boarders were at home) children involved, they began to feel they were imposing too much. So Claire Leneghan moved back to the house again while Paddy tended to stay with cousins in the Falls after the pub closed. Mary stayed overnight with university colleagues more often.

Violence was escalating in the Ardoyne. Bricks and stones were replaced by guns. Gerry Kelly, a Catholic who had a sweet shop not far from the Leneghans' house, was murdered on 11 November 1972. His killing had a huge impact on the Leneghan family. By then they were back in 657 again and, especially as it was coming up to Christmas, Claire Leneghan was deeply reluctant to impose her nine children on any of her extended family.

It was around that time that Mary had a dream.

'Shortly after Gerry Kelly's death I had a dream in which I saw a gunman at our window. I would say everyone in Northern Ireland had a dream like this.

But I got so upset over it that I said to my sister Nora that we will have to get Mammy out of the house because it could be our turn next,' the President says.

She had been invited to a curry party at Queen's, hosted by a member of staff, Rajeev Dhavan, to be held on 7 December 1972. Mary wanted to go but was reluctant to leave her mother without her support. So she devised a strategy. Knowing that her mother was unlikely to stay in the house without her two eldest daughters, Mary asked Nora to come to the party with her and said they could stay overnight with friends. Nora agreed. They told their mother and she said she didn't want to spoil their fun. She would take the rest of the children to stay the night with their aunt.

A car was parked outside the gate of the house that night, which was rare. Paddy Leneghan always parked his car around the back. He remarked on the car and that it didn't seem a sensible thing to do – to park on a road where there had been so much violence. Paddy took the other children to their aunt's as Mary and Nora went to the party in Queen's. Lights were left on in the bedrooms at 657, to give the impression that the family were at home. The car outside probably added to that impression.

The next morning, on the Feast of the Immaculate Conception, the Leneghan family went to first Mass in the parish church and then returned to their own house. Mary and Nora were still at Queen's with their friends when they got a phone call from their mother who was deeply upset. She told her daughters to come home quickly. They did. But nothing prepared them for what they saw on arrival.

'The house had been absolutely riddled with bullets. I can still remember walking through the garden, seeing all the shells emptied from two machine guns. They had shot only into the rooms with the lights on. There were bullet marks on the dressing table and the chest of drawers. It was the most chilling thing,' the President remembers.

Nora's bedroom was to the front of the house, in the direct line of fire. Her bed had been riddled like a colander. The furniture in her room was pockmarked from bullets which had ricocheted. 'That was the last day we ever stayed in the house.' The family moved immediately. 'We were scattered around all the relations, yet again, until my father was fortunate enough to be offered a house.'

Though the police and army were soon on the scene that day there was never any follow up, nor was the case ever brought to closure. However, an RUC officer subsequently told an aunt of the President's that it was their belief that two UVF gunmen had been involved and that one of them had been murdered by his associates in an internal feud later. But no one knows for sure whether that is true or not.

The house offered to Paddy Leneghan was at Fruithill Park in Andersonstown, in west Belfast. It belonged to an order of nuns who were planning to demolish it and build a nursing home on the site. 'So we moved to this abjectly derelict house. There were nineteen broken windows. It had been set fire to and so was completely blackened, but anyway my parents put that to rights and that's where we ended up for the next couple of years, in this house which the nuns were kind enough to offer to us.'

They did their best to transform Number 20 into the semblance of a home but even there the Leneghans were not to find peace. In that nationalist ghetto they were seen as strangers, outsiders, big shots in the big house. A large garden at the back of the house was used as a throughway by locals, even occasionally by soldiers. Youths would loiter there. They would light fires, even use it as a toilet. They would shout at family members they saw through windows and write obscenities on the walls. They would turn on the garden hose and put it through an open window or the letterbox. They began throwing stones at family members. Claire Leneghan was hit several times. Soon this persecution made it seem that, in moving to 20 Fruithill Park from 657 Crumlin Road, the Leneghans had gone from the frying pan to the fire.

It provoked Paddy Leneghan to write a letter to the *Andersonstown News* explaining that the family had been driven from Ardoyne after an attempt to murder them in their beds and that they had moved to Andersonstown to be safe. He concluded his letter by asking 'Can any reader explain to me why we have once again become victims, in the middle of west Belfast, in the heart of the biggest and so-called safest nationalist stronghold of them all?' A few evenings later two men came to the Leneghan house and told Paddy that they were there to make sure the family had no further trouble. They sat in a car outside the house for hours. It was the first night since they moved into Fruithill Park that the Leneghans had peace. Before they left, the two men gave Paddy Leneghan a guarantee that the family would be left alone by the youth of the area. There was no further trouble.

Asked whether the violence perpetrated on the family, or the comparative indifference of people in the Republic when they sought refuge there, had instilled bitterness in her or any of the Leneghans, the President is unequivocal, 'We just don't do bitterness'. She thinks the family inherited that trait from their parents. As for herself, she doesn't carry grudges. She moves on to the next thing. She can get cross and, sometimes, righteously indignant. But it is not carried further. It is the same where all the events of those years are concerned. She no longer even remembers the name of the man who tried to kill her brother John and she hopes that will remain the case. 'The people who put us out of our home, they have gone from memory.'

She has never heard her parents express any bitterness. She has seen them lose confidence but she has never heard them express resentment even though they lost a lot, including their business and their home. 'I never ever heard — no matter what happened, no matter how bad it got, the worst it ever got — a word of recrimination, of bitterness, of anger from my parents. They were so heartsick. They had no space for bitterness.'

But they were set back, never to regain lost ground. And when Paddy Leneghan bought a pub in Rostrevor, County Down a few years later, he was only there a short time when his health broke down. Life was not easy for Claire or Paddy Leneghan. They lived modestly, worked hard and raised nine children for whom they provided as many opportunities as they could. 'They are just people who get on with things and make the best of things,' the President says. She also believes that it was her parents' example and their faith which helped all the Leneghan children escape any feelings of sectarianism, despite their experiences. 'We all became peacemakers, very staunch peacemakers, every one of us.'

A Path Less Travelled

The young Mary Leneghan was absolutely addicted to Perry Mason. The TV series featuring the defence attorney character created by Erle Stanley Gardner was one reason why she did law. But there was a more serious one.

To grow up as a Catholic in Ardoyne was to feel an outsider. Government politicians at Stormont talked about Catholics in appalling terms. You could read it in the newspapers every day. It made Catholics feel like the scum of the earth, lesser human beings. Mary absolutely refused to accept that. It contributed to her feeling a boiling sense of social justice. As it later emerged, law was in the family background – a granduncle of her father's had been a county judge in Chicago.

Patrick Banaghan Flanagan left Ireland as a teacher, and didn't qualify as a lawyer until he was in his forties. First he worked in Chicago for a trade union, and as a bailiff. He studied law through night classes and was later appointed a Cook County judge. The President had never heard of him until after she was elected in 1997, when relations emerged from all sorts of places.

Her paternal grandmother, Annie Flanagan, lived with her father's family in Roscommon when they were growing up. Patrick Banaghan Flanagan was her brother. Both were said to be related to *the* Fr Flanagan, the priest who led the prayers at the meeting of the First Dáil in Dublin's Mansion House on 21 January 1919.

The Dominican sisters prepared their pupils for just two professions, teaching and nursing. Of the over 200 pupils in Mary Leneghan's year, by far the vast majority are teachers. 'Their pupils were being trained for the service and vocational professions. Though the nuns never discouraged us

Judge Patrick Banahan Flanagan, the President's great grand-uncle

from trying something else,' she says. Her English teacher, a Miss Beckett, asked the class what they were hoping to be when the left school. She went down through a list of things, asking if they had ever contemplated being nurses, for example. Mary put up her hand, as that was one of the careers she had considered. A lot of her aunts were nurses and her primary school was right beside the Mater hospital, where her aunts worked. But Miss Beckett had other ideas. '"Why would you want to be a nurse?" she asked. She said that if I ever contemplated a medical career, I should think about being a doctor.' Miss Beckett told her she must understand her own brain power. Mary was taken aback that anyone would think she had the brains to be a doctor. But Miss Beckett was wrong if she thought her pupil lacked ambition. 'From about the age of fourteen it was fixed in my mind that I would do law,' she says.

'The Dominicans did embed in us girls a culture of ambition and of being independent women, being financially independent and professionally independent.' They were certainly not anxious for them to leave school at sixteen to go into factory jobs and marriages. The nuns had figured out where women could get their feet into the professions, and they were helping to guide their pupils to those places. What they really wanted for their girls was a third level education, the basic platform from which to launch a professional career. And it's what the vast majority of that class ended up doing – most of them the first in their families ever to go on to third level.

However, the Dominicans were a very tough breed of nuns. Mary envied her sisters who went to the Louis nuns in Kilkeel, County Down. The Louis nuns would help her sisters choose lipsticks. The Dominicans had no time for that stuff. 'They wanted to focus their pupils on intellectual pursuits and were scathing about any deviation or distraction from that. Then all these orders have their own different charisms,' she says. The Louis nuns seemed a far less muscular bunch than the Dominicans or the Mercys, especially the Mercys.

But there were some terrific role models in the Dominicans. One such was the headmistress, Mother Urban, now in her 90s. In her 50s she decided she wanted to go to the missions and off she went to Africa, Angola and South America. She ended up working in Portugal. Mary McAleese says she has never come across anyone so open, so radical, so refreshingly easy-going. She couldn't be shocked. She was so measured. 'She was one of those people you could really talk to about anything. A very open, liberal woman, and is to this day. She has a great sense of humour.' The President is still very friendly with her.

But the nun who succeeded Mother Urban was a different character. Mother Helena was narrow, very traditional, very caring, but her way of caring was to get into your life and try and control it. Mother Helena is deceased, but right up until she died she would send letters to the President chiding her for things she had said or done. 'You know how much I love you, but did you have to say... such and such? Did you have to take Communion? [referring to the Christ Church Eucharist]. Did we teach you nothing?'

When Mary Leneghan was thirteen or fourteen she attempted to join the Communist party. Her mother opened the letter sent to her daughter from the Communist Party with the application form. She arrived at the school in a state. Where Mrs Leneghan was concerned, she might as well have found cocaine under her daughter's bed. That was how Mother Helena

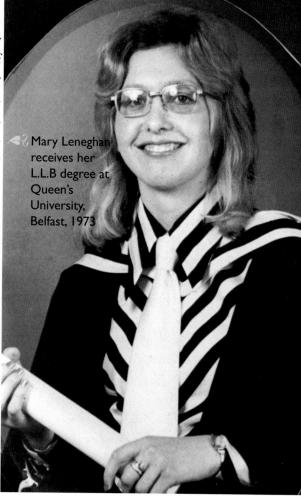

Mary Leneghan receives her L.L.B degree at Queen's University, Belfast, 1973

responded too. So every morning from then on, before class started, Mary had to go to her for counselling. The nun would go through everything on her young charge's desk, repeating 'Do you see that inkwell, God is in that inkwell.' God was also in the ink. God was in the pen with which she wrote. And this was meant to help the young would-be communist and then convinced atheist before her!

This went on for some time until Mary figured out the best thing for her was to agree that God was in the inkwell, God was in the ink etc, and once she rehearsed all those things back to Mother Helena she was happy she had succeeded. Thereafter she kept a very wary eye on her wayward pupil.

Mary Leneghan got A levels in English, History and Spanish at St Dominic's. Three A levels were enough to get into Queen's University.

The staff and students in Queen's were predominantly Protestant and Unionist. But there were exciting things going on. Although it was an establishment place, it was also a locus for the People's Democracy group, which had been established in the late 1960s. Mary had become a member at secondary school and had been going up and down to their meetings at Queen's. Many of that first generation of young, educated, Catholic radicals were there at the time – Bernadette Devlin [McAliskey], Eamonn McCann, Michael Farrell – people she already knew and admired enormously. For her, Queen's was the place where the ambitions of Catholics and nationalists were being articulated, most loudly and most vociferously. 'And the vast majority of the Protestant students that I became friendly with at Queen's were all up for civil rights, with very few exceptions. They were interested. They saw themselves as part of that 60s generation, as in Paris and elsewhere, who believed in human rights and civil liberties.' There were a few, of course, who probably took a different view, but it didn't get in the way of friendships. It was also while at Queen's that Mary became a member of the SDLP for the first time.

There were few women in law in those days. When she went to Law School at Queen's, about 10 per cent of her class was women. 'At that time there were no women practising at the Northern Ireland Bar. A number had been called to the Bar but no women were attempting to practise.'

The class was small, not more than sixty. They had very different political perspectives. 'The ethos of a university allows you to test yourself, your views and your perspective against people who are as equally articulate as yourself. Also, for that generation in the late 1960s, university was a blessed liberation,' she recalls. They were fascinated by each other. They loved and relished every opportunity to get to know people from right across every possible divide. 'We mixed and mingled. The rugby crowd went to GAA matches. The GAA crowd went to the rugby matches. It was a wonderful place.' She loved those years in Queen's. Yes, there were bitchy politics from one day's end to the next, but there were also fabulous friendships.

Learning the Law by Professor Glanville Williams was the primary introductory text which the students used when starting Law School. All these years later that book still rankles with the President. She has quoted from Glanville Williams frequently in her speeches, and not out of admiration. Delivering the Arthur Cox Memorial Lecture at UCD on 4 March 1999, she said that 'male students might be disappointed to hear his opinion that "men cannot improve the beauty of their countenances" but all is not lost if, when choosing a suit for job interviews, you "avoid wide lapels, buttons on pockets and fancy trimmings".' But, she continued, 'You fare better than women, whom he largely ignores, except to advise that they should "dress conservatively, without sexual display, in a way that betokens quiet efficiency rather than fashion". This was clearly written in the days before Ally McBeal. But it is at least preferable to his other advice to women, namely that along with non-whites, we should think long and hard before attempting to practise at the Bar. Sadly, this advice was based on evidence submitted to the Royal Commission on Legal Services in 1977 that many chambers limited the number of tenancies given to women, due to their irritating tendency to have children and skive off full-time practice.'

She returned to the book again at the launch of the Centre for Advancement of Women in Politics on 28 September 2001. 'If anyone ever

Called to the Bar, 1974. Patricia Kennedy, Mary, Eilis McDermott

asks why we need a centre for the advancement of women in politics please feel free to tell them this story! In the summer of 1969 – over thirty years ago, yes – but not exactly the Dark Ages, I was getting ready to come to Queen's to do law. Like all my fellow and sister undergraduates, I received a letter from the Faculty with strict instructions that we were to prepare ourselves for our studies by buying and reading a book called *Learning the Law* by one of the most eminent legal scholars of the day, Professor Glanville Williams. I did as I was bid, knowing this book was Holy Writ, probably Holy Grail – the key to all that was to follow. The reading was going well until close to the end, on page 192, I ominously came to a section entitled very simply "Women". There was no corresponding section entitled "Men". The section opens with the following words "It is difficult to write this section without being ungallant. Parliament, it is said, can do everything except make a man a woman or a woman a man. In 1919, in the Sex Disqualification (Removal) Act, it went as far as it could to perform the second feat. The results so far have not been striking."' Glanville Williams went on: "Practice at the Bar ... is difficult enough for a man: it is heartbreaking for a woman. She has a double prejudice to conquer: the prejudice of the solicitor and the prejudice of the solicitor's lay client. Combined, these two prejudices are almost inexpugnable". And there was more "It is not easy for a young man to get up and face the court; many women find it harder still. A woman's voice does not carry as well as a man's." 'But thank God, we women had some glimmer of hope, for, according to the eminent Professor, "the technical Bar qualification is a good enough stepping stone to posts that do not demand actual practice at the Bar. Most women barristers, if they do not marry, take this way out."'

The President recalled that 'Five years later in 1974 when I and two other undeterred women were called to the Bar of Northern Ireland, without a trace of irony, the gift presented to each of us by the Benchers on the day of our call was a specially bound copy of – yes, you guessed it – *Learning the Law* by Glanville Williams.'

'What was true of the law then, was true of many, many spheres of life and in particular spheres of public influence, among them the sphere of politics which profoundly shapes so much of our lives. It is a story that is changing, but a story of much unfinished business."

One of her lecturers at Queen's was David Trimble. He taught Property Law, which was not one of her strong points. She says that he 'drew the short straw. It was just a very tough subject but he was a very fine teacher'. He has 'no strong recollection of her' from that time, but 'she was a good student, attentive, also active'. He met her more often outside the lecture hall, at meetings involving the faculty and its students.

David Trimble was not one of the people who would have shared an enthusiasm for civil rights in those days, though other members of the faculty did, including Kevin Boyle and one of the great champions of civil rights, Colin Campbell. The Law faculty also included Professor Claire Palley. A South African who helped draw up the South African Constitution and the new Cypriot Constitution, she has been involved with the ongoing debate there on how to facilitate the two parts of Cyprus. When the President went to Queen's it had an eminent faculty, with people who had been at the top of their field, such as Professor William Twining, Dean of the Law School. He set up a group with Claire Palley at the time the Emergency Powers were introduced. Mary Leneghan became a member of that group which debated the Emergency Powers. 'It was wonderful, as a young student, to be invited to join such top academics, to hear them and debate with them. And also to have the comparative law fed in from the jurisdictions that they would have worked in and written about. It was a very stimulating environment. Queen's was a fantastic place to be.'

Called to the Irish Bar, the King's Inns, Dublin, 1978. With Martin and her parents, Claire and Paddy Leneghan

Mary did well academically at Queen's. In their first exams in 1970, she came first in her class, and finished in 1973 with an honours degree in Law. After her degree she did a one-year post grad course for the Bar. She was called to the Bar and then devilled, for a year. Her master was a man called Peter Smith, better known in more recent times for the work he did with the Patten Commission. He was then chair of South Belfast Unionist Association and very much associated with the Ulster Unionist Party. He had been a tutor of hers at Queen's. He offered to become her master as she didn't know any barristers. Just three women were called to the Bar in her year. Women had been called to the Bar before but nobody had attempted to practise for about twenty-five years.

Law was a hard place for women then. It wasn't geared to women. Even when they got a letter telling them what to wear for their call day, it described the morning suit right down to the trousers and the wing collars. Mary went to the under treasurer, the administrative officer of the court, and asked whether the women should wear the little collars that women wore at the English Bar. He was immovable. He said the letter set out the proper attire for barristers and the women would have to wear it. Asked then if he would be happy that the women turned up in trousers he said, "No, No, No". Eventually skirts were permitted but still the women had to wear wing collars. 'The entire business illustrated that in Belfast they had not got their heads around women being at the Bar. They were probably hoping they would never have to get their heads around it. They were probably hoping, as elsewhere, that the women would disappear. But they didn't!' she says.

During her university years she also took part in other extra-curricular activities. She was president of the College Law Society. She did some debating and she was involved with the people who set up a Women's Aid group, the first to be established in Belfast. Queen's gave them a house. Sport took up a lot of time, too, particularly GAA.

She has always been a keen GAA follower and a Down supporter. Down was her McManus grandparents' county but, probably as significant, Down won two All-Ireland football finals, back to back, in 1960 and 1961 when she was nine and ten. Martin had played as a minor for Antrim, and played for Queen's while studying Physics. Mary played on a mixed hockey team.

Famously, she was once selected 'Man of the Match' following a controversial GAA game in Dublin. She wasn't even a player. The match against UCD was supposed to be played in Croke Park, but then was changed to UCD's home pitch and Queen's weren't at all happy about that. And if that wasn't suspicious enough, UCD supplied the referee. It was a very tough match. On the day, Martin McAleese was 'abused, assaulted, what-have-you' by the man marking him. He was physically beating the lard out of Martin when she ran onto the pitch with her umbrella. Apparently she looked like a cross between Mother Teresa and Mary Poppins. She was dragged off before she got a chance to wrap the umbrella around the referee. At that stage Martin had been really injured, but the referee had done nothing. She was furious. Queen's lost the match, badly. On the way back to Belfast on the bus she was unanimously declared Man of the Match by the team. But it didn't end there. Peter Quinn [later President of the GAA] has claimed, apparently, that one of the most embarrassing episodes in his entire time with the GAA was when he had to write a letter of apology for her incursion onto the pitch that time at UCD. He was then secretary of the GAA club at Queen's where he was also an Economics lecturer.

But those years at Queen's were among her happiest, even allowing for the sectarian violence which her family was being subjected to at home. Queen's was her happy place, where she had great friends and a great life.

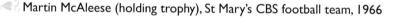 Martin McAleese (holding trophy), St Mary's CBS football team, 1966

Blessed Trinity

In 1975 Mary Leneghan was appointed Reid Professor of Law at Trinity College, Dublin. At twenty-four she was the youngest person to hold the post. She had applied for the job at the suggestion of Professor Robert Heuston, of Trinity's Law Department. She succeeded the then Senator Mary Robinson in the post, who she would also succeed as President of Ireland twenty-two years later.

Robert Heuston was an eminent Tort lawyer and a shy man, except in front of an audience when the natural born actor would come out. They just hit it off, a very unlikely combination – the girl from Ardoyne and an elderly eccentric academic, a Pembroke College, Oxford-educated man.

Trinity was 'different from Queen's in that it was a university where a lot of people lived in. They didn't have to go home at five o'clock,' the President says. Dublin, too, was a big change. Initially she stayed in a bedsit on Waterloo Road in the same building as her sister Nora, who was working in Dublin. Later they moved to an apartment near Mount Argus in Harold's Cross. She loved Dublin. Coming down from the North in those years she always felt as soon as she hit Swords that a great burden lifted from her and she was entering 'party land'. As well as the family's brief stay in Kilmacud in 1969, all during the Troubles she had been up and down to Dun Laoghaire where their McKenna cousins lived. 'I associated Dublin with a normality and an openness to the world that Belfast lacked. Belfast was more parochial and increasingly becoming more absorbed with the Troubles and was also becoming more and more dangerous. Dublin had just fun and normality. I adored Dublin and Trinity,' she remembers.

At the beginning, however, she was very lonely and was on the road a lot, visiting Belfast and Rostrevor, to where her family had now moved. Gradually she became more involved in life at Trinity. A friend of hers and also from Ardoyne, was Professor Vincent McBrierty of the university's Physics Department. He went out of his way to help her settle in. It was around then too that Trinity had its first ever Catholic chaplain and Mass began to be celebrated daily on campus. She and Professor McBrierty attended daily Mass there throughout her twelve years at Trinity.

Along with David Norris, she co-founded the Campaign for Homosexual Law Reform. 'I had become friendly with David Norris and had then seen a notice in the university for anyone who was interested to go along and discuss gay issues,' she recalls. But she had already been involved in other civil liberties issues and had talked about them in public meetings. She had also done a number of radio interviews on gay rights. In those interviews she said that in the Republic of Ireland the State was structuring, through the use of criminal law and taboo, a situation in which gay men and women found it very, very difficult to enter into the humanly uplifting, loving, life-time

President McAleese with Senator David Norris at the Bloomsday Breakfast, North Great George's Street

relationships that were available to heterosexual people. As soon as gay people set up home together their visibility would immediately label them. Society was therefore, in a sense, colluding in the pressures that were on gay people. Many gay people didn't like gay bars and the gay scene that they were forced into. Back then, over thirty years ago, she said in an RTÉ interview that Irish society had to contemplate formal gay relationships, like marriage.

In August 2007 the President delivered an address at the twenty-fourth world congress of the International Association for Suicide Prevention, held in Killarney, County Kerry. She said that suicide was the 'biggest killer' of young men in the State; they accounted for 40 per cent of all suicides. 'Although Ireland is making considerable progress in developing a culture of genuine equality, recognition and acceptance of gay men and women, there is still an undercurrent of both bias and hostility which young gay people must find deeply hurtful and inhibiting. For them, homosexuality is a discovery, not a decision and for many it is a discovery which is made against a backdrop where, within their immediate circle of family and friends, as well as the wider society, they have long encountered anti-gay attitudes which will do little to help them deal openly and healthily with their own sexuality.' As a result they were driven into silence. 'And we know that silence is a very dangerous place'.

Her own awareness of the plight of gay people arose during a student summer spent on the west coast of the USA in the early 1970s. She was about twenty-one and working in a company that made food for airlines. One of her supervisors was a charming, lovely man. A fellow worker warned her that he was gay – not in a nasty way – she was just being alerted not to get romantically interested. She and he became great friends. He was a refined, sophisticated man who was deeply wounded that he had been excluded by his family. In San Francisco, which many would have identified as the gay capital of the world, he was still a lonely person. The gay scene didn't appeal to him. He felt it was overwhelmed with a lot of predatory people and all he wanted was a loving relationship, happiness and peace. They talked a lot.

'At school or university I was never aware of ever meeting a gay person, such were the taboos at that time. As a heterosexual I had wondered what it must be like for those who are outside of that mainstream, the self discovery, when you can reveal it to no one.' That man in California was her first introduction to the world of the suffering of people who are gay. 'When I came back to Ireland I made it my business to do something about it,' she says.

Divorce was another issue with which she became involved in those Trinity years. At a Law Society annual meeting in University College Galway in 1979 she spoke in favour of the introduction of divorce legislation. She said, '…anti-divorce lobbyists often argue that divorce damages children, yet the truth is that what damages children is not the *de jure* dissolution of marriage but the process of rows, scenes, violence, bitterness, recrimination and upheaval which *de facto* break it up.'

Yet in 1986 she opposed the referendum which would have introduced divorce to Ireland. She has described her change of stance on divorce between her 1979 Galway speech and her 1986 view as 'more of a left turn than a U-turn'. The difference between what was debated in Galway in 1979 and what it was planned to introduce in 1986 was the type of divorce on offer. The speech in Galway was delivered in the context of divorce and annulment. No-fault divorce was what was put before the electorate in 1986, which she would also have opposed in 1979. It couldn't be argued that divorce had no social ramifications, she said. She sees divorce as a civil facility and has pointed out that it is not listed in any UN document as a human right.

She did not like the shape of the legislation being proposed in 1986. She didn't like a lot of the claims that were made then – such as the second chance for happiness, the exclusion of the interests and rights of the children. But she felt she was open to persuasion. At the end of the day, she felt it was about making one of the biggest social changes that has ever been made in the Republic and was deserving of the very best and deepest thought. It was no longer a topic simply for debate. In a debating context you can argue both sides. By the time it came to the issue as a referendum though, it was no longer just a debating point. It meant she was more cautious. She was no longer living in the Republic by the time of the second and successful divorce referendum in 1995.

Where divorce is concerned in the Republic today, she sees it from two perspectives: 'It is a civil right that has been afforded to people. That is the beginning, middle and end of it. For me, though, it would never be an option. I have made a binding covenant for life.' But divorce is there. It is a civil right that people in the Republic now have. It is part and parcel of everyday life. It is a facility the people of Ireland decided to accord each other and that's it. Which she honours, absolutely.

In early 1981 she chaired a meeting on abortion in Dublin's Liberty Hall, organised by the Women's Right to Choose group. One of the reasons she was asked to chair it was because she had, shortly beforehand, presented the first RTÉ programme on abortion. It featured a young woman going to

England for a termination. Among those on the panel were journalists Anne Marie Hourihane and the late Mary Holland, as well as trade unionist Anne Speed. The organisers have always insisted that this was a pro-choice meeting. The President has, as adamantly, continued to repeat that she understood it was a public meeting to discuss the issue of abortion and that it was promoted as such. It was not a pro-choice meeting. She felt very offended when at the end it was clear that there were people there who were using the meeting to start a pro-choice movement.

Ironically, the President, who has always been opposed to abortion, and who strongly supported the right to life of the unborn in the 1983 abortion referendum campaign, found herself on the opposite side to the pro-life movement in the 1992 referendum.

In that 1983 referendum two-thirds of voters rejected the legalisation of abortion in Ireland. However that decision was thrown into turmoil in 1992 when the real life complexities of issues surrounding abortion intruded forcefully, with the X case. 'X' was a fourteen-year-old girl who was pregnant after rape and whose parents intended bringing her to England for an abortion. Then Attorney General Harry Whelehan went to the High Court to stop them. It decided 'X' could not leave the State if her intention was to have an abortion. This was appealed to the Supreme Court where it was argued that 'X' was at risk of suicide if forced to continue the pregnancy. The court allowed her permission to go to England and in its judgment strongly criticised the Government for the absence of adequate legislation dealing with the complexities surrounding abortion.

Forced to act, the Government held a referendum on 25 November to decide on three matters: (i) the availability of abortion in Ireland; (ii) the right to travel for an abortion; and (iii) the right to distribute information on abortion services.

On the substantive issue, it was proposed that no one would have the right to terminate the life of a foetus except where that might be necessary to save the life of the mother, as distinct from preserving the health of the mother. The substantive issue was rejected by voters while (ii) and (iii) were passed. Though Mary McAleese had been out of the Republic and working in Belfast for over five years, she became involved in the 1992 referendum campaign. She supported the referendum and called for a 'yes' vote on the grounds that its wording was 'pro-woman and pro-unborn'. In a letter to the *Irish Press* which she signed with the anti-abortion campaigners Patricia Casey, UCD professor of psychiatry, and Cornelius O'Leary, political science professor at Queen's, they urged a 'Yes' vote in the abortion referendum and criticised the Supreme Court decision in the X case.

'The Supreme Court decision in the case of the Attorney General versus X contradicted the express will of the Irish people as well as decades of medical and legal practice by permitting the direct abortion of the unwanted child. Since that decision many voices have argued against another constitutional referendum, claiming that the matter is too complex and divisive. They have stated their preference for dealing with the matter by legislation, even though to do so would enshrine the X judgment in Irish law, thus making for easy access to abortion. In spite of such opposition, the Government has courageously chosen to provide the Irish people with an opportunity to overturn the Supreme Court decision. We particularly welcome the government's recognition that threat of suicide provides no medical justification whatever for abortion,' they wrote.

Taoiseach Bertie Ahern and President McAleese at the GPO, O'Connell Street, during the 92nd Anniversary Easter Rising Commemoration ceremony

She even advised the Catholic bishops to call for a 'yes' vote. They decided to leave it to people's conscience, though the then Archbishop of Dublin and later Cardinal Desmond Connell, as well as Bishop John Magee of Cloyne and the then Bishop of Killala Dr Thomas Finnegan, issued pastoral letters advising a 'no' vote.

A 'Late Late Show' special on the referendum issue took the form of a court hearing, with retired Judge Peter O'Malley presiding. Counsel presented the arguments for and against. Mary McAleese was a witness for the 'yes' side.

The Most Difficult,
The Darkest, The Worst Time

In March 1979 Mary McAleese secured a job in RTÉ as a presenter/reporter in television current affairs.

Her first position was on the 'Frontline' weekly current affairs programme. There was a great crew on the programme, people like the producer, Peter Feeney. She interviewed Mary Robinson about the Diplock Courts in Northern Ireland. Before Christmas that year she and Charlie Bird worked on a programme about abortion in which they accompanied a young pregnant woman on the boat to Liverpool. She was also involved in coverage of the PAYE workers' strike in January 1980, the Fianna Fáil Árd Fheis the following month, and an item on the proposed new women's prison at Clondalkin in Dublin. Then, on 9 September 1980, the last 'Frontline' programme was broadcast and what she has described as 'the most difficult, the darkest, the worst time of my life,' had begun. In making that observation years later she added, 'In saying that, I am taking into account the years of the Troubles in Belfast. Without a doubt, it was the most traumatic period of my life – bar none.'

She became a reporter on the new 'Today Tonight' current affairs programme. In fact she took part in the very first 'Today Tonight' broadcast on 6 October 1980 from outside Dublin's Gate Theatre where Brian Friel's new play *Translations* was having its opening. Bizarrely, she had not been told about her 'Today Tonight' appointment; she read it in a newspaper. A senior manager on the programme later told her, candidly, that if she had Irish (which she has now) she would have been put on the Irish language current

Mary McAleese presenting RTÉ's 'Frontline' programme, 1979

affairs programme 'Féach' instead. He made it very clear he did not want her there. Very soon it was apparent she was being treated by her bosses on the programme as an IRA sympathiser, in an atmosphere where that guaranteed maximum hostility. As she wrote later, 'I was a Catholic, a Northerner, a Nationalist and a woman – a quadruple deviant in the eyes of many influential people in RTÉ.'

According to some who worked in current affairs at RTÉ then, it was a place where people were very quickly labelled politically, added to which there was a lot of begrudgery and professional jealousy. There were many would-be prima donnas and it was a very stratified, sexist place. Production assistants, for instance, tended to be women and were considered lower down the pecking order. The attitude towards people with degrees was that they tended 'to lord it', that they felt entitled to deference. People also seemed very conscious of grades and seniority levels, rather than acting as team players. 'Today Tonight' was said to be particularly like that. 'The bosses there had been given little in the way of management training and knew nothing about motivating staff,' says one source who worked on the programme then. It is a view that was widely corroborated by others.

'Today Tonight' was to be RTÉ's flagship current affairs programme. It was to be broadcast four nights a week and had been given considerable resources, with Joe Mulholland as its editor. It was well staffed, with ten producers, ten reporters, ten production assistants, and a strong presentation team in Brian Farrell, Barry Cowan and Olivia O'Leary. There were three camera crews, and according to Gerry Gregg, who worked on the programme at the time and defends it staunchly, competition to get a camera crew was 'massive'. Production meetings were regular and frequently torrid as analysis of programmes broadcast was frank, as was the examination of ideas for new programmes. 'Joe Mulholland was a bit like Alex Ferguson. We all got the hair dryer treatment from him one time or another,' Gerry Gregg says.

Shortly after it began broadcasting it was being claimed that the Workers' Party had an undue influence on 'Today Tonight' content. The Party had evolved from an IRA/Sinn Féin split in December 1969 which resulted in both an Official and Provisional Sinn Féin/IRA, with Official Sinn Féin members, known as 'Stickies', having a class-based Marxist agenda. The Party was also heavily influenced by the 1972 book *States of Ireland* by Conor Cruise O'Brien, which vigorously challenged the nationalist and republican view of

The President with playwright Brian Friel and his wife, on his election as Saoi of Aosdána

Irish history. Always deeply hostile to Provisional Sinn Féin/IRA, Official Sinn Féin changed its name to Sinn Féin the Workers' Party in 1977 and to the Workers' Party in 1982.

By the late 1970s and early 1980s Sinn Féin the Workers' Party was believed to have deeply infiltrated student bodies at the universities, the trade unions and the media in Dublin, including RTÉ current affairs programmes, where they were said to exercise an influence which far exceeded their number in RTÉ or Irish society. Asked whether the Party influence was overt in 'Today Tonight' at that time, a member of the then programme team responded 'Absolutely. That was one of the things that made me so uncomfortable and why I eventually left. The programme was absolutely agenda driven. I found it very difficult to work there, knowing that under the terms of the Broadcasting Act we were obliged to be fair to all the parties. It became increasingly difficult to live up to that statutory requirement in that environment. There were a lot of problems on that programme, but agenda was one of them. Other people observed it from outside, but we could feel it very much inside.'

Gerry Gregg, who was a Workers' Party sympathiser at the time and later became a member, says the 'Today Tonight' team was 'absolutely, a campaigning group of journalists, pro the liberal agenda.' He also agrees it was revisionist in its approach to Northern Ireland. The key dynamic of the programme, in whatever subject it addressed, was to 'challenge the consensus both from a programming and a political point of view'. He concurs with the view that some people on the programme were treated roughly, including Mary McAleese. 'Joe Mulholland never thought he had a future President of Ireland on his hands.' But he has no doubt that the programme's approach helped make possible much of what has happened on this island since. 'Who would've thought we would ever see the day when Bertie Ahern would be serenaded at the Boyne by Orangemen,' he says, as an example of what he means.

He remembers Mary McAleese from those days as 'intelligent' and 'always sociable'. He also remembers observations from her then that the programme seemed to be out of touch with what was happening on the ground in Northern Ireland. 'It was true', he says, 'that there was a sense among some on the programme team that she was sympathetic to the Provos.' He also remembers an awareness at the time that a relative of hers took part in the 1981 hunger strike.

It was in relation to 'Today Tonight's' coverage of the 1981 hunger strike particularly, that matters came to a head between the President-to-be and the powers-that-were at the programme. Republican prisoners in the H-Blocks in Northern Ireland had organised a series of protests seeking to regain special category status and not to be subject to ordinary prison regulations. This began in 1976 with the 'blanket protest' when they refused to wear the prison uniform and covered themselves in blankets instead. This escalated to the 'dirty protest' of 1978 when repeated beatings led to prisoners smearing excrement on the cell walls. The first hunger strike was in autumn 1980. It ended when the British Government appeared to concede to the prisoners' demands. However when that strike was over the Government reverted to its previous stance. The 1981 hunger strike began when Bobby Sands refused food on 1 March. He had decided that other prisoners should join the strike at staggered intervals, to maximise publicity as the prisoners steadily deteriorated one by one over several months. The hunger strike centred around five demands: (i) the right not to wear a prison uniform; (ii) the right not to do prison work; (iii) the right of free association with other prisoners, and to organise educational and recreational pursuits; (iv) the right to one visit, one letter and one parcel a week; (v) full restoration of remission lost through the protest. The striking prisoners' aim was to be declared political prisoners (or prisoners of war) and not be classed as criminals. Some, however, saw the primary purpose of the exercise as an attempt to gain international publicity rather than political prisoner status. By the time the hunger strike was ended, ten of the men, including Bobby Sands, had died.

A constant visitor to family and friends in Northern Ireland, Mary McAleese was keenly aware of the effects the 1981 hunger strikes were having on the ground there, particularly the impact of Bobby Sands' election as an MP, and then his funeral. On Northern Ireland affairs generally she felt she was not listened to at 'Today Tonight'. She was not the only one. When another reporter on the programme, generally regarded as a first-class journalist, brought back a programme from Belfast about the impact of the hunger strikes, which included an interview with Fr Des Wilson, a priest whose politics and views were not liked by the programme, he was accused by a colleague at a programme meeting of being a Provo. In fact, he was accused of being 'a fucking Provo'.

So annoyed was Mary McAleese at this abuse of a colleague with whom she had also worked on 'Frontline' that she intervened. According to witnesses, it was unforgettable. She said she was astounded that such language would have been used by one colleague to another. She was also astonished that the boss would not intervene and say 'Stop this. You cannot treat another colleague like that.' It was intolerable and outrageous that his superiors would allow a member of staff to be subjected to that. It was in breach of every decent human resource practice in the book and it was highly libelous. And she warned, before anyone started extending such labelling to anyone else there, that if she ever heard anyone using such language to or about her she would take them to court. She said that this was because nobody was protecting anyone's right to their good name at the programme.

Asked whether the tenor of such exchanges and meetings involving Mary McAleese ever threatened to become physical, a colleague from those days remarked, 'If you heard Mary McAleese you would understand that there was no need to get physical.'

Mary McAleese has said elsewhere of those days that 'the bigotry in RTÉ was an extraordinary phenomenon. It was very different from bigotry in the North; bigots in RTÉ were the most righteous self-styled liberals. It was bad enough when the revisionists in the 70s were telling us that nationalism was dead, but then the Provisionals came along to tell us that they, and only they, were the real nationalists, the super-nationalists. Whatever ordinary poor nationalists were left after all that were now being attacked by "Today Tonight", a programme of our national television station.'

There were people at 'Today Tonight', who, it was felt, were clearly 'in' with the powers-that-be, and others who were just tolerated and who received no protection, even from libel. So a number of those on the team felt very exposed. Mary McAleese, although aware that she was among the exposed, continued to make her points at programme meetings. In March 1981, at one such meeting, she asked what coverage was planned for the Fermanagh/South Tyrone election on 11 April in which hunger striker Bobby Sands was a candidate.

The election was on a Thursday and the results were expected the following day, but 'Today Tonight' did not broadcast on a Friday. To do so it would need to make an application to the RTÉ authority. She asked if an election special was planned for 12 April as she felt the result was going to make the headlines.

Independent Republican MP Frank Maguire had died of a heart attack on 5 March 1981, precipitating the by-election in Fermamagh/South Tyrone. Bobby Sands was the only candidate on the nationalist side, against the Ulster Unionist Party candidate Harry West. The SDLP had not put forward a candidate, to avoid splitting the nationalist vote. What Mary McAleese was predicting at the programme meeting was that Bobby Sands might win the seat.

It was not such a remarkable call. She simply looked at the number of Catholics and Protestants in the constituency and concluded that Bobby Sands could win. She told the meeting, 'It looks to me that Bobby Sands could win this election by possibly 500, 600 or 700 votes. If he does it will be a major upset. So are we going to have a programme?' One person at the meeting says, 'She was ranted at. Absolutely ranted at and told she didn't know what she was talking about. That it was absolute nonsense. Harry West was going to win the election and there was no need for a special programme.' Some concluded from her comments that she must be a Bobby Sands supporter. Such events led her to say afterwards that 'Today Tonight' 'was really a very awful environment to work in, a very depressing one.'

At lunchtime on Friday 11 April news came through to RTÉ from a freelance reporter in Fermanagh/South Tyrone that Bobby Sands had won the election by 30,493 votes to Harry West's 29,046. There was all-out panic at 'Today Tonight'. Sources have recounted how Joe Mulholland came out of his office, went directly to Mary McAleese's desk — which was in an open plan area — and announced, '… your man won'. She responded that on no account was Bobby Sands 'her man' and that she took great objection to that sort of language. All she had done was her job. She had pointed out that Bobby Sands could possibly win the election and that, if he did, it was their job as people who were about the business of bringing current affairs and news to the Irish people to bring that news to them properly. She did not shout it. She could be forceful in asserting her point, but she never shouted. Joe Mulholland was furious. He said to her that he needed to get a crew to Fermanagh/South Tyrone and that she should go with them. She said that she had already made plans for the weekend.

He sent a crew, but without a Production Assistant. Under union rules agreed at RTÉ they could not broadcast without a PA. A few of the 'Today Tonight' team, including Mary McAleese, got together and decided that union rules would have to be observed. Joe Mulholland then sent a PA but she didn't reach the count centre in time. He had to do a deal to get footage of the count from somewhere else. It was a scandal and elsewhere heads would have rolled. They didn't at RTÉ. Instead that was the day Mary McAleese decided she was leaving.

But that was not the end of her troubles. Bobby Sands died the following month, on 5 May. He had been on hunger strike for sixty-six days. It was action replay at 'Today Tonight'. During a programme meeting where plans for coverage of Bobby Sands' funeral were being discussed, a member of the team commented that there would be more cameras and camera crews than mourners at the funeral. Mary McAleese disagreed. She said that it was going to be a very important showcase of the extent to which the hunger strike had both polarised and politicised nationalists in Northern Ireland. She had garnered this from talking to people fairly widely in Belfast, including SDLP supporters. Those she had been in contact with in Northern Ireland spoke of the increased politicisation taking place as a result of the hunger strike. People were being drawn into polarised positions. The attendance at the Sands' funeral was going to include many who had never in their lives gone to an IRA funeral. It was repeated to her that the best information the programme had from Northern Ireland was that the camera crews would outnumber the mourners. On the day, over 70,000 people attended the funeral.

The day afterwards she was heard to say to a 'Today Tonight' colleague '... I didn't notice 70,000 camera crews!' They had been wrong again. They had served the Irish people badly, again. They were being paid a salary and they were not delivering the goods. It did not make her any more popular with some colleagues, while others agreed with her.

Former 'Today Tonight' colleagues from those days say that the Workers' Party influence was at the root of it all. There were people on the programme who simply wanted to filter the news their way. They wanted to tell the story they *wished* was happening rather than what was actually happening. 'That really was the essence of the problem at "Today Tonight" in those days, big time,' says one person who observed what was going on.

While that Workers' Party influence was rarely overt, there were incidents. A team member walked back into the office at lunchtime one afternoon to collect a forgotten item and found a colleague placing copies of an *Irish Independent* editorial on their desks which was very much in tune with the Conor Cruise O'Brien/Workers' Party viewpoint. People on the programme regularly returned from breaks to find Workers' Party tracts on their desks. This was always done discreetly. It was unusual for anyone to be caught in the act, as on that occasion, and it was never clear whether the same person was distributing the other tracts.

It did not help Mary McAleese that a first cousin of hers, IRA man John Pickering, nicknamed 'Pickles', was in the H-Blocks at the time. He was serving a life sentence for murder and a further twenty-six year sentence for his part in a siege. The life sentence was for killing William Creighton, a seventy-one-year-old Protestant man who owned a filling station on Belfast's Lisburn Road. On 19 August 1976 his filling station was raided by four men and he was shot dead when he resisted. A bomb was placed there and when it exploded the British army were quickly at the scene. Two of the four men escaped and were followed to a nearby house where they were soon under siege. They held an elderly man hostage there, but were captured. One of the men was John Pickering. The leader of John Pickering's IRA active service unit was Kieran Doherty, who would die during the H-Block hunger strikes on 2 August 1981. He had been elected TD for Cavan-Monaghan in the Republic's June 1981 general election. John Pickering began his hunger strike on 7 September 1981. He would be the very last of the hunger strikers to accept food, over a month later.

The fact that she had a first cousin in the H-Blocks was something that Mary McAleese was very troubled about. She had no time for what he stood for and less for what he had done. In all of his seventeen years in prison she never once visited John Pickering. Indeed, before he was jailed she had met him at a funeral where she was overheard to ask him about his job plans and when he said he was 'a freedom fighter' she let him know just what she thought of so-called freedom fighters and what she thought of their version of freedom. She told him it would be more in his line if he got a job to help his mother raise her other eleven children and not have her continue to risk her health as she was doing.

It also irritated her that people could be so stupid as to deduce that because one of her sixty first cousins in Belfast had done what he did, and because he held a particular political view, she must share such views too. She was close to John Pickering's mother, her aunt Bridget Pickering. A warm, generous woman, she worked all her life as a cleaner in St Joseph's Teacher Training College near her home in Andersonstown. She had no time for her son's politics or his membership of the IRA. She was also fiercely opposed to the hunger strikes. She was the first person ever to stand up at a meeting of hunger strikers' parents and lambast what they were doing. That took a lot of courage. Some of the parents were made an offer by the authorities that if their hunger striking sons lapsed into unconsciousness they would be given an opportunity to have them force-fed. Bridget Pickering said that if that happened to John she most certainly would avail of the opportunity. There was uproar. Her windows were broken by Provo supporters.

Joe Mulholland grew up in Stranorlar in east Donegal and went to Finn College, a secondary school that was both co-educational and ecumenical. After various jobs in Ireland and England, he began work on 'Féach', the RTÉ Irish language current affairs programme, with Eoghan Harris, Prionsias MacAonghusa, Breandán Ó hEithir and Eamon Ó Muirí. It was where he came into contact for the first time with Eoghan Harris's thinking.

The programme team 'were a group of almost subversives'. He felt 'the odd man out. Like a duck out of water. This was my political education. I was getting to know Irish politics and culture. Donegal was very isolated. With hindsight, I hadn't a clue about politics in Ireland.'

In 1980 he was offered the post of assistant controller but opted to remain at programming's coal face and was charged with overhauling television current affairs at RTÉ. It was to be 'utterly changed'. Front-of-house presenters were crucially important, he felt. Such presenters 'defined the programme, determined its credibility and authority, as in the old "7 Days" where you had David Thornley, Brian Farrell, and John O'Donoghue.' He wanted a similar team to front what was to become 'Today Tonight'. 'Unfortunately Mary McAleese became a casualty. I decided she was not strong enough. It had nothing to do with her politics. I don't think I was that politically aware at the time. Probably left of centre, due to the "Féach" team.'' Instead of Mary McAleese he appointed Olivia O'Leary, Barry Cowan and Brian Farrell as his team of presenters. Later there was also Pat Kenny.

'It must have been quite difficult for Mary McAleese, thinking back. I certainly didn't handle any of this with a lot of the sensitivity which, with experience and age, one would have done. It was not easy. It wasn't easy for a very intelligent woman like her. No doubt, from that point of view it was difficult. But I emphasise, politics had nothing to do with it. I had no idea what Mary McAleese's politics were.'

He had never been a member of the Workers' Party but was 'ferociously anti-violence'. Because of his Donegal background he would have 'a huge sensitivity' to ordinary Protestant people. He had made a programme in the early 1970s about former Harland and Wolf dockers from East Belfast and had also made a documentary titled 'The Sash My Father Wore' about the Orange Order 'to show they hadn't two heads. I might have been naïve but it was hugely criticised by nationalists here [the Republic].' Above all he was 'utterly opposed to violence and what the Provisional IRA were doing.' But he is not sure 'whether one paid enough attention to nationalist feelings in the 1980s. Thinking back I could have been more sensitive to the nationalist position but I was determined current affairs would not be used as a propaganda weapon for violence. That applied to the hunger strikes.' He believed that a full range of views was represented among the programme team, including those of the Workers' Party, but that 'the general view of presenters and reporters was that there should be no truck with violence.'

There were also the limits applied by Section 31 of the Broadcasting Act which banned interviews with paramilitaries. They tried to get rid of it, and despite its provisions, had, for instance, interviewed Owen Carron, Bobby Sands election agent 'under the guise of his being a Catholic nationalist' during the April 1981 Fermanagh/South Tyrone by-election campaign. Carron would stand for the seat vacated on the death of Bobby Sands. Barry Cowan also did a report on the H-Blocks 'which was not totally propaganda or one-sided. Such was the climate at that time, flags everywhere, it could easily have become a disaster.' He has 'huge respect' for the governments of the 70s – Cosgrave, Lynch and Hillery, and later Garret FitzGerald. Those were 'hugely difficult times, extremely emotional.' He recalled that in his early years at RTÉ many there were sympathetic to the republican cause. He was 'not sympathetic. Violence was going nowhere.'

He shared certain of the Workers' Party views, 'that bombing working-class Protestants of Northern Ireland was not going to serve anything. But I was totally opposed to any illegality in which they [Workers' Party] might be involved. These were also the views of the establishment here and of the SDLP and Alliance in Northern Ireland.'

'Today Tonight' 'certainly presented the Protestant view. Harold McCusker was always available. Ken Maginnis was another who provided the decent Protestant view.' John Cushnahan another. They also had Fr Denis Faul, Fr Raymond Murray, Fr Des Wilson on the programme, who probably felt it was too much on the Protestant side. 'Maybe we didn't get it right against the background of murder and violence, but it is easy to be wise after the event,' he says. But he 'deeply felt that unless we understood their [Protestant] views you could not foster trust. It was difficult to do so with bombs and guns going off. It was the only way forward, as it has turned out to be, and only when the violence stopped.'

'Today Tonight' meetings were 'extremely open forums' which sometimes went on for hours and where whole programmes were reviewed. 'I suppose I never had communications with Mary McAleese, the way things happened. I suppose it was my fault I didn't have the sensitivity and that I didn't understand where she was coming from. I do understand in the atmosphere on the programme how she might feel the way she did. It was a time of unprecedented violence and atrocity. It was kind of difficult to hold an anti-violence line and to stay censorious in the other direction. Section 31 was a very blunt instrument, which allowed no nuance. I felt I was acting out of integrity and concern for the island of Ireland and where it was going. I was determined that one of the most popular current affairs programmes ever wouldn't become an instrument to excuse hunger strikes and violent republicanism. I was implacably opposed to the Provisional IRA.' Yet when the peace process started 'and John Hume showed me on the back of an envelope what he was telling Gerry Adams, I applauded it.' And 'once Section 31 was done away with I took the view that Provisional Sinn Féin should be welcomed as comprehensively as possible.' Later, as RTÉ director of news, he 'opened channels to the Provisional IRA, but didn't tell the upper echelons at RTÉ, who would have been nervous about such things.' His own attitude to Provisional Sinn Féin was based on his attitude to violence, which he saw as 'futile, destructive, unfair, counterproductive.'

'Because of the overall atmosphere arising from my own attitude, I can well see how it wasn't a very congenial place for her [Mary McAleese] to work. She was from the North and I, to my discredit, didn't talk to her about the North. We didn't discuss it. I took the view that the programme was very open. I don't remember Mary McAleese having a great input or whether she had decided to withdraw. It is easy to be wise after the event. One would be more sensitive again. It was a tough time for anyone working in current affairs. It wasn't easy. But it is hurtful to hear someone was so unhappy.'

He has met Mary McAleese since but they have not discussed those days. She wrote to him in 2002 to congratulate him on winning a Donegal Person of the Year award. He wrote back to thank her and expressed the hope she would run for a second term as President. 'I have nothing but respect for her presidency. She has done a terrific job. She is such a people person. It makes one think that one missed an opportunity. But what's done is done and cannot be undone.'

Mary McAleese had been speaking to friends about leaving RTÉ and this was heard on the grapevine by Professor Heuston, her former boss in the Law Department at Trinity College. He wanted her to come back. She agreed and returned there in the autumn of 1981, to be as warmly welcomed as a prodigal daughter. She continued to do part-time work with other programmes at RTÉ, in both radio and TV. For television she worked on a programme called 'Europa' with people such as Conor Brady and Michael Ryan, who were co-presenters. Noel Smyth produced. The atmosphere was similar to what it had been on 'Frontline' – collaborative and very respectful of one another.

Conor Brady remembers her as 'a person with a very strong sense of her own independence. She wasn't going to fit in with any of the stereotypes that some of the RTÉ factions liked to identify. She knew that people were very anxious to label her but she was such a mixture of differing views and convictions that it wasn't really possible. She knew that this baffled and irritated some people and she didn't care one whit.' As a colleague he 'liked her enormously. She was great fun. I found she had a great sense of humour and she had the warmth that later became a defining characteristic of her presidency. She was patient and professional. Making TV programmes in those days was a slow, painstaking business. I always remember that even though we might be cheesed off at doing repeated takes late at night, she never showed the slightest impatience or discourtesy to the production staff, which is probably more than I could say for myself.'

They never discussed her 'Today Tonight' experiences at 'Europa', nor was her Northern, Catholic, nationalist background ever an issue there. 'Europa' was a monthly programme which examined cultural, political and social issues across Europe. Though her background was never an issue at 'Europa', Brady did observe that it might have been elsewhere in RTÉ. 'I noticed that if we went to the canteen for a coffee we weren't exactly swamped with people wanting to join us. RTÉ was deeply polarised politically. There were "closet" Provos and "closet" Stickies (Workers' Party supporters) who were basically socialist/internationalists who were virulently opposed to the narrow nationalism, as they saw it, of traditional thirty-two county Ireland people. Mary was seen as a product of her background and she didn't embrace the socialist/internationalist position. Many of those who held that position would also have been hostile to the Catholic Church – often with good reason. The fact that Mary worked with the bishops [at the New Ireland Forum in 1984] was gall and vinegar to some and she attracted a lot of hostility for that.'

She also did a lot of radio work at the time, everything from court reports, theatre and film reviews to current affairs, which gave her welcome flexibility. She continued to work during the summer at RTÉ until 1985 while also full-time at Trinity.

But her troubles with RTÉ journalist colleagues had not ended. On 2 February 1984 Mary McAleese appeared with the Catholic Church delegation at the New Ireland Forum. The Forum had been set up by then Taoiseach Garret FitzGerald at the instigation of John Hume, with a brief to look at ways in which lasting peace and stability might be made possible in a new Ireland. Those wishing to make submissions to the Forum could do so either in written or oral form. These were considered and those making oral submissions were then questioned in open session by politicians from Fianna Fáil, Fine Gael, the Labour Party and the SDLP at hearings in St Patrick's Hall, Dublin Castle. The Forum first sat on 30 May 1983 and published its report on 2 May 1984.

The Catholic Bishops' written submission to the Forum had not been well received. Its principal author was the irascible and very traditional Bishop of Limerick and former President of St Patrick's College Maynooth, Dr Jeremiah Newman. The bishops decided to make an oral submission as well, to 'clarify' matters in their written submission. At the end of January 1984 the then Archbishop of Dublin, the late Dr Dermot Ryan, invited Mary McAleese to join their delegation to the Forum. She agreed on condition that Bishop Newman was not part of the delegation and that she was not tied to the bishops' written submission. The delegation included Bishop Cahal Daly of the Down and Connor diocese in Northern Ireland, Bishop Joseph Cassidy of the Clonfert diocese in the West of Ireland, Bishop Edward Daly of Derry, Auxiliary Bishop of Dublin Dr Dermot O'Mahony, Fr Michael Ledwith, vice-president of St Patrick's College Maynooth, and Matthew Salter, a lecturer in Education at Queen's University Belfast.

At the hearing Mary McAleese spoke in favour of the separation of Church and State and of pluralism in society, where harmony in diversity was the ideal.

'The Church does not want a Catholic State for a Catholic people,' she said. 'The Church believes in marriage as a sacrament, as an indissoluble union, as a contract for life. It is entitled to hold that view and to preach that view to its flock. Its sole jurisdiction is in relation to its flock.' She continued, 'It does not seek to have any jurisdiction beyond that. It is not entitled to, nor does it seek to tell any government that the Catholic view of marriage should be enshrined in legislation because it is the Catholic view.' It had the right to comment and state its views, but not to dictate. On integrated education and in answer to a question from Senator Mary Robinson on the rights of minorities, she said there was a suggestion this referred to the constitutional ban on divorce and that it was 'a pity that civil and religious liberty almost invariably revolves around solely the question of divorce because certainly if divorce and contraception are to be seen as the hallmarks of a liberal society then Northern Ireland was a very liberal, pluralist society a long time ago.' Her strongest statement was on interdenominational schools. 'The notion that consensus comes from contact or even that understanding comes from contact is wrong. It is a dubious and simplistic notion ... I myself lived in an area, which is often described as a flashpoint area, known as Ardoyne. It was a mixed area as I was growing up. I had tremendous contact with Protestant neighbours, played with them. They were in and out of my home, but it did not stop one of them from becoming a member of the UDA and now doing a life sentence for killing five Catholics.' A Catholic education 'arises in the context, not out of a desire to create a sectarian education system but out of a genuine desire to extend the home vision, the vision of a Catholic way, the way of life simply to the school,' she said. 'I have very grave doubts from my own direct experience about the ability of the school to break down sectarian prejudice.'

Her appearance with the bishops at the Forum did not go down well with some colleagues at RTÉ. In March 1984, a month after her appearance, a special meeting of the Broadcasting Branch of the National Union of Journalists was convened to discuss a motion calling for her suspension from the union on the grounds that two-thirds of her income was not from journalism – a criterion for NUJ membership. In a letter read at the meeting, she pointed out that she had no problem with the NUJ rule, but did not understand why she was the only one in her situation at RTÉ being called to task by the Branch. It was pointed out that Brian Farrell was in a similar position to her, but he was not being called to account. No one else in the same situation at RTÉ was. Her membership of the NUJ was suspended, but she continued to work there.

In an *Irish Times* interview in February 1986, almost two years later, she said she had 'no doubt whatever about it' when asked if some officers of the NUJ were prejudiced against the Catholic Church. 'It could be that there is a personal prejudice against me but my opinion is that if I had gone to the Forum with a Church of Ireland or with a Jewish delegation there would not be a word about it.' In the same article the then chairman of the NUJ

Broadcasting Branch, Patrick Kinsella, dismissed what she said as groundless. Questioned about the Brian Farrell case he agreed that 'yes, there are anomalies' when it came to the NUJ rule and some who worked at RTÉ. Mary McAleese wrote to him to correct the inaccuracy. 'You were not correct when you said there were anomalies. There is just one anomaly – and I am it.'

She has since said, 'It was a case of absolute bigotry. I was given no opportunity to defend myself at that meeting. I am convinced that the whole issue arose out of my appearance with the bishops at the New Ireland Forum. It was a disgraceful act on the part of those who initiated it. The worst aspect of it is that nothing was ever done to rectify the situation, or to bring it to a proper conclusion.' She is still suspended from membership of the NUJ.

Her faith is very important to her and is rooted in her sense of being Irish. She has said that for a good part of her life it was 'chosen for me' but somewhere along the way she made a conscious decision to stay with it. Where Irish history is concerned for her, as for a majority of Irish Catholics, there can be no doubt that past experience of being a Catholic in Ireland as lived by antecedents has left a deep impression on the living generation which underscores their sense of identity. As Northern nationalists will tell you, it is a strand which is hard to untwist. A deep sense of justice has been forged out of an experience which saw seven million out of the eight million who once lived on this island treated abominably. It cost generations of them dearly.

'A Good Recruit'

In 1984, Mary McAleese was asked by Fianna Fáil women to address a conference in Galway, at which Charles J Haughey was guest of honour. As part of her speech, she spoke about the miscarriage of justice case of the Maguire Seven.

Shortly afterwards she was approached by two members of Fianna Fáil to ask if she would consider joining the party and running for election. The two men who approached her were Liam Lawlor and Frank Dunlop. She told them she would discuss it with her husband, Martin. They brought a message from Charles Haughey to say that he thought she would be a good recruit to Fianna Fáil, a good candidate in the future and that, if she was mindful to have a political career, they would encourage her. If she was interested they would talk about the right kind of positioning and cumann. She talked to Martin about it and they decided to give it a try.

She had already been approached by Fine Gael but decided against. Former Fine Gael TD, and later a member of the Progressive Democrats party, Michael Keating, made the approach. She had a lot of regard for him but she realised her natural affinity lay elsewhere. It might also have been because her first experience of government in Dublin was the coalition government of 1972 to 1977, which involved Conor Cruise O'Brien who was not perceived as sympathetic to Northern Ireland nationalists. It soured her attitude to the Labour Party. Her father had been a leader in the trade union movement before he became a publican. Her politics fell somewhere between Fianna Fáil and Labour but she could not get her head around the Irish Labour

Party's bizarre twist on history as enunciated by Conor Cruise O'Brien. She couldn't see herself as a member of that party, although there were people for whom she had great respect in the party, for example, Dick Spring and his leadership. While there were some very good people in the Labour Party, in government they managed to switch off any interest she may have had in them in terms of active party politics.

So she joined the Fianna Fáil Markievicz Cumann in the Dublin South-East constituency and became active there. She spoke at meetings and was involved in various committees. She didn't support the 1985 Anglo-Irish Agreement negotiated by Taoiseach Garret FitzGerald with British Prime Minister Margaret Thatcher. Fianna Fáil was opposed to it, too, and Charles Haughey said the party would try to change it if returned to power. Senator Mary Robinson resigned from the Labour Party in protest at the Agreement, as she felt it didn't have broad enough support. It didn't have unionist support. There were too many people excluded. Although history would show that it was a very important step, but as something that was going to work and as a framework that was going to stick and hold, Mary McAleese knew that it was never going to happen because 'the people who were obliged to work it had not bought into it. And they hadn't been asked to buy into it.' That was the problem. Garret FitzGerald was right when he said that it moved the debate on very considerably. People learnt from it and when it came to the Good Friday Agreement 'so many recognised that there had to be a buy-in from a very wide constituency. There was a learning element that has been profoundly useful in the long run.' It was a wake-up call to a lot of people in Northern Ireland about what was coming down the line. 'Ironically many of those who didn't buy into it subsequently bought into something which was

**MARY
McALEESE**

DÁIL CANDIDATE
DUBLIN SOUTH-EAST

Please Vote 1, 2, 3, and 4 in order of your choice for Fianna Fáil Candidates — Gerard Brady T.D., Cllr. Michael Donnelly, **MARY McALEESE** and Cllr. Eoin Ryan.

Thank You For Your Support on Feb. 17th.

Dublin South-East election campaign poster

considerably more advanced, and that was the Good Friday Agreement. Particularly the unionist side,' she says.

In 1986 she opposed the Single European Act (SEA), as did Charles Haughey. He feared it would have negative implications for Ireland's neutrality and its native industries. Mary McAleese opposed it because she felt it would encroach on the sovereign powers of the Irish people in the formulation of foreign policy and because it was to be ratified by the Dáil and not by referendum.

At a convention in early 1986 she did not succeed in being selected as a Fianna Fáil candidate for the Dublin South-East constituency, but when a general election was called for 17 February 1987, the party's national executive announced that she and Councillor Eoin Ryan were being added to the Fianna Fáil ticket there. It was a four-seat constituency where the incumbent Fianna Fáil TD was Ger Brady. It was also the constituency of outgoing Taoiseach Garret FitzGerald and outgoing Minister for Labour Ruairí Quinn of the Labour Party. Fine Gael's Joe Doyle held the fourth seat.

She had no expectation of winning the seat; it was about trying to establish a presence. She was parachuted in. She has said since that she would never allow such a thing again. It is such an untidy way to go into politics. There was a young woman coming up through that constituency at the time and she didn't get through the nomination procedure because Mary McAleese was parachuted in. That was Mary Hanafin, who was born and reared in Fianna Fáil. Mary McAleese says she was not happy about that. It was not a pleasant thing to have been part of. She knows that this is a part of politics and that people make judgment calls and leaders have to make tough decisions, but at a human level she doesn't like it.

But she enjoyed most of that election campaign, especially the canvass. She didn't like the fact that, in a multi-seat constituency such as Dublin South East, you could be so much at odds with party colleagues. There were strains then, not between candidates who got on well, but there were strains between supporters of each candidate. She received 2,243 first preferences, placing her seventh out of sixteen candidates on the first count. Garret FitzGerald was elected first, followed by Ger Brady and Ruairí Quinn. She was eliminated after the eleventh count and the last seat went to Michael McDowell of the Progressive Democrats.

She wasn't disappointed. 'I was pleased with the outcome, but the process itself started to shape my view of a life in politics. There were other things. Martin had graduated and moved into a dental practice in Northern Ireland, first as an assistant and then he was offered a partnership. And if he went down that road to make his professional life in Northern Ireland it had implications for the family. By then we had three small children and had to decide whether he was going to continue to commute up and down, which he was doing, at a lot of physical and emotional cost,' she says. To be closer to where he worked, they moved to Rostrevor, County Down.

But she continued her opposition to the Single European Act. Though a deeply committed supporter of the EU, Mary McAleese agreed to join the campaign against ratification of the SEA with well-known Euro-sceptics such as Anthony Coughlan and Raymond Crotty. She and John Carroll of the Irish Transport and General Workers' Union became joint chairs of the Constitutional Rights Committee. By then the SEA had been ratified in all other EU member states. The FitzGerald government had been anxious that ratification in Ireland be done by New Year's Day 1987. The Constitutional Rights Committee, however, made an application to the High Court seeking an injunction preventing the Dáil from ratifying the SEA before Christmas 1986. The injunction was granted on Christmas Eve, placing Ireland in a now familiar position as the EU member State which prevented implementation of an EU Treaty.

On 18 February 1987, the day after the general election, the High Court decided that the Constitutional Rights Committee case for a referendum had no basis in law and that the Dáil was free to ratify the SEA. The Court did, however, allow for an appeal to the Supreme Court.

Charles Haughey was returned to power and changed his stance on both the Anglo-Irish Agreement and the Single European Act. He received a visit from the then President of the EU Commission, Jacques Delors, chequebook in hand and offering largesse to Ireland. Soon Mr Haughey had become an enthusiast for the Single European Act and wanted its immediate ratification by the Dáil.

However, the Constitutional Rights Committee went ahead with their appeal to the Supreme Court which, in early April 1987, decided in favour of a referendum on the Single European Act. RTÉ came to the Committee looking for a spokesman or woman to take part in a programme on the SEA and the Supreme Court decision. The late *Sunday Independent* journalist Veronica Guerin had become involved with the campaign in disillusionment at Charles Haughey's volte face, though a long-time Haughey supporter herself. She had been handling publicity for the Committte and told them that RTÉ had said to her it would accept any spokesperson for them '... but not Mary McAleese'.

The referendum took place on 24 May and was passed overwhelmingly. But Charles Haughey remained displeased with his former protégé. Just prior to the referendum he was asked by a *Sunday Tribune* reporter about what was described as the obvious disagreement between himself and 'one prominent member of the party clearly not following the party line' on the SEA. Charles Haughey's caustic response was '… did you say "prominent"?'

Mary McAleese found Haughey very polished, but in an arched way. In dealing with him you would always be aware that you were dealing not with an equal, but a superior. 'He was the boss. He always had that aura of leadership. He was always friendly and funny,' she comments. She wasn't close enough to him to see what kind of lifestyle he lived. There were stories doing the rounds but they didn't over-exercise her. She didn't know, anymore than anyone else. 'I was in Kinsealy once … and did a brief interview with Maureen Haughey, who I found to be a lovely lady who couldn't have been nicer.'

President and Dr Martin McAleese sympathise with Maureen Haughey and her family at the funeral of former Taoiseach Charles Haughey in 2006

Becoming Mrs McAleese

Belfast, 19 March 2008. The President and Martin McAleese were chatting with reporters as an RTÉ camera crew set up for an interview. Just moments earlier in the Black and White Hall of the Lanyon Building at Queen's University, Queen Elizabeth II of Britain and President McAleese had met publicly for the first time on the island of Ireland. The occasion was the centenary of the university. Queen Elizabeth unveiled a centenary stone in the Black and White Hall to mark the occasion. It was inscribed with a specially commissioned stanza by poet Seamus Heaney, who was also present along with approximately 100 other dignitaries. The lines read:

Still red brickwork
Remains our bulwark
Here exercise
Of mind has stood
To us, for us
These hundred years
And will, for good.

As the President waited for the camera crew to be ready, the mauve flowers on a eucalyptus tree beginning to bloom behind her, Martin commented jokingly '… this is where she chased me … almost forty years ago.' She nodded in his direction with a 'would-ya-just-listen-to-yer-man' look. They are an

Mary and Martin at a
dinner dance in 1970

extraordinarily close couple, though never lovey dovey. Many of her football jokes at public functions that he attends with her are directed at him, or his county, Antrim. She also frequently issues dire warnings to other counties about her own dear Down, though why remains a mystery to all but herself, as that team has rarely risen to meet her expectations.

She and Martin began going out together when they were teenagers. Martin first saw her at a debate in St Dominic's where she was speaking. He has said he 'fell in love with Mary that evening. I was sure she was the girl I wanted to spend my life with, and I was never more sure of anything in my life.' But not so with her. She was more interested in his friend, Peter O'Keeffe, and invited both to her eighteenth birthday party at 657 Crumlin Road, as they were always together and she was sure Peter wouldn't go unless she asked Martin also. However, it was Martin McAleese who made the biggest impression at that party and by the end of the night they had agreed their first date. It was the beginning of a relationship that was frequently turbulent, with its break-ups and get-togethers and, not infrequently, with her own family taking Martin's side against her. He was constant. She less so.

Martin's family lived on the Albertbridge Road in Protestant east Belfast. His father, Charlie, was from Portglenone, County Antrim and his mother, Emma McElgunn, was from Lisnaskea in County Fermanagh. They met and married in Derry where Charlie worked with Short Brothers and Harland, an aircraft manufacturing firm. When he was transferred to the firm's main factory in Belfast the couple moved there. The factory, whose workforce was almost entirely Protestant, was located in east Belfast and, being unfamiliar with the sectarian demographics of that city, Charlie and Emma found themselves living there among Protestants, many of them loyalist. Charlie worked a six-and-a-half-day week, with a half day off on Saturdays.

Martin attended primary school at Ballyhackmore and secondary school at St Mary's Christian Brothers at the bottom of the Falls Road. There were five McAleese children. Martin, the second eldest, was born on 24 March 1951. They grew up in an atmosphere that was full of fear, intimidation and sectarianism, combined with a great sense of marginalisation and isolation. They were made aware that they were second-class citizens. This was long before the Troubles began in 1968/69.

Going to school, even at the age of four and five, the children would be verbally abused. Terms like 'Fenian bastard' would be thrown at them. They were spat upon. His parents were ridiculed about contraception and about the Pope. They, too, were spat on. They would be afraid to go to the shop

Young Martin

around the corner. What it taught was great street wisdom. You would never turn back when you walked down the street. You learned when to cross the road and go down the other side. You knew when to take a right or left turn. You developed a keen sense of anticipation and of how to handle certain situations on the street. Martin was often involved in fights and had to run away. The children did the 11-plus at a Protestant primary school locally, as was the practice at the time for Catholic children. So they went into a totally alien environment. He failed the exam but has insisted that the circumstances were not a factor. But the fact that you couldn't even go to your own comfortable school to do the exam was very stressful. When Martin went to the Christian Brothers, he felt very conscious of the uniform and tried to hide the badge. He would bring a hurley stick to school, which itself was difficult to hide. His first twenty years were laced with that type of thing.

What that sort of atmosphere did was to make you keep your head down well below the parapet. You tried to fade into the background and become unnoticed, walk away and avoid things. It contributed to a lack of confidence. Martin McAleese has been very conscious of that where his own kids are concerned. Having confidence, developing confidence, is one of the greatest things you can have at that age. The young McAleeses of East Belfast had it driven out of them. It was tribal. There were no friendships. You could never have a conversation about anything there.

During that time there were two things to which Martin clung, to preserve a sense of identity. Those were the GAA and the Catholic Church. His whole life as a young man revolved around the GAA. He joined the O'Donovan Rossa GAA club. At sixteen he was playing minor football for Antrim and did so in 1968 and 1969 as well, by which time he was the minor team captain. In 1967 he played at under-16 and under-21, as well as on junior and senior sides for the O'Donovan Rossa club, usually in midfield, sometimes centre-half forward, sometimes centre-half back. He was also doing well at school and secured A levels in physics, chemistry, pure mathematics and applied mathematics. He continued his footballing at Queen's where he studied physics, and in 1971 was on the Queen's team which won the Sigerson Cup, the highlight of his playing career.

Back home in the heartland of Loyalist east Belfast the intimidation continued. The McAleese family had to have grilles fitted on the windows, front and back, and for at least the last six months of living on Albertbridge Road one of them had to stay up all night in case a petrol bomb came through the front window or over the backyard wall. One night was particularly bad. There had been a lot of activity in the streets and the family was very frightened. Martin went down to the local RUC station. He knocked at the counter and told the policeman that the family was having huge problems and that they were terrified. He was laughed at. He walked out, feeling like nothing, and when he got home he had to tell them that nobody was coming to help.

The McAleeses lost their home the night internment was introduced in Northern Ireland, Monday 9 August 1971. Martin was on a summer job in Blackpool at the time. His mother and father, two brothers and sister were in the house. People were very tense that day. A mob of loyalists arrived at the back and the front door. They gave the McAleeses five minutes to leave. The police arrived. Charlie McAleese asked the police if they could help them retrieve some of their belongings. There was no help. So they gathered two suitcases and left. Charlie McAleese said later that they were lucky that all that was thrown after them were insults and curses. The house was ransacked. The McAleeses were dispersed among extended family for a few months and eventually were offered an alternative house in Rathcoole, a place as dangerous for Catholics as east Belfast. It was where a lot of Protestants ended up as a result of the redevelopment of the Lower Shankill. The McAleeses spent two and a half years there and eventually had to leave that house too. It was in Rathcoole that Martin's younger brother Kevin was attacked. He was eleven at the time and on his way home from school when he was jumped on by a gang who attempted to scrape the letters UVF on his arm with a broken bottle. It was a very difficult time for the family.

Eventually they got another house near Finaghy. When they left the house in Rathcoole the McAleeses consciously decided to start life anew. They would not refer back to those childhood days. There were so many bad memories and the things that happened to their father and mother were such that they never recovered. Even now, memories of their childhood remain obscured and masked by an over arching ambiance of intimidation and fear and suspicion.

But it is ironic. It seems sometimes that in life everything has a purpose. Because some thirty-three years later when Martin McAleese met the inner council of the UDA their conversation centred on their turf. Sitting around a table they talked the street talk – the pubs, the clubs, the YMCA hall, the shops, the schools, the churches and all the geography of east Belfast. His street cred was beyond doubt in their eyes. The greatest asset he brought to that first meeting with them in 2003 was the experiences of those first twenty years of his life, which he had pushed away, but which came to have a huge impact on the type of work he would do.

He secured an honours Physics degree at Queen's but then decided he wanted to do accountancy. When he graduated in 1972 he went straight to Dublin and joined the Stokes, Kennedy, Crowley accountancy firm. In autumn 1974 he began working at the firm's Belfast office. By the following February he and Mary Leneghan had split up again, this time apparently irrevocably. Meanwhile, just the previous month, January 1975, the Leneghan family had moved to Rostrevor where Paddy Leneghan had bought the Corner

House pub in November 1974.

In the summer of 1975 Mary Leneghan began going out with Rory McShane, who was older than her and had been very active in civil rights and student union politics at Queens. From Neigh, just outside Newry, he was a founder member of People's Democracy and was on the executive of the Northern Ireland Civil Rights Association. He was a high profile figure in Northern Ireland during the late 1960s. He graduated from Queen's in 1968 and had left before Mary Leneghan began there. By the time they met, in the summer of 1975, he was practising as a solicitor. They met at the courthouse in Newry and he invited her to lunch. It went from there. The word 'whirlwind' seems inadequate to describe the pace of events that followed, but she was engaged to Rory McShane within three months of breaking off with Martin McAleese after a six-year relationship. Hearing the news, Martin has said, 'I was destroyed. I couldn't believe what I heard. Within three months of leaving me, she was engaged to another man. It was very hard to take.'

He decided to brazen it out. Pretend nothing had happened. That he wasn't in the least bothered. They bumped into one another on a Belfast street in mid-July. He wished her and Rory well. She said they were going to honeymoon in Italy. He said he was heading to Tenerife with friends. They talked for about ten minutes, by which time Martin was convinced he would get her back, not through anything she said, but by her body language, the things left unsaid. Even then he could read her like a book, he has said. That meeting was a fateful episode which 'bounced her back from whatever sort of catatonic trance she was in'. But not just yet! Mary Leneghan had applied for the post of Reid Professor of Law at Trinity and was determined to live in Dublin. Rory McShane would not consider leaving his busy solicitors' practice in Newry. She would not let him buy her an engagement ring. In September 1975, and three weeks before she was due to marry Rory McShane, she was questioned, very closely and very honestly, by her friend Jo Thompson about what she intended to do. She became upset. Jo called Claire Leneghan. 'And who says you have to go ahead with the wedding. Who says you have to if you don't want to … Come on home, Mary, and we'll talk about it,' said her mother. And she did. Everything had been arranged. Priest, chapel and hotel had been booked and the invitations sent out, presents received, honeymoon arranged. By that night the wedding was off.

To show that they were still friends, Mary Leneghan and Rory McShane went ahead with plans they had made for that October to host a Hallowe'en party for family and friends at the Rostrevor cottage where they had intended to live. The day following that party Paddy Leneghan had a bad heart attack and was taken to Daisy Hill hospital in Newry. It was a week before Martin McAleese heard about this. He was very fond of Paddy, not least as he had been such a help to the McAleese family when they were put out of their house in August 1971. He went to see him at Daisy Hill. Claire and some of the younger Leneghan children were there. She invited him back to Rostrevor for dinner. 'Look who's here for dinner, Mary,' she announced into the kitchen on arrival. Mary embraced him. They have not turned back since. A party had been planned by friends of Mary for the following night. The Leneghan children pleaded with Martin to stay over with them for it. He did. At that party he and Mary did some talking. They danced to 'their' song, Simon and Garfunkel's 'Bridge Over Troubled Waters'. Before Martin left

Wedding day, 9 March, 1976

Rostrevor on that visit he and Mary Leneghan were engaged and they had set a date for their wedding, 9 March 1976.

They planned to have the reception at the Golden Pheasant in Lisburn. It was owned by two brothers from Ardoyne, Tony and Myles O'Reilly, who were old friends of Mary Leneghan. It was to be a small wedding, seventy or eighty guests. 'I can't imagine your mother being satisfied with a wedding of that size ... I know your mother,' Myles said to Mary. He pencilled in the date but said if the numbers grew and they had to change later, there would be no problem. And they had to change later. As the guest list became ever longer they had to seek a bigger venue and ended up booking the Ardmore hotel in Newry, which was owned by the Scallon family, one of whom, Damien, would later marry Eurovision winner, later MEP and presidential candidate, Dana.

Martin and Mary were married in the Star of the Sea church in Rostrevor. The reception was a huge success, but, as the evening wore on, the couple noticed a shift in mood among guests. And there was unusual pressure from the families to get them on the road to begin their honeymoon. It was strange. Some people seemed to be crying. As they were leaving, Claire Leneghan advised them to go off and enjoy themselves and not to be depressing themselves with newspapers or watching the news for the following fortnight. They were at Drogheda before Mary McAleese remarked on what a strange thing it was for her mother to say. They were on their way to Kerry, but would first spend a night at Sachs hotel in Dublin, which was owned by Hugh Tunney, for whom Martin had done some accountancy work.

By then Mary was very anxious about what had been really going on as they left the wedding reception. She rang home. Her sister Claire answered. 'Is Mammy sick? Did Daddy have another heart attack?' she asked, adding that she knew something was wrong and that if they didn't tell her she was going home. And Claire told her that Tony and Myles O'Reilly had both been killed that day. Three UVF gunmen entered their Golden Pheasant restaurant and ordered everyone – thirteen people – into the storeroom. They then forced the two brothers to crawl out on their hands and knees. Four shots were heard and a few moments later the building shook as an explosion went off. Those in the storeroom, in defiance of the gunmen's orders, ran for their lives. Had they not done so they too would have been killed in the second explosion which demolished the building. The bodies of the O'Reilly brothers were later found in the rubble. Part way through Claire's story Mary McAleese fell back in her chair and the phone fell from her hand. She had difficulty breathing. Now she understood why the O'Reillys hadn't made it to the wedding. Martin heard the remainder of Claire's story while simultaneously attending to his young wife. She wanted to go home. He would do whatever she wanted, he said. But the Leneghans were adamant that the pair should continue with their honeymoon. So they deliberated and deliberated and decided to carry on to Kerry, but it was useless. She was distraught. And there in Killarney, as they had breakfast one morning in the Aghadoe Heights hotel, they heard on the news that the Ardmore hotel in Newry had itself been damaged by a bomb. Mary McAleese would describe those two weeks as 'our honeymoon from hell'. A member of the UVF was later sentenced to two

The O'Reilly brothers. Myles (left) and Tony (right) were murdered on the McAleese's wedding day, 9 March 1976. The President keeps their picture in her office

life terms for the murder of the O'Reilly brothers. The trial judge described the crime as 'among the most abominable committed by terrorists in recent years.'

On holiday in Florida some years later the McAleeses met members of the Clubsound band, Protestants, who were staying at the same resort. In conversation with Ann McKnight, wife of one of the band members, Mary McAleese was telling her about the events surrounding her honeymoon when Ann McKnight began to cry. It turned out that on the day after Tony and Myles O'Reilly had been murdered, her father was drinking in the Homestead Inn pub near Lisburn when two men burst in and began shooting indiscriminately. Ann's father, Robert Dorman, was killed and six people were wounded. The killers shouted that the shooting was in retaliation for the murder of the O'Reilly brothers. A man was later tried and convicted for Robert Dorman's murder, and for membership of the IRA.

When she married, Mary McAleese was lecturing at Trinity College. For the first months of their marriage the couple were together only at the weekends, in a house they had bought at Eglantine Avenue in Belfast. Martin applied for and was successful in securing a post as financial controller of the Aer Lingus travel subsidiary Blueskies, based at Westmoreland Street in Dublin and began work there in January 1977. He and Mary rented a house in Rathfarnham while selling their home in Belfast. Eventually they bought a house at Mooretown, in the countryside between Dunshaughlin and Ratoath in County Meath. They named the house 'Rostrevor'.

In 1978 Martin McAleese became financial controller of Enterprise Travel which comprised ten Belfast travel agents in consortium with Aer Lingus. Its headquarters was in Belfast, but it had an office in Dublin.

But Martin was restless. In the spring of 1980 he decided to change careers; he wanted to do dentistry. He and Mary discussed it and she encouraged him, though it would mean them living on her salary for his four years at Trinity while he studied. He was allowed a year off the five-year course because of his Physics degree from Queen's. He began his studies at TCD in October 1980, the second oldest in a class of twenty-nine. Their first child, Emma Claire, named after her two grandmothers, was born at Mount Carmel hospital in Dublin on 21 September 1982. Six weeks later Mary McAleese was back at work, but exhausted. Emma accompanied them to the crèche in Trinity each morning, but then there was a strike. Charlie McAleese was now living alone at Finaghy in Belfast as his wife Emma had

Martin's graduation as a dentist, TCD, November, 1984

died. He was lonely, so they decided to kill two birds with one stone and asked him would he stay with them for a while where he could also look after Emma. He did so and returned to Belfast a few months later. They missed him and asked him to come to live with them fulltime. He agreed and was with them until his death in Áras an Uachtaráin, eighteen years later.

In early autumn 1984 Mary McAleese discovered she was expecting twins. Her aunt, Bridget Pickering had twins after her tenth child. Mary was their godmother. By then Martin was coming to the end of his dentistry course in Trinity. He had arranged to work as an associate dentist with Des Casey in Bessbrook, County Armagh, with the intention of getting sufficient experience to secure a position in the Republic. After four months Des Casey offered him partnership in his practice and Martin accepted. Shortly afterwards they opened the first permanent dental practice in Crossmaglen, hometown of then Catholic primate Cardinal Tomás Ó Fiaich.

Martin spent two days a week in Bessbrook where a large proportion of his patients were Protestant and Unionist. His Crosssmaglen patients were Catholic and nationalist. With the Protestant patients the conversation tended to be superficial, about irrelevant things like the weather and football matches, to be sure of not giving offence, even inadvertently. There was no engagement with the hard things of politics. In Crossmaglen the conversation covered all grounds, including politics. Martin has since concluded that this was one of the problems with the Northern Ireland issue. People tended to have a superficial or dishonest conversation with perceived stereotypes of the other side rather than engage fully with the real human being. Even today he feels there is still a lot of work to do in that area, because those superficial relationships can feed on ill-informed misconceptions of each other. They can keep reinforcing prejudices.

It was a busy practice and Martin rented a house at Warrenpoint where he stayed when too exhausted to face the journey to Meath. It was from there that Mary was taken to Daisy Hill hospital in Newry for the delivery of twins Sara and Justin on 6 April 1985. She spent her maternity leave there too, just miles from the Leneghan clan in nearby Rostrevor. By the time Martin left the practice it had thousands of patients, who came from every county on this island. The significance of this widespread patient base became

Mary with twins Justin and Sara at Daisy Hill Hospital, Newry, 6 April, 1985

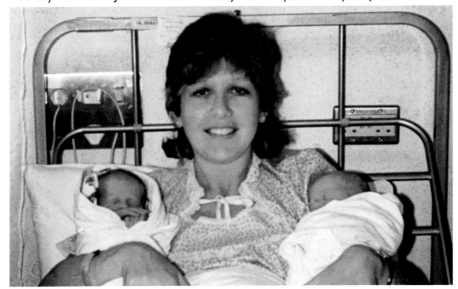

apparent in the presidential election campaign of 1997, when patients turned up at every rally and meeting throughout the Republic.

The effect of Mary McAleese's election on her immediate and extended family was almost beyond description. They had spent all those years in the North, looking south. The South was a place where they felt at home and where there was a value system with all the benefits of a Republic accruing. That was the background and context. But there was a sinking feeling over the years that it would never happen. The stories have been heard before. About Croke Park on All-Ireland final day and that feeling as the national anthem is played. It is hard to contain the emotion. These were the things Northern nationalists had been deprived of and were cut off from in Northern Ireland, because of the system that operated there.

Then, as Martin McAleese recalls of that morning of the inauguration, 'you are in the Republic and your wife is President. It was such a huge honour and privilege. The day the family travelled in from the Portmarnock Hotel where we had been staying until the inauguration was one we will never forget. We were in that old Rolls Royce with the tricolour on the wing. We drove into Dublin Castle. We drove up to Áras an Uachtaráin. The emotion of seeing the tricolour flying on the house was so intense it cannot be described.'

And it is probably Martin who has been most affected by his wife's election. When she became President it just wasn't feasible for him to continue with his dental work in Northern Ireland so he eased himself out of it over a number of years. But he doesn't see this as a sacrifice. 'It is only when you live here that you realise the affection and regard that people have for the office and the office-holder. When you see that being expressed in so many ways as you travel around the country with Mary, you become more conscious of the sacred trust and responsibility [placed on you]. But with that also comes a tremendous freedom. You dream up something that is very laudable, of integrity, but seemingly impossible to do – and then you make it happen. The reference point, of course, is that you don't do anything that would demean the office or the office-holder. Everything would be discussed with Mary and then I would go off and try and make things happen. So it was with wholehearted enthusiasm that I immersed myself in Mary's presidency. Nothing would be considered a sacrifice because it is an absolute privilege to be here.'

Back in Belfast

No longer 'prominent' in Fianna Fáil, though still a party member, effectively blackballed by RTÉ and the NUJ there, with three young children and studying for a PhD on women in prison while still lecturing at TCD, it seemed a change of pace and scene was called for. Also, the dental practice in Crossmaglen and Bessbrook, County Armagh of which Martin was a partner, was growing. By early August 1987 the family had bought a house in Rostrevor, County Down.

Reflecting on the Dublin she had left and would not return to again for another ten years, Mary McAleese has said she never felt a complete outsider there. In certain circles in Dublin, yes, but not at all in the same way as in the North. And, after all, she was no stranger to the South. Her Leneghan grandparents lived in Roscommon and she was there at Easter, Christmas and during summer holidays. She had family and friends living in Dublin, but, more importantly, her brother John had gone to school there, a school for the deaf. It meant she was in the city once a month from the time when John was four years of age. However, arriving in Dublin and into a certain middle class ambience in 1975, and into the milieu of revisionism, she did feel an outsider. She couldn't understand the place at all. It was like some surreal planet; things that she knew to be true were regarded as untrue in Dublin. Things that she knew to be real were being denied. So it was a time when she felt out of focus. But she thinks, quite frankly, that Dublin was out of focus with reality. It wasn't all of Dublin, because Dublin 4 is not all of Dublin. The revisionist media was not all of Dublin, or all of Ireland for that

Justin, Sara, Martin, Mary, Charlie
McAleese (Martin's father), Emma,
in Rostrevor, 1991

matter. That has been put to rights long since.

In the North it was different. There you knew that in perpetuity you were going to be regarded as a lesser human being by virtue of having been born a Catholic. That was the ambience and it was articulated in so many ways. Nowadays people don't want to admit that because it was the genesis of the Troubles.

The McAleeses had hardly arrived in Rostrevor when she was contacted by Professor Des Greer of the Law Department at Queen's University in Belfast, who had lectured her when she was a student there. He told her that there was a vacancy for the position of Director of the Institute of Professional Legal Studies, which was attached to Queen's. It had been set up in 1976 to provide training for law students in drafting, advocacy and client care. The job of director had been advertised months previously and she had not applied for it. She was happy at Trinity and, besides, the advertisement stipulated that a successful applicant would be a practising lawyer. Professor Greer told her that none of the applicants had been successful and that the selection board was itself putting together a list of likely candidates. They had also reserved the right to appoint an academic lawyer if they saw fit, he said. He invited her to apply for the position. Another applicant was her former law lecturer, David Trimble, who was then Acting Director of the Institute.

She was not aware of Trimble's application. She knew there had been internal candidates for the position on the previous occasion and that they were now out of the frame after the first round of trying to fill the post. She

 David Trimble

was in with a chance. Following a gruelling interview she got the job and was delighted.

'I liked the idea of a new challenge. There was certainly a lot of work to be done and I was really looking forward to doing it. I felt well placed to make a contribution.'

Mary McAleese was the first Catholic and the first woman to be appointed to the post. As she had to work out three months' notice at Trinity, she did not take up her new job until January 1988. Her appointment was not well received in certain quarters. David Trimble was by then a rising star in the Ulster Unionist Party. He was chairman of the Lagan Valley Unionist Association. Rumour began to circulate among Unionists that Mary McAleese had been appointed under the terms of the Anglo-Irish Agreement at the behest of her Fianna Fáil party leader and then Taoiseach Charles Haughey. This provoked fury. The belief was further reinforced when it was noted that the original advertisement for the director post had stipulated that the successful candidate would be a practising lawyer. It was pointed out that Mary McAleese had practised for just one year in Northern Ireland and never in the Republic. This suggested to them that being a practising lawyer was no longer a criterion for the post, which underlined still further the question as to why David Trimble, Acting Director of the Institute for a year by then and also an academic lawyer like Mary McAleese, was unsuccessful. Unionist suspicion could not be allayed. The matter ended up in the House of Commons. Four Unionist MPs, Cecil Walker, Roy Beggs, Clifford Forsythe and John Taylor, colleagues and friends of David Trimble's, put down what is termed 'an early day motion'. Such motions are rarely debated in the Commons but are a way of calling attention to issues and getting publicity for them, under parliamentary privilege.

John Taylor

The motion read: 'That this House, believing in the principles of merit, equal opportunity and fair employment, shares the concern among members of the legal profession and others regarding the appointment of Mary McAleese as Director of the Institute of Professional Legal Studies at Queen's University, Belfast; and calls for an early debate, to establish if the post was advertised for a semi-retired or retired practitioner of several years standing; if Mary McAleese has practical legal experience; if on graduating from

Queen's University, Belfast, she went to live and work in another jurisdiction, namely the Republic of Ireland; if she has ever practised in the jurisdiction of the United Kingdom; if she now spends two days per week on average in Belfast and still lectures in Dublin; the level of salary afforded to the Director of the Institute of Professional Legal Studies at Queen's University, Belfast; the number of lectures given by Mary McAleese since her appointment at Queen's University, Belfast, to date; whether there is validity in the speculation that Mary McAleese was nominated by the Premier of the Republic of Ireland, Charles Haughey, and appointed for political reasons rather than merit; and the number of applications made for the position of Director of the Institute of Professional Legal Studies at Queen's University, Belfast, and the qualifications of each applicant.'

Many on the nationalist side felt that all the questions in the motion could be boiled down to one: 'Why did this Catholic get this job when it is supposed to be the exclusive reserve of Protestants?' That is basically what they were asking and suggesting that she had got in as a result of some sub-deal done with Charlie Haughey between the two Governments. Once the matter was on the order paper of the House of Commons it was out in the public domain and Queen's was asked for a comment. The vice-chancellor of Queen's, Professor Gordon Beveridge, was anything but pleased. He sent off a letter saying that Mary McAleese was the best candidate. That's how she got the job – no great mystery, and that the rest was rubbish. The questions never came up on the floor of the House. They were never followed through. Asked about this motion recently, John Taylor couldn't recall it. 'Someone must have put me up to it,' he says.

Mary McAleese herself did not comment on any of this publicly for seven years. Then, in 1995, she was on a BBC programme called 'If I Should Die', hosted by Rev Dr John Dunlop, a former Moderator of the Presbyterian Church in Ireland and a regular broadcaster. It was a kind of pre-death obituary programme. David Trimble was on it, too. It was broadcast a month before he was elected leader of the Ulster Unionist Party. He commented on the fact that she had got the Institute job and insinuated that it was for reasons that had nothing to do with her merits. She was asked to comment on his remarks. She replied that she would not comment on the story of the job except to say there were two candidates shortlisted. She was one and he was the other. She was successful and he wasn't, and that she would let people judge for themselves the merits of what he had said.

David Trimble does not recall knowing of her application for the directorship of the Institute of Professional Legal Studies at the time. He, too, had been encouraged to apply for the post though aware that preference was for someone with experience of practising law. He didn't know that Mary McAleese had been invited to apply for the post and when he found out that she had applied he was surprised, as, like him, she was an academic lawyer, though she had practised for one year at the Bar in Northern Ireland. He only became aware of the House of Commons 'early day motion' after the event. Thereafter the matter was never discussed at Queen's, where he continued to lecture until 1990. There was no debate there about her appointment, post the event.

Mary McAleese's departure from the Republic did not go unnoticed. On 4 October the *Sunday Independent* published an article which was in the form of an open letter. It began 'So farewell Mary McAleese, publican's daughter, self-publicist, professor and conscience of the "set menu" rather than à la carte Catholics.' Probably its most libellous paragraph read, 'Those nasty people in RTÉ called you "our Provo lady" and gave you the boot for double-jobbing, while more acceptable double-jobbers (like Mr Brian Farrell) continue to grin at us from the goggle box.' As someone who had already received death threats, this article caused Mary McAleese to fear even more for the security of herself and her family. That upset her as much as she was angered at the libel associating her with the IRA.

Her fears were not the stuff of fantasy. She was back in a society where rumour, gossip, a libel could kill. Miriam Daly, a lecturer at Queen's and chair of the Irish Republican Socialist Party, was shot dead by the UDA at her home in Andersonstown, West Belfast, on 26 June 1980. Edgar Graham, a law lecturer at Queen's and a colleague of David Trimble's, was a UUP member of the Northern Ireland Assembly when he was shot dead by the IRA as he got out of his car outside Queen's on 7 December 1983. Further back, in 1974, Mary McAleese had been in the Bar library in Belfast one day when she heard a colleague ask Judge Rory Conaghan if he had bulletproof glass in his windows and steel sheeting in his doors. He said he had not; if terrorists wanted to kill him he could not stop them. His only defence was to keep his soul in a state of grace. Two months later, on 16 September 1974, he was shot dead by an IRA gunman as he answered the door to his home on Belfast's Malone Road. She took his advice on living with danger and would say her best strategy in such context was 'to keep my soul in a state of grace'.

Shortly after she took up her appointment at the Institute of Professional Legal Studies in January 1988, she began receiving telephone death threats.

After a time she became convinced her caller was going to go no further. 'However, and as a precaution, I made a point of never travelling the same route to my office or of arriving at the same time on consecutive mornings. I would also examine my car every morning before getting into it.'

That was the context in which she sued the *Sunday Independent*. On 17 November 1988, senior counsel Fred Morris (later President of the High Court) and senior counsel Garrett Cooney took her case against the newspaper to the High Court. There was a last-minute, out-of-court settlement resulting in a front page apology accompanied by a photograph of her, chosen by her, costs, and a generous award. At the time it was believed to be the highest award ever given in a libel action. The amount was never disclosed but it was sufficient to allow the McAleeses put a deposit on an apartment in Dublin's Ballsbridge as well as to afford holidays for relatives and to donate some money to charity.

In the midst of that action much the same libelous material was repeated by *A Belfast Magazine*, an ultra right-wing publication, in its August/September 1988 edition. It said that Charles Haughey had got her the job as director of the Institute of Professional Legal Studies. It also lifted material from the *Sunday Independent* article. When she saw how a libel had travelled into a second one, Mary McAleese decided she could not afford to allow that kind of story to go further. She sued them, too. The magazine was cited on nineteen counts for defaming her. The resultant action put it out of business.

Promotion in (Relative) Tranquillity

Mary McAleese was about to enter one of the more productive, fulfilling and peaceful periods of her life. Away from public life and controversy, and away from media, whether as participant or performer, she now concentrated her considerable energies on her new job, the academic life of Queen's University, and her family.

The Institute of Professional Legal Studies itself was then about 100 metres from the university. Its physical situation reflected its relationship with the university. She set about bringing it to the centre of Queen's academic life. She introduced job-sharing, then unheard of in the university, and soon widely practised there. She introduced new training methods in advocacy, client counseling, mediation and then innovative computer-based learning. The Institute's reputation began to grow, not just in Northern Ireland but abroad also. It meant that she, as director, began to receive invitations to lecture abroad. She did so at the George Washington University and the Catholic University, both in Washington, and the William Mitchell School of Law in Minneapolis. She lectured at the Institute of Advocacy in Oxford, as well as at Bristol and Newcastle universities. She was advisor to the Joint Forum on Legal Training in Dublin and soon became an external examiner for the School of Law in Nottingham and the Law Society of England and Wales. She made useful contacts in the US, Britain and the rest of Europe, and, as a result, international leaders in the field of Advocacy and European Law were guest lectures at the Institute in Belfast.

She also became a member of a plethora of Queen's committees, including its Academic Council. Such was her success and industry at the Institute and on the university's committees that in 1993 Queen's gave her the title Professor of Law. Then, in 1994 the University appointed her pro-vice Chancellor, the first woman and second Catholic to hold the post. The University Chancellor, now US Senator George Mitchell, has a nominal role and acts as chairman. The vice-chancellor acts as chief executive, with three pro-vice Chancellors as deputy chairmen/women. Being chancellor of a university is an unpaid honorary. So at Queen's the pro-vice Chancellor position is a type of assistant chief executive.

But almost immediately she assumed the role, Mary McAleese was in the firing line. In her new post she had responsibility for the University's communications and public relations. Shortly before her appointment as pro-vice Chancellor a working group of the University's Senate had recommended that a tradition involving an RUC band playing 'God Save the Queen' at University graduation ceremonies be discontinued. Though the President became an ex-officio member of the University Senate on her appointment as pro-vice Chancellor, she had not been a member beforehand. However the coincidence of that appointment and the Senate decision on the anthem simply resurrected old suspicions about her in Unionist circles. That her new job made her the public face of the University at that time simply underscored those suspicions.

Belfast Telegraph journalist Alf McCreary was Head of Information at Queen's University at the time and worked alongside the President in her pro-vice Chancellor communications and public relations role. He says that the University was going through a difficult period, with bad headlines about its fair employment policy concerning the ratio of Catholics on its staff in comparison to Protestants. There was a media obsession with this when the anthem issue arose. It had been a contentious one for some time at Queen's graduation ceremonies as some nationalists would pointedly remain seated while it was being played. 'This annoyed many unionists, and others of no particular political persuasion who felt that this was not so much a political gesture on the part of nationalists, but simply bad manners,' he says. The anthem had become a political football and there was never going to be an easy time or way to dispense with it, without a hostile reaction. 'When the University Senate decided to do so, there was uproar. It was taken as a sign by many in the Protestant/Unionist community as yet another example of the deliberate erosion of Unionism, at a time when that community felt that too many of its cherished and symbolic links with Britain were being whittled away.'

The senior management team that had approved of the decision to drop the anthem needed to make it acceptable to the widest possible audience. In his opinion they did not 'fully comprehend the potential (and real) pain which that decision would cause in the majority community.' He also feels that 'at that time Mary McAleese, like many another nationalist, may have failed to appreciate fully the depth of feeling it would cause, among even fair-minded unionists. To that extent she and the others misjudged the potential and inevitable extent of the public outcry that would ensue. It could and should have been handled better in terms of public presentation, and the blame for that rested collectively with the university's senior management.'

More generally, he says that at Queen's Mary McAleese was regarded as 'astute and well able to flourish within the complex political minutiae of university life. She had a chameleon-like ability for survival and progression, and she even dressed in the anonymity of female academia, when necessary – sensible shoes, steel-rimmed glasses and a sometimes unflattering hairstyle. She had her own agenda, and no one would have been surprised if she had gone on to higher things in the university world. She might even have become a university Vice-Chancellor, though not necessarily at Queen's. She was tough, and more than able to fight her corner. She could be charming, but beneath her affability there was a core of steel. There was an element of surprise when newspaper reports began to speculate that she was a possible Fianna Fáil candidate for the Presidency, though her "green" credentials were already well-known, north and south. This "surprise" was partly due to the fact that she had apparently left active politics, and her roots as a Northerner could have made her an outsider in the contest for the Presidency.'

As pro-vice Chancellor, Mary McAleese was determined to extend Queen's distance learning programme to those areas of Northern Ireland where people did not have ready access to third level institutions. The first of these programmes was established in Armagh where an outreach campus of Queen's University was set up, with specially designed distance-learning programmes for part-time mature students. At the opening of the Armagh campus, local Unionist MP John Taylor, one of the four MPs who had signed the House of Commons 'early day motion' on the appointment of Mary McAleese as director of the Institute of Professional Legal Studies, complimented her on the wonderful job she had done in founding such an institution in his city. 'I was very, very impressed by her dedication to that cause. She had worked hard on Armagh,' he says. 'I could relate to her as a Protestant and a unionist. She is a very strong nationalist and a very good Catholic, not a nominal one like so many these days. We worked well together.'

She also established an outreach programme in Omagh, a town she would visit in 1998 in a very different role and in the most appalling circumstances. And she set up the first cross-border degree course involving Queen's and Dublin City University. More locally in Belfast she developed a relationship between Queen's and its Protestant neighbours in Sandy Row and its Catholic neighbours on the Ormeau Road through organising visits to the university and a 'Good Neighbour' project whereby students at the university helped children in those deprived areas with their studies.

In 1995 she had the first of many meetings with Queen Elizabeth of Britain. It was at St James's Palace in London at a dinner to celebrate the founding in 1845 of the Queen's Colleges at Belfast, Galway and Cork. She had been asked to introduce the guests to Queen Elizabeth. Not long afterwards she was invited to lunch with the Queen at Buckingham Palace. She was surprised at the depth of Queen Elizabeth's knowledge of Northern Ireland affairs.

Apart from her academic and academic-related activities at that time, Mary McAleese was applying her skills in some unexpected quarters. She was appointed to the board of Northern Ireland Electricity as a non-executive director in 1991 and in 1992 she was appointed to the BBC Broadcasting Council of Northern Ireland, a position she held until her appointment to the board of Channel 4 Television in 1994. She was there until her election as President of Ireland. She was also appointed to Northern Ireland's Royal Hospitals' Trust as non-executive director. It supervised three of Belfast's bigger hospitals and its dental hospital. She was honorary president of the Northern Ireland Housing Rights Association and a board member of Flax Trust, a voluntary cross-community business agency based in her native Ardoyne. Throughout all of this time she avoided party politics, though when the SDLP needed a hand locally in Rostrevor, she would have helped out.

As crises over Orange parades erupted in Drumcree in County Armagh and at the Ormeau Road in Belfast, she was invited by the Catholic bishops in the autumn of 1996 to be a member of its delegation which would make written and oral submissions to the North Commission for Contentious Parades. The Commission consisted of Dr Peter North, former Presbyterian Moderator Rev Dr John Dunlop, and Fr Oliver Crilly. Other members of the Catholic Church delegation were the then Archbishop now Cardinal Sean Brady, Cardinal Cahal Daly, Monsignor Denis Faul and solicitor Martin O'Brien.

That year also, she began a far more significant involvement with the drive towards peace in Northern Ireland through the Redemptorist Peace Ministry based at the Clonard monastery near the Falls Road. She had become involved at the core of what was to transform relations in this island, and relations between this island and its neighbour, in the most profound way. Back then, in the mid-90s, most of what was happening took place in secret. It had

Fr Alec Reid, who established the Redemptorist Peace Ministry

begun some years earlier with Fr Alec Reid, a Redemptorist priest based at the Clonard monastery. In early 1996 he and the then Redemptorist provincial Fr Brendan Callanan came to Mary McAleese and asked her to join their Peace and Reconciliation Mission. Around the same time they approached Jim Fitzpatrick, publisher and managing editor of the *Irish News* daily in Belfast.

'By then it was already becoming clear that the Redemptorists' peace initiative was a chance to reconcile, for the first time in Irish history, the two traditions of Irish nationalism and to diffuse them around the concept that its articulation was infinitely better served by democratic dialogue than it was ever going to be by the use of violence. The degradation of human dignity experienced over the thirty-odd years of the Troubles in Northern Ireland bore witness to the false claims of those who asserted that the gun and the bomb were capable of solving the problems. It wasn't a matter of saying "give up your weapons because it is immoral to use them". That argument had been tried for hundreds of years and had made no impact at all. It was about saying "give up your guns because the ambitions you have are achievable in much more effective ways. Try it and see," ' she says.

'What Jim Fitzpatrick and I were being asked to do at those meetings with SDLP figures and others was to sell a product, the political product that is democratic dialogue. We would argue that if it was tried they would see that it would deliver a democratic construct where they could flourish. Which was manifestly not the case then. They lived in chaos. The dialogue was a way out of that chaos. But there would have to be an element of compromise because that is the nature of democratic dialogue. It was the old argument ... that mantra repeated endlessly in discussions, that "90 per cent of something is better than 100 per cent of nothing".'

Fr Alec Reid had been facilitating dialogue between Sinn Féin President Gerry Adams and SDLP leader John Hume. The priests spoke about the intentions behind the ongoing dialogue between Hume and Adams and of how they wanted to push it out among the broader nationalist community and try, once and for all, to end the two traditions in Irish nationalist politics, the warring tradition and the democratic tradition which went back to Daniel O'Connell and before him. Fr Reid was absolutely convinced of the powers of persuasion of John Hume and of the commitment of Gerry Adams to go down the democratic and constitutional route. 'Fr Alec could see endless opportunity for the healing of that longstanding, centuries-old division in the politics of Irish nationalism, the two sides which shared an ambition but

John Hume

had very, very different modus operandi. He told me he wanted a female input and that he wanted a lay input. He also wanted a number of other facilitators to help support the dialogue,' the President says.

He knew that dialogue between Adams and Hume would not be enough. They would have to bring their respective constituencies with them. This was where he felt Mary McAleese and Jim Fitzpatrick could help.

At the time and beforehand John Hume had been taking a lot of abuse, not least from within his own party, for talking to Gerry Adams. Fr Reid felt he cut a very lonely figure, as most visionaries do, and precisely because they are leaders who lead from the front. He saw Mary McAleese and Jim Fitzpatrick as having the job of both facilitating the Hume–Adams dialogue and, having listened to that dialogue and seeing where it was going, then to try and encourage others to go the same journey. Their job was to give and encourage backing for the journey. This was not an easy task. Some senior figures in the SDLP were scathing about Hume. Those in contact with him at the time had some sense of the tremendous loneliness surrounding him but also of the extraordinary moral fibre which enabled him to continue to be as strong and as focused and as faithful and as believing in his vision as he was, while being simultaneously assailed from within and without. For much of the time there was hardly a civil word written in any newspaper about him or the dialogue. Some just stopped short of suggesting he was the paramilitary. To those in closer contact he was, in fact, the O'Connellite figure. They had the privilege of listening to him explain his philosophy over and over again and of hearing Gerry Adams's response to it and of seeing the moral integrity of John Hume's position take hold so strongly and root itself strongly in Adams's thinking. By then Gerry Adams had already gone on his own journey down that road.

Fr Alec Reid and the Redemptorists were the facilitators. It was Fr Alec who first realised that within the prisons the IRA was tired. It was he who was first to have the intuition that Gerry Adams was on a different journey because he (Adams) could see that there was no stomach for the war in the next generation. By then the IRA knew they could neither win nor lose. There was a space opening up for new thinking and Fr Reid was among those who realised this first on the nationalist side in Ireland.

Meetings between Fr Reid, Mary McAleese and Jim Fitzpatrick took place regularly and secretly at the Clonard monastery. While not directly involved in the dialogue taking place between John Hume and Gerry Adams, they were briefed regularly so they could help garner further support for the dialogue, particularly within the SDLP, the constituency both Mary McAleese and Jim Fitzpatrick were closest to themselves. 'We tried to help others understand where John Hume was leading. We went around seeing members of the party. We explained what the dialogue was about and tried to open members' minds to the possibilities it offered. Hume and Adams were both very courageous men in their own right, but there could be no doubt that Hume particularly was suffering greatly because of the things which were said and written about him,' she says. It was very evident. And, though Gerry Adams was battleworn, he had always lived in an embattled atmosphere and was probably better able to cope with the onslaught. The critics simply could not see, or refused to see, where the dialogue was leading.

Both governments were kept informed and up to speed with what was going on. Martin Mansergh was most involved as a conduit to the Irish Government. Mary McAleese's involvement with the Clonard initiative continued until autumn 1997 when the presidential election campaign began. In October 1997 leaks about her involvement, and her inability to speak about it because of a commitment not to do so publicly, precipitated the greatest crisis of her presidential election campaign.

She was not directly involved with the peace ministry at the time when the first IRA ceasefire was called in 1994. It has been described as the foundation stone of the peace process. The IRA bomb at Canary Wharf in London on 9 February 1996 was the worst moment of that process. It killed two people, injured over a hundred more and caused colossal damage. Fr Alec Reid rang to assure her all was not lost. 'Look, the Holy Spirit retired to the subs bench too soon, we have to get him back and working again,' he said. The priest's faith was absolutely unshakeable. So the talks started again, the participants knowing that the wrath of heaven and hell was going to be on top of them now, from all sides. If Hume continued the dialogue with Adams it would be war for him, while Adams was, obviously, under a lot of pressure too. But after Canary Wharf there was an absolute determination that this thing had to be put right as quickly as possible. If it was the case that a second ceasefire was established, everything would have to be done to plug all the possible holes.

Fr Alec Reid joined the Redemptorists in 1949. In 1957 he was ordained by the then Bishop of Galway, Dr Michael Browne. In 1961 he was appointed to the Clonard monastery in Belfast and was there for forty-four years, until 2005. His accent, however, has remained pure Tipperary, a county he supports in hurling – a game from which he still draws his metaphors. When the subject of his Belfast parishioners comes up he remembers Tommy Rice who was a bricklayer and 'a saintly man'. When he died he left Fr Alec All-Ireland tickets for a decade in his will. They stopped conducting missions at Clonard in 1970/71, 'when the Troubles began'. There was rioting and shooting outside the door. An army officer lost a leg when an IRA bomb attached to a lamppost nearby was detonated. Fr Reid noticed that one of those taking part in those early riots was a teenager who had been a senior altar boy at Clonard and he thought to himself that if a sensible young man like him is leading a riot there must be good reason. He had to find that reason and gain access to those who organised the riots if he was to stop them. At that time, the Official and Provisional IRA were involved in 'a vicious war' with one another.

He and Fr Des Wilson got involved. He gained experience of dealing with the IRA, IPLO, INLA leadership. He learned he could trust the IRA leadership. It appeared to be reciprocated, as either Officials or Provisionals would come to him to check out with the other side whether it was safe for them to go home, or whatever. One Holy Thursday night there was rioting and shooting and the IRA opened fire at soldiers and a pregnant young woman was shot at the gates of the church. He anointed her and complained to the IRA about shooting in the streets, where they were endangering civilians. Years later he met a woman in the Poleglass area of West Belfast who said to him, 'You anointed my mother when she was shot'. The young woman had been the child she was carrying at the time.

He visited Long Kesh every Sunday and said Mass for the prisoners there. It was where he first got to know Gerry Adams, who was a leader among the prisoners. They would get to know one another better on the ground, as Fr Alec tried to address ongoing feuds. He remembers thinking at one point that if he, Fr Des Wilson and Fr Gerry Reynolds made a concerted effort they might stop them from shooting one another. He felt they had a responsibility to try.

For him that necessity crystallised at the wake of a young man killed by loyalists. They were saying the rosary over his open coffin as the young widow wept and wailed her grief loudly. It went to the heart of everyone there and

Fr Alec remembers saying to himself *this kind of thing should not be happening in a Christian, civilized society*. It persuaded him to redouble his efforts to try to end it. He began by trying to get the IRA to stop. He wrote to the papers proposing a peaceful way forward and called for an all-party conference. 'We had to take the conflict away from the streets,' he says. He proposed an all-Ireland peace conference. He recalls Gerry Adams saying about this afterwards that it had been very helpful when he first began sowing the seeds of such ideas with the IRA leadership.

It was also helpful that he could say, 'It is Fr Alec's idea' rather than his own. However, the blanket protests, which began in the late 70s and continued into the 80s, distracted from all that. They led to the two hunger strikes, in 1980, and again in 1981 when ten men died. 'Sinn Féin didn't want the hunger strikes but when they went ahead they had to support them publicly,' Fr Alec says. In his view, had they not taken place 'We could have had the ceasefire in 1984 and not in 1994. It would have meant 1,500 less dead.' Cardinal Ó Fiaich, who mediated in the first hunger strike, said that the British Prime Minister Margaret Thatcher thought the IRA were just trying to prove their virility. The Cardinal had met the Prime Minister to persuade her that the issue was clothes and political status. He had argued with her and eventually he understood that she was prepared to allow the prisoners wear their own clothes. It was broadcast that this was the case on a London radio station news bulletin. The Cardinal had been told to wait in a particular government office. There was a delay of an hour to an hour and a half in preparation of the document the government planned to release and which he was to have sight of. Eventually he received the document. It said the prisoners could wear their own clothes but that these would have to be supplied by the prison authorities. It was an offer that would be rejected by the prisoners. Fr Alec believes that the Northern Ireland Prison Service had heard the news from the media that 'the IRA had won' and immediately got on to London. Hence the change in the British Government's position as it had earlier been understood by Cardinal Ó Fiaich. Fr Alec has often wondered since what the Irish Government was doing then when it should have been keeping the British better informed about what was really going on.

Fr Alec spent an hour and a half one day with Bobby Sands, trying to talk him out of going ahead with the second hunger strike. He recalls that the leader of the first hunger strike, Brendan 'The Dark' Hughes, who died in February 2008, was a 'very intelligent, very moderate man'. He was on hunger strike for fifty-three days. Cardinal Ó Fiaich had told Brendan

Hughes then that there was nothing he could do to help secure the hunger strikers' demands if the IRA continued to kill prison officers. It was stopped, and so was the hunger strike. But Bobby Sands was 'very determined'. He couldn't be stopped. Fr Alec remembers how Bobby Sands went into a state of shock as they spoke. 'He started to shake.' He has regretted since that he didn't spend longer with Bobby Sands. It soon became the case that even if Sands wanted to get off the hunger strike he couldn't do so. But, looking back, Fr Alec realises he didn't appreciate the situation he himself was in at that time. He knows now that had he succeeded in persuading Bobby Sands not to go ahead, ten lives would have been saved, as well as the sixty who were killed in the week after Bobby Sands died. 'The whole thing was very tragic. Sinn Féin and the IRA outside did their best. Failure to prevent the second hunger strike meant ten more years were added to the Troubles. Meanwhile the British and Irish Governments wouldn't deal with the IRA on the ground. They didn't understand them, so they couldn't work with them.'

The day after he spoke to Bobby Sands, Fr Alec became sick as he waited for the prison van to take him from the H-Blocks. He was very ill. He had diabetes and almost died. He was taken to Our Lady of Lourdes hospital in Drogheda. After which, in April 1981, he was sent to Rome for five or six weeks' recuperation. He was in St Peter's Square on Wednesday 13 May as Pope John Paul was being driven through the crowd during his weekly audience. Fr Alec was taking photographs when he heard a bang and a woman in front of him began to tear at her hair. A man had his hands up at the back of his head. Someone shouted, 'The Pope's been shot' and a man right beside Fr Alec was shouting 'Allelujah'. Had known who he was, he believes now he would have tackled him. Swiss guards vaulted over a barrier and grabbed the man. Fr Alec thought he must be an accomplice, but recognised him later from photographs as Mehmet Ali Agca, the man who would later be jailed for trying to assassinate Pope John Paul.

As Fr Alec's health improved he was told by his superiors he could return to Belfast on one condition – that he would not get involved in politics. He didn't, for a year. Then the IRA captured a UDR man. He went to the IRA and asked 'can nothing be done about saving this man?' They agreed to help get him released. They went down to South Armagh to 'a big house. I found that wherever I met leaders of the IRA or ETA it was in a big house.' They were too late. The man had already been shot. One of his killers told them he was 'sorry, but it's too late. He's dead.'

On his return to Belfast, Fr Alec went to Gerry Adams who said the Church

was the only organisation with the credibility and status to do anything about the situation. 'Gerry Adams knew more about what the Church should be doing than the Church did.' So he set up the Redemptorist Peace Ministry, as an official ministry, at Clonard. He returned to Gerry Adams who said, 'If you want to stop the IRA get an alliance between Sinn Féin, the SDLP, and the Dublin Government. Without that you won't stop the IRA. You have to have a powerful strategy to stop the armed struggle.'

No one was talking to the IRA in those days but Fr Alec felt that Gerry Adams must talk to the SDLP. The priest wrote a fourteen-page letter to John Hume addressing what he felt was an opportunity to persuade the IRA to stop. It also included a 'very good CV for Gerry Adams, as very capable and honourable.' He sent it off, thinking, this is the last throw of the dice. And 'Fair play to the man, in the morning John Hume phoned and said he would see me the following day. He didn't even know me. He was the leading politician in Ireland. Gerry Adams always said he was head and shoulders over any other [politician] in Europe.'

The next day at Clonard, John Hume agreed to meet Gerry Adams. 'He opened the door for Gerry Adams where the IRA was concerned. He opened the whole door then to a reconciliation between the physical force tradition going back to the French Revolution, Wolfe Tone, Robert Emmet, the Young Irelanders, the Fenians, the IRB, 1916, the IRA, and the political tradition of O'Connell, Parnell, Redmond. John Hume represented the political tradition. Gerry Adams represented the physical force tradition.'

Soon word got out about the Hume/Adams talks. Both men were seen going into a house together in Derry. John Hume was subject to terrible abuse. He collapsed at one point. 'It should be remembered that John Hume did this at great personal cost. It still affects his health, what happened him at that time. It was very symbolic. The physical force tradition knocking on the door ... and he suffered this incredible amount of abuse from all the media, the British politicians and Government, Irish politicians and Government ... this man who opened the door which allowed Gerry Adams in.'

Fr Alec recognised that they needed the Dublin Government onside. In 1986 he went to see the Opposition leader, Charles Haughey, who listened to him for an hour and a half. 'He never asked a question. It's a great sign of a politician that he didn't offer a counter-argument.' At Kinsealy the following day, a Saturday, Fr Alec met Martin Mansergh. 'I knew he was the man. Very brilliant, understated, perfectly republican, not a civil servant. He could do things a civil servant couldn't do.' He was to be the political contact of the Irish Government with the Hume/Adams dialogue.

'Charlie Haughey deserves great credit. He was a complete blessing. Albert [Reynolds] was brilliant. He'd say, "I couldn't meet the IRA but if you give me a message from them I'll have a reply for you within half an hour." Albert played a key role in getting the peace process going. That should be remembered about Albert. He said he was prepared to sacrifice his political career and his government if he could save just one life. When you are dealing with a man like that you're in business. He was a key person in getting the whole peace process going and in persuading the IRA to stop. Bertie [Ahern] was brilliant, too. I was at his mother's funeral. She had a republican background. Both his parents are buried in the republican plot in Glasnevin.' When Charles Haughey became Taoiseach in 1987 he contacted Fr Alec who was to be the intermediary between Martin Mansergh and Gerry Adams.

But it was on Saturday 19 March 1988 that Fr Alec Reid came to the attention of a wider world. He was at the funeral of IRA man Kevin Brady, who had been killed as he attended the funerals in Milltown cemetery of Sean Savage, Danny McCann and Mairead Farrell, known as the Gibraltar Three, who had been shot dead in Gibraltar by British SAS forces on 6 March. Sean Savage had once been an altar boy at the Clonard monastery and Fr Alec had attended his funeral. He was standing behind Gerry Adams at a graveside when the commotion started, fifty to sixty yards away. UDA man Michael Stone had fired on the mourners and killed Kevin Brady, John Murray and Thomas McErlean. Fr Alec saw Michael Stone being chased and said to Gerry Adams, 'Someone should go down there or someone will kill him.' To which Gerry Adams replied '... are you mad?' Fr Alec anointed a wounded man nearby and accompanied him to the Royal Hospital in a car while a nurse tried to keep the man alive. But the victim died on the way. In the hospital Fr Alec anointed the two other men who had been killed. He remembers the wife of one of them arriving at the hospital and how 'she disintegrated when I put my arm around her shoulder. That's what the Troubles did to people.'

That night, Kevin Brady's mother got in contact with the priest to inquire whether her son had been anointed. He assured her that he had been. He went to Brady's funeral to meet her and reassure her. But another reason for his presence was that he had a document arising from the Hume-Adams talks which he was to pass to Sinn Féin's Tom Hartley there.

As he made his way to Mrs Brady, a car backed towards the mourners at speed. Fr Alec thought it was another attack, similar to the Stone episode at Milltown cemetery a few days previously. He saw people banging at the car and one man beating at it with a wheel brace. The car windows were smashed. One of the men in the car fired into the air. There was something about the two men which led Fr Alec to believe they weren't dangerous. He went to talk to them. The back of the car was being kicked. By now the two men had been taken from the car and what looked like two rugby scrums surrounded each of them. Their hands were being held in case they had guns. Neither was being abused. They were both brought to the side of nearby Casement Park where they were placed lying on the ground. Sensing what might happen, Fr Alec lay down between them and placed an arm around each. They were 'dead still. I remember thinking they must be soldiers, they were so still.' He shouted for an ambulance. And someone shouted at him, 'Get up or I'll fucking shoot you as well.' By then, with so much experience of the Troubles, he knew how far he could go. He had an instinct for it and, 'as a priest, you could get away with things.' He felt they were probably going to take the men away in a black taxi. Next thing, the two men were dropped over a wall. He ran around and saw a black taxi pulling away. He thought the men would be taken away for interrogation. It could be a big propaganda coup. He ran into a side street where his own car was parked and was just opening the car door when he heard two shots. He went to a street corner where he saw people looking up towards waste ground. 'I realised then that they had shot them. All I could do was anoint them.' One man was still breathing. He gave him the kiss of life. *Irish Times* journalist Mary Holland came up to him 'Father, can I do anything?' she asked. 'Do you know how to give the kiss of life?" he asked her. She didn't. He asked her to go down to the nearest shop and call an ambulance. An army ambulance was soon at the scene, but both men were dead by then.

Fr Alec was annoyed with himself. He really thought the men were being taken for interrogation. He believed that if senior Sinn Féin or IRA people had been there they would have intervened and saved their lives, 'I know they would.' He learned from senior Sinn Féin figures later that when the car backed into the funeral it was thought to be a decoy and part of a plan aimed at the assassination of senior Sinn Féin figures. That was why Gerry Adams and others were whisked away. Gerry Adams told Fr Alec later that had he or senior colleagues been there, the two men would not have been shot. They had fallen into the hands of a local IRA unit, and not long after three of their people had been killed in Gibraltar.

Fr Alec recalls how, in the ongoing talks, it was John Hume who first mooted the strategy whereby the Irish Government, the SDLP, Sinn Féin and the IRA would agree a joint statement which would be joined by the British Government. It would agree the right of the Irish people in both parts of the island to exercise their right of self-determination on the basis of consent, freely and concurrently given, North and South, to bring about a united Ireland, if that was their wish. The statement would also include an assertion by the British Government that it had no selfish strategic or economic interest in Northern Ireland.

John Hume wrote the original draft of such a statement which then went back and forth between Dublin, London, Sinn Féin and the IRA for more than a year. The IRA often could take up to six weeks to come back with answers to queries. It was proposed and agreed that there would be a joint statement by both Governments and that the IRA would declare a ceasefire within twenty-four hours. British Prime Minister John Major was dependant on unionist votes for the support of his Government in London and began tinkering with the statement. There was, as Fr Alec recalls, 'a stand-up row' between John Major and Albert Reynolds before the statement was agreed and, generally, as originally proposed. The kerfuffle meant, however, that though the statement, known as the Downing Street Declaration, was presented jointly in London by John Major and Albert Reynolds in December 1993, the IRA did not declare a ceasefire until April 1994.

'Gerry Adams was the genius behind all of this. He said the Church was the only organisation which could do something, but the Church didn't know what to do. So he told them what to do. Gerry Adams is an extraordinary man,' reflects Fr Alec. He recalls how Gerry Adams used to go to the 10 o'clock children's Mass every Sunday at Clonard. Once, in what may have been an assassination attempt, a strange car was spotted outside the church door, so he was ushered out a different door. Fr Alec assured him he didn't have to go, but he insisted on being there every Sunday. The priest used say to people, 'Gerry Adams in the only man who goes to Mass every Sunday at the risk of his life.' Martin McGuinness was also a weekly Mass-goer. Fr Alec had heard how he would walk out of Mass in Derry if the IRA was condemned. So he found an Irish Mass he could attend where, even if the IRA was being condemned, he wouldn't understand it as he didn't have Irish. Both men were 'perfect gentlemen' who had Christian principles, which Fr Alec believes was another very significant factor in the peace process.

Gerry Adams had been arguing from the beginning that if the IRA was to stop, the peaceful alternative had to be credible. Prior to that first ceasefire in 1994, the IRA had been told there would be an all-party peace conference within six months. Seventeen months passed and there was no conference. Gerry Adams then went to both the British and Irish Governments, asking them to name a date and publicly commit themselves to it. 'The Governments refused and a few days later we had Canary Wharf. It was a protest by the IRA, by the physical force people using their methods to persuade powerful people to use their methods,' says Fr Alec.

Had Canary Wharf not happened there was a danger the IRA could have split. Its leadership had pointed out that it had split in the 1920s, 30s … in almost every decade up to the 1990s. Such organisations were always difficult to manage, particularly where its less seasoned nineteen and twenty-year-olds were concerned. It was in danger of splitting, which would have resulted in more violence. 'Canary Wharf was about keeping the IRA membership quiet. It was about avoiding a split. A week later the two Governments announced peace talks. The leadership of the IRA told Gerry Adams he had been trying to bring this about for seventeen to eighteen months and that they had done it in a week. It was stupidity to do that with people like the IRA,' Fr Alec says.

Everyone had been upset and depressed by Canary Wharf. He felt they had to strengthen the peace ministry team. He had been very impressed by Mary McAleese's 1984 performance at the New Ireland Forum in Dublin Castle, where she had accompanied the Catholic bishops. Further, one lesson he had learned from the peace process was that the most powerful dynamic, after the grace of God, was when male and female combined in dialogue. Insights were deeper, as was consensus, when reached. Ideally the proportion should be 40/60 in male/female participation, weighted either way. He also believed this should apply to the Church. He was 'very strong on that'. He mentioned her to his provincial at the time, Fr Brendan Callanan, and he agreed. They went to meet Mary at her home in Rostrevor and she agreed to be involved, as did Jim Fitzpatrick, editor and owner of the *Irish News*. He was 'completely committed to peaceful means and had a lot of connections in the loyalist community.' Their job 'was to speak to the SDLP and Sinn Féin about organising a peaceful strategy to persuade the IRA to stop.'

Mary McAleese played 'a big role' in the success of this approach. She was 'central to the efforts and objective of the Redemptorist Peace Ministry to take the gun out of politics.' She was 'totally committed to the talks. It was like having Christy Ring on the team. She was very, very articulate and completely committed to the peaceful alternative. She was extraordinary and very persuasive where the value of the strategy was concerned. Her endorsement, support and enthusiasm for the Hume–Adams dialogue and resulting strategy meant that those who had opposed it began to agree with it as the way forward.'

The President visits Pope Benedict XVI in the Vatican

A Contender

How Mary McAleese won the Fianna Fáil nomination for the Presidency of Ireland in September 1997 is one of the more remarkable stories of recent Irish political history. From a jurisdiction other than the Republic, where she hadn't lived for ten years and where her profile was such by then that she wasn't known at all to many members of the Fianna Fáil parliamentary party, she still went on to beat a former Taoiseach and a former European Commissioner in the battle to be the party's nominee. Even today, recollection of that event arouses anger, sometimes bitterness, among some in the party, though it is never directed at her. Its object remains former Taoiseach Bertie Ahern, at whose door total responsibility is laid. However, it was not as simple as that.

As far back as the 1990 presidential election campaign Harry Casey had been thinking that Mary McAleese would have made an ideal candidate. He had been her director of elections when she stood for Fianna Fáil in the Dublin South-East constituency in 1987. A former seminarian, he was a member of a prayer group to which she belonged when the McAleeses lived in County Meath during the 1980s. He was a teacher in Navan at the time and became close to both Mary and Martin McAleese. So when President Mary Robinson announced on 12 March 1997 that she would not be seeking a second term, he rang Martin McAleese and said 'Martin, don't think I'm crazy, but ...' Martin laughed and said, 'Put it to her yourself and see what's her reaction.' Harry advised Martin to think about it for a few days and maybe they'd meet to discuss it. They met the following Sunday and decided that

Prof Paul McNelis S.J., Sara, Mary, Martin, Harry Casey, Justin, in Meath, 1997

Harry would ring Mary McAleese the day afterwards. And he did. As to why he went to Martin first, he said that, knowing the couple so well by then, he had learned that there was no point in talking to Mary about such an idea unless Martin was 100 per cent supportive. 'Mary is a woman of extraordinary vision and energy, but Martin is the powerhouse,' he says.

She was in her car driving home from Belfast to Rostrevor when Harry Casey rang her on her mobile phone that March evening in 1997. 'Don't put the phone down … and I'm not joking about what I'm going to say … but I want you to give this suggestion some consideration. Would you consider throwing your hat in the ring for the presidency?' he recalls saying, or something on those lines. He remembers her reaction. 'She didn't seem to pay too much heed.' She didn't because, as she has since said, 'I was stunned. I remember the impact more than the details. The idea, once it was articulated, hit me like a blow. My breath was taken away. When I came to myself again after several seconds, I was convinced that the whole thing was pure nonsense.' But Harry Casey persisted. He met the McAleeses in Rostrevor the following weekend. By then Martin McAleese was also an enthusiast. Other friends of theirs began to come up to them openly and suggest she should run. Included were Jim Fitzpatrick of the Redemptorist Peace Ministry, solicitor Denis Moloney and his sister Maria who were long-time friends.

The arguments of this ad hoc group had begun to crystallise. She should run, they said, because she was a Northerner and one who had worked and lived for substantial periods in the south. She also had such strong connections to the Republic from childhood. Her election, should it happen, would be a tremendous boost to the confidence of Northern Ireland nationalists, and would most likely, therefore, have a positive effect on the ongoing peace process. As the first President of Ireland from the province of Ulster she would be in a unique position to bring together the ever growing gaps between the two parts of the island. She could help overcome a deepening and mutual ignorance, they argued, and she was uniquely placed through her own life experience to do so. They pointed out that she had a natural, family bond with both parts of the island. She also had family abroad, in the US, Canada, New Zealand and would therefore have affinity with Ireland's far-flung Diaspora. It was also a burgeoning time in the Republic, with a rapidly growing economy. With her background in education and the experience of business she had gained since her return to Belfast, she was ideally placed to represent this new Ireland and its bright generation of energetic, entrepreneurial young people on trips abroad. They believed she had both the confidence and the communications skills to represent this dynamic Ireland well. They succeeded in convincing her that the idea of her seeking to become President of Ireland was not 'nonsense'.

But, inevitably at that stage, the conversation turned to John Hume and his intentions. His name was being widely discussed as a possible next President of Ireland. Mary McAleese made clear to her enthusiasts then and has since repeated her view that 'John Hume was the only Ulster person I would have considered for the job of President of Ireland.' Then too it was being speculated that should John Hume choose to run he would probably secure all-party support in the Republic and would therefore become President without an election. The idea had its own attractions for all political parties in the Republic at the time, heading, as they were, into a general election. None relished the prospect of a presidential election campaign so soon afterwards, or its expense. So Harry Casey, Mary and Martin McAleese, Jim Fitzpatrick, the Moloneys and others of like mind ended their discussions those last weeks of March 1997 in wait-and-see mode. They would wait to see what John Hume would do.

But the friends of Mary McAleese were not idle. They began spreading her name around among personal contacts, north and south of the border. They urged those friends to spread the word also and to write or speak to their Fianna Fáil councillors and Oireachtas representatives in support of Mary

McAleese's candidacy. But no politician was yet approached. Spring passed, summer came. Not much happened in between, though that April Fr Alec Reid suggested Mary McAleese's name to Martin Mansergh as a possible Fianna Fáil candidate for the presidency. Martin Mansergh seemed taken by surprise and said something to the effect that nothing like that would be addressed until after the general election.

The June general election saw Fianna Fáil returned to power in a shaky coalition with the Progressive Democrats and with the support of four Independent TDs. Bertie Ahern was Taoiseach for the first time. The result would have a significant impact on Mary McAleese's prospects of securing the Fianna Fáil nomination for the presidency. Still the uncertainty remained about John Hume's intentions. And still the job was his for the asking. However, by then, too, former Taoiseach Albert Reynolds was being hotly tipped to get the Fianna Fáil nomination. This was no great surprise. His success in establishing the first genuine relationship of mutual respect and regard between a sitting British Prime Minister, John Major, and himself as Taoiseach, went a long way towards establishing a normalisation of relations between and within these islands. And the role of that relationship in bringing about the Downing Street Declaration of December 1993 and an IRA ceasefire the following April, has been seen since as a crucial stepping stone towards a stable peace on the island of Ireland. Albert Reynolds had also succeeded in building a relationship of trust with Sinn Féin and through them with the IRA, again something of a first in contemporary Irish history and equally significant where the evolving peace process was concerned. That relationship continued even after he resigned as Taoiseach and leader of Fianna Fáil in December 1994, and would prove something of ballast in the immediate years ahead.

Albert Reynolds had by then been approached twice by his party leader, Bertie Ahern, to stand for the presidency. The first time was in January 1996 when the two men met for lunch at Dublin's Berkeley Court hotel. Reynolds did not commit himself as Mary Robinson had yet to decide on whether she would stand for a second term. The two men met again early in 1997 at McGrattan's restaurant, near Government Buildings in Dublin. Reynolds was encouraged by his successor to stand again for the Dáil in the forthcoming general election. There had been rumours he might step down. It was put to him that his son, Philip, might stand and hold the seat in Longford/Roscommon should Albert win the presidency. Again Mary Robinson's intentions were still unclear at that stage. Nothing was decided.

It was left at that, even after 12 March 1997 when Mary Robinson announced she would not be standing for a second term. A significant factor at the time was Albert Reynolds's family's attitude. They were not keen on him standing for the presidency at all. Regardless, there was a general election in the offing and that was the priority. Fianna Fáil was determined to get back into power and all the party's energies were absorbed in making sure that would happen.

By early July 1997 Harry Casey was becoming impatient. The general election was over, a Government had been formed, and no one among the McAleese supporters had yet approached a single Fianna Fáil TD or Senator. Harry Casey felt it was high time a move was made. But John Hume's continuing indecision remained the obstacle to everything. Then there was an American Independence Day celebration at the residence of the US consul to Northern Ireland in Belfast. Among the guests was John Hume. Martin and Mary McAleese, Fr Alec Reid, and others keen on a McAleese candidacy for President were also there. Soundings were made about whether or not John Hume would be running and at the end of the evening the consensus among those present was that he would not. This was conveyed to Mary McAleese and she was urged to act. Returning home to Rostrevor, where the patient Harry Casey was waiting, she drafted a letter to Taoiseach Bertie Ahern expressing an interest in being the Fianna Fáil candidate in the presidential election later that year. Three copies were printed. One was sent by registered post to the Taoiseach's office in Government Buildings. Harry Casey personally delivered the second to the Taoiseach's St Luke's office in Drumcondra and the other to Fianna Fáil headquarters on Dublin's Upper Mount Street. The response, the following week, was a simple formal acknowledgement of receipt from Fianna Fáil headquarters. No more.

By mid-July the Taoiseach had received an eleven-page curriculum vitae of Mary McAleese's career to that point. By then, too, the psychiatrist Patricia Casey (not related to Harry Casey), who had been involved in the 1993 abortion referendum campaign with Mary McAleese, had come on board. She advised that the curriculum vitae be sent to every member of the Fianna Fáil parliamentary party, to TDs, outgoing senators (the 1997 Seanad election campaign was still in progress) and MEPs, except for Albert Reynolds, though he had yet to declare himself publicly, and MEP Brian Crowley, who had already declared for Reynolds. Accompanying the McAleese CV, Casey sent a personal letter to each Fianna Fáil representative. She contacted people she knew in the media about the possibility of Mary McAleese standing for the presidency. Most were dismissive. She contacted her local Fianna Fáil TD in

Bray, Dick Roche, for whom she had canvassed the previous month and who had been a supporter of her Pro-Life stance.

He was enthusiastic and assured her he would spread the word. 'When Patricia Casey contacted me about Mary McAleese I felt she [Mary McAleese] was absolutely perfect. She had been born and reared in the Six Counties and had a Fianna Fáil background. A bright, articulate woman, so capable.' He 'spoke to Bertie several times about it', and twice the Taoiseach told him 'e was 'staying out of it'' ... 'He was always positive but you never quite know what Bertie is thinking. A sphinx is always a sphinx.' He liked Albert Reynolds. He was 'a good man', but 'there was a lot of opposition to him in the party' and there was 'the urban/rural divide'. He did not relish the prospect of 'the savage attacks' to which he felt Reynolds and his family would be subject were he to succeed in securing the party's nomination. For that reason too, to avoid such hurt, he was 'anxious that Albert not run. It was a car crash that could be avoided.' And it was 'clear that a lot in the party were very, very worried about Albert [succeeding in being elected], and these would be people who would not be hostile to him.'

By mid-July it was becoming clear that Albert Reynolds was intent on running. Equally clear was the ever-growing anxiety about this in Fianna Fáil. Part of the reason was that the new Government's majority was slender but, even more significantly, the new Tánaiste and Progressive Democrat leader Mary Harney had let Bertie Ahern know that her party would not, in any circumstances, support the nomination of Albert Reynolds for the presidency. Neither she nor her party had forgotten that Albert Reynolds had publicly described her predecessor and Progressive Democrat party founder Desmond O'Malley as 'dishonest' in 1992, precipitating the fall of that Fianna Fáil/PD Government. Soon word began to seep out that it was not certain that Fianna Fáil would hold on to Albert Reynolds Longford/Roscommon seat in the by-election which would have to take place were he to win the presidential election. This was rejected by his supporters, who pointed out that there was always a Fianna Fáil seat in Longford. The same argument – about the danger of losing the seat – would be used successfully to dissuade David Andrews, a Fianna Fáil TD in Dun Laoghaire, from seeking the party's nomination for the presidency. But, much more basically, there was genuine anxiety within the Fianna Fáil party about whether Albert Reynolds was electable as President, an office the party was determined to 'get back' and which it had sensationally lost to President Mary Robinson in 1990.

Mary Robinson was the only President of Ireland not to have had Fianna

Fáil support, either as an agreed candidate or through being elected as a Fianna Fáil candidate. Party stalwarts then and since have never acknowledged that she won the 1990 presidential election campaign. Their claim is that they lost it. As one Fianna Fáil source put it, her election was 'a fluke win'. They point out that despite the disasters inflicted on their candidate, Brian Lenihan, in that election campaign, he still secured a higher first preference vote than Mary Robinson, who was elected on Fine Gael candidate Austin Currie's transfers. Fianna Fáil stalwarts have also continued to refuse to accept an analysis of Mary Robinson's election which presents it as a watershed moment in contemporary Irish politics and which wrought a socio-political sea change, or realignment. Winning back the office had become of huge symbolic importance to them in 1997 and the more they thought about it the less likely it seemed to them that Albert Reynolds would be the one to do it.

He had been Taoiseach for a brief twenty-two month period between February 1992 and December 1994. It may have been a time marked by great achievement where the Northern Ireland peace process was concerned and in laying the basis for the Celtic Tiger economy, but it had also been marred by deep division, both within his own Fianna Fáil party and in relations with his Coalition colleagues. The row with the Progressive Democrats precipitated their withdrawal from Government and the general election of November 1992, but also led to Fianna Fáil's worst performance in a general election since 1927, with a loss of nine seats and 20 per cent support. The following Coalition, which Albert Reynolds also led and which involved Fianna Fáil and the Labour Party, lasted only until December 1994 when Labour withdrew and he resigned as Taoiseach and leader of Fianna Fáil.

Within Fianna Fáil itself he had made powerful enemies when, on becoming Taoiseach in February 1992, he sacked some of the most formidable Fianna Fáil ministers in the Government he had inherited from Charles Haughey. Among those he removed from office were Ray Burke, Mary O'Rourke, Rory O'Hanlon, Michael O'Kennedy, as well as then junior ministers John O'Donoghue and Dermot Ahern. All would figure in his failure to get the Fianna Fáil nomination for the Presidency in 1997. On the return to power of a Fianna Fáil/Progressive Democrat coalition under Bertie Ahern as Taoiseach in the June 1997 general election, the new Government included Ray Burke as Minister for Foreign Affairs, Mary O'Rourke as Minister for Public Enterprise, John O'Donoghue as Minister for Justice, Equality and Law Reform, Dermot Ahern as Minister for Community, Social and Family Affairs, while Rory O'Hanlon was appointed Leas Ceann

Comhairle of the new Dáil and was also chairman of the Fianna Fáil parliamentary party. O'Hanlon would preside over the meeting to select the party's candidate for the presidency on Tuesday 16 September.

Michael O'Kennedy had lost his seat in that disastrous 1992 general election. O'Kennedy had been Minister for Labour in the Government Albert Reynolds inherited from Haughey in February 1992. He was replaced in that ministry by the current Taoiseach Brian Cowen, then a minister for the first time. Apart from Cowen's own natural ability, his father, Ber, was a personal friend of Albert Reynolds who had stayed at the Reynolds apartment in Dublin the night before he died suddenly and precipitated the by-election which saw Brian Cowen first elected to the Dáil in 1984. Michael O'Kennedy was re-elected to the Dáil in the June 1997 general election.

Albert Reynolds's enemies were waiting in the long grass. They had been waiting a long time. Their opportunity had come. They were about to seize it, but stealthily. Besides, they knew their man. They knew that if Albert Reynolds suspected what was afoot, it would simply spur him to redouble his efforts. More neutral party members had also begun to worry. They could see the media having a field day if Albert Reynolds was their presidential candidate. There would be re-runs of the Beef Tribunal, of the *Sunday Times* libel action where he was awarded a penny damages, of the TV clip from the 1980s where he had dressed up in a cowboy outfit to sing the country number 'Put Your Sweets Lips a Little Closer to the Phone', of the 'that's women for ya' comment in the Dáil … and from a man hoping to succeed Ireland's first woman President. To make matters worse for Fianna Fáil, that summerm there were already rumblings about the appointment of Ray Burke as Minister for Foreign Affairs in the new Government. It wasn't looking good. Burke would be forced to resign on 7 October 1997 during the presidential election campaign, as allegations of corruption against him intensified.

Indeed, had he known the depth of these concerns earlier and what was likely to happen, Albert Reynolds might very well have withdrawn there and then. Recalling that time eleven years later, he says 'The family were against it. They said it wouldn't suit me.' His own thinking was 'If the party wants me to do it, I'll do it.' The notion of the presidency was not something he had been wildly enthusiastic about, but like Mary McAleese, who hadn't really thought about it at all before it was put to her, he warmed to the idea as more and more people encouraged him to stand. Among those were some of the strongest ministers in the new 1997 Government. If Albert Reynolds had powerful enemies in that Government, he also had deeply loyal and just as powerful friends. This feature of strong, divisive leadership was no less a reality in his case than it had been where his predecessor as Taoiseach and leader of Fianna Fáil, Charles Haughey, was concerned. As well as the new Minister for Health & Children, Brian Cowen, his staunch allies among Fianna Fáil Ministers in the new 1997 Coalition under Bertie Ahern included its Minister for Finance, Charlie McCreevy, the Minister for the Environment and Local Government, Noel Dempsey, Minister for Agriculture & Food, Joe Walsh, and Minister for Defence, David Andrews. All of them had been raised to full ministerial rank for the first time when Albert Reynolds became Taoiseach in February 1992.

It meant that those who believed Albert Reynolds was unelectable as President and those who were simply opposed to him, as well as those who were both, had to tread very warily indeed. Which is what they did. In fact, they hoped the decision would be taken out of their hands by John Hume.

Meanwhile Albert Reynolds' difficulty was recognised in 'Kairos', the name of the McAleese home in Rostrevor (from the Greek, meaning 'opportunity'). Harry Casey was very much in tune with what had been happening in politics in the Republic, particularly since the 1987 general election in which he had been so involved. And he knew Mary O'Rourke, who was now again back in Government and also deputy leader of Fianna Fáil. Mary O'Rourke, sister of Brian Lenihan and aunt to his sons Brian and Conor, also knew Mary McAleese from the days when both served on Fianna Fáil's Women's Committee in the 1980s. So it was arranged that the McAleeses would go to see Mary O'Rourke at her home in Athlone. Mary O'Rourke pledged her support. 'I said she would make a very good candidate,' she recalls, 'it went on from there. I never doubted she would get a terrific vote. I believed her warmth would shine through. I would love to be as expressive as that. Did you ever meet her parents? That's where she got it from. Lovely people.' She suggested the McAleeses contact Rory O'Hanlon and Dermot Ahern, and that she get her name 'out there'.

The McAleeses met both Dermot Ahern and Rory O'Hanlon, who were polite though non-committal at that early stage. Harry Casey spoke to Mary Hanafin, then just made a TD for the first time. They had attended NUI Maynooth at the same time. However, she said she would be supporting Michael O'Kennedy, whose name was being thrown in the ring about then, as he represented Tipperary North, her father's constituency. But she promised to assist in whatever way she could. And she did, through her advice. Other TDs and party members they met or contacted at the time included Mary Wallace, Eamon Ó Cuív, party general secretary Pat Farrell, John O'Donoghue and Frank Fahey, but there was nothing stirrin', except polite encouragement and advice. It was still only July and John Hume had yet to declare his hand. Fianna Fáil was fervently hoping that he would decide to seek the Presidency and the Reynolds issue would not have to be dealt with. And, at that point, Mary McAleese was not really seen as a serious contender, even by those in the party who knew anything at all about her. And they were few.

In August John Hume went on holiday to France. Days later, on 9 August in Belfast, and following a memorial lecture in honour of civil rights solicitor Paddy McGrory, Albert Reynolds made it clear publicly he was seeking the Fianna Fáil nomination for the Presidency. On 11 August David Andrews said that he himself was 'extremely interested' in seeking the nomination. He would decide later. On 16 August, at the MacGill Summer School in Glenties, County Donegal, Michael O'Kennedy announced his intention to seek the party nomination. None of this was good news for Albert Reynolds. David Andrews had been a supporter of his and so would attract votes which would have normally gone to him, while Michael O'Kennedy would further fragment the Reynolds vote as another Reynolds ally, Michael Smith, who he had promoted to full cabinet status as Minister for the Environment in February 1992, would now be voting for his Tipperary North constituency colleague instead. It may have been the vista of further subdivisions in the party which prompted PJ Mara, who had been Fianna Fáil director of elections in the June general election, to pronounce at the Humbert Summer School in Ballina, County Mayo on 28 August that John Hume was the outstanding candidate for the Presidency. But three days later, on 31 August, that sentimental man, Minister for Finance Charlie McCreevy, was not for turning. He said he had been on the back benches for fifteen years before Albert Reynolds appointed him to the Cabinet and that he would support him for the Presidency 'without equivocation, whether he asked me or not'.

Returning from France, John Hume announced on 8 September that he would not be seeking a nomination for the Presidency. Speaking recently on that decision he said, 'I couldn't leave the peace process. It was not a big decision.' Nor has he regretted that decision. 'Mary McAleese has been a very good President. She has presented a very good image of Ireland and is highly regarded, highly respected in Northern Ireland.'

But in early September 1997 she wasn't at the races where the Presidency in the Republic was concerned. An opinion poll published on 2 September in the *Irish Independent* didn't even mention her name. It found that John Hume was still the most popular choice, with 31 per cent support (this was six days before his announcement that he would not seek the nomination), Albert Reynolds was next at 13 per cent, then David Andrews on 8 per cent, Dana on 6 per cent and Michael O'Kennedy on 3 per cent. At that point Dana was still hoping for a Fianna Fáil nomination.

On 8 September, Harry Casey heard on the RTÉ radio news that John Hume would not be standing. Shortly afterwards he received a phone call from the Taoiseach's office inviting Mary McAleese to meet Bertie Ahern in Government Buildings the following afternoon. Escorted by Martin Mansergh, who met them in the foyer, Mary and Martin McAleese were taken to the Taoiseach's office where the then Fianna Fáil chief whip, the late Seamus Brennan, was also in attendance. She was invited to make her pitch and did so for about fifteen minutes after which she was questioned about being a Northerner in a southern election, about her Catholicism and the degree to which it was influencing her decision to seek the nomination. This was a question that had come up before when speaking to other members of Fianna Fáil in the previous months. As one party member put it, 'We were trying to establish whether they were Catholic right-wingers with an agenda.' The McAleeses laid that to rest and left the Taoiseach's office feeling positive, but they were no more certain of where they stood as far as Bertie Ahern was concerned. As they left, Seamus Brennan reminded them that they had a short time left before nomination day, 18 September. Since then, both Seamus Brennan and Martin Mansergh have been high in their praise of Mary McAleese's performance in the Taoiseach's office that day. Another would-be candidate, Dana, met the Taoiseach the same day, and it was Dana the media was interested in.

Behind the scenes, senior party figures were now totally convinced that neither Albert Reynolds nor Michael O'Kennedy would be elected. PJ Mara made a last ditch approach to former Tánaiste Ray McSharry, but McSharry declined to put his name forward. Then, as confirmed by reliable sources, and with the tacit, though not overt approval of Taoiseach Bertie Ahern, they set about discreetly canvassing support for Mary McAleese. They focused on those thirty-eight new members of the parliamentary party who had been elected for the first time the previous June, as well as on those known to be floating and those who would not vote for Albert Reynolds. From the beginning there was a determination to keep this as low key as possible; above all else, the leadership did not want another split in the party, while it also wanted to avoid any further alienation of existing factions. Mary McAleese may have suspected what was going on through the manner in which she was now being received and advised by senior party figures, but she was kept outside the loop. That way, she could not be blamed later for what might happen, or be identified as a divisive figure within the party.

Meanwhile Harry Casey had been busy. He prepared a personal letter detailing Mary McAleese's curriculum vitae and recommending her for the position of 'First Citizen'. Information was also supplied about her to the national and local media, with a particular emphasis on the weekend papers. Mary and Martin McAleese began to canvass within Leinster House itself, focusing on those who were known to be uncommitted, particularly on members of the cabinet. Soon her supporters felt that, as well as Mary O'Rourke, they had Dermot Ahern, John O'Donoghue, Síle de Valera, Jim McDaid, Micheál Martin, junior minister Eamon Ó Cuív and chief whip Seamus Brennan onside. It was believed that by then, too, the party general secretary Pat Farrell was a supporter.

A major fillip was the news on Sunday, 14 September, that Adi Roche of the Chernobyl Children's Project was to be the Labour Party presidential candidate. It placed an emphasis on gender as an issue in the election. And next day David Andrews, on his way home from Calcutta where he had represented the Government at Mother Teresa's funeral, said he would not be standing. Dana had by then decided she would seek the support of four county councils so she could stand as an independent candidate, and increasingly it looked as if Mary Banotti would secure the Fine Gael nomination.

It meant also that there were now three candidates seeking the Fianna Fáil nomination: former Taoiseach Albert Reynolds, former European Commissioner Michael O'Kennedy, and Mary McAleese, whose one bid for a Fianna Fáil seat had failed in Dublin in 1987. On the surface even then it wasn't thought she would have much of a chance. But the factors which had been building in her favour would soon make her seem 'unstoppable'. That was the word used by Bertie Ahern in his last interview as Taoiseach with RTÉ's Gerald Barry in May 2008.

It helped that, late in the day, Michael O'Kennedy sensed he was in trouble. He confronted Dermot Ahern in the members' bar in the Dáil and just stopped short of accusing him of treachery as word reached him of what had been going on behind the scenes. He was tempted to withdraw his name then, but family members persuaded him not to do so. He didn't, but he knew his race was run. Not so Albert Reynolds, not then, even as senior Government

Ministers were, at the eleventh hour, canvassing support for Mary McAleese by phone. But that night he, too, got a phone call. It knocked his confidence. 'I was told what was going on,' he says. 'I knew if the people mentioned to me were involved [in canvassing for Mary McAleese], she had to be successful.' As to whether Taoiseach Bertie Ahern knew about this at the time, he says, 'Of course he did. His people were canvassing for her ... I thought about pulling out that night ... I knew my fate was sealed.' But he stayed in 'to see whether people were telling the truth or not.' It was 'a bitter blow' and he wondered 'what was it in aid of? It would have been a decent thing [for someone] to come and tell you.' But no one ever did, then or since.

Earlier, another man who received a similar phone call that night was *Irish Independent* journalist John Cooney, then working with *Independent Network News* (INN) which was broadcasting hourly bulletins to the regional radio stations. In his last report that night he forecast that Albert Reynolds would win the nomination the following day, with Mary McAleese coming second. He recalls that 'shortly after the report's transmission, I received a call from a close aide of Taoiseach Bertie Ahern who told me that I was off-track and that support was swinging heavily towards McAleese, who would win. The source's curt though friendly guidance was that I should correct the forecast in the morning's bulletins. While this tip-off sounded authoritative, I got back onto Albert to check it out. Without betraying the identity of my "Deep Throat", I found that Albert remained confident that he had the vote in the bag.

'I had a restless few hours slumber. Overnight, I wrestled with the dilemma of what was really going on behind the scenes in the Fianna Fáil hinterland. It was inconceivable, I reckoned, that a Taoiseach would be organising a *coup d'état* against his predecessor. It was equally unthinkable, however, that Fianna Fáil would be going for McAleese without either Bertie's connivance or even encouragement through intermediaries. Yet, my source was adamant that McAleese, a failed Fianna Fáil Dáil candidate, had gained the upper hand over a former Taoiseach ... I wondered, too, if I was being used by the Bertie faction within Fianna Fáil to influence wavering members of the Fianna Fáil parliamentary party, many of whom would be listening to the morning bulletins on their car radios as they drove to Dublin for the crucial vote. Tipping McAleese to win could send a strong signal to them to get on the winning side. In my early morning bulletins, starting at 6am, I moved McAleese up the field, calling it a neck-and-neck race with the former Taoiseach. But I felt uneasy afterwards that I had been too cautious and should have called it in McAleese's favour.'

The McAleeses arrived at Leinster House on Wednesday, 17 September without either a proposer or seconder. Mary O'Rourke and Dick Roche had discussed this and discovered neither had been asked. Harry Casey says that asking Mary O'Rourke to do so 'would look like an act of revenge' on Albert Reynolds and he didn't want the McAleese candidature to have that sort of flavour. He had thought of asking local Meath TD Mary Wallace to propose and Dick Roche to second, but that didn't happen. That was the situation when Martin and Mary McAleese arrived alone on the fifth-floor Fianna Fáil room in Leinster House. They have recounted a number of times since how difficult an experience it was before the meeting began as members of the parliamentary party filed into the room, barely acknowledging their existence. It was a secret ballot and no one wanted to give hostages to fortune by being too friendly. It was a cold house for the McAleeses during those moments.

That morning, Albert Reynolds had a phone call from his party leader at home before he left for Leinster House. Bertie Ahern asked if he was happy he had the numbers to get the nomination and Albert Reynolds said he was. Both then discussed who Reynolds would like as his director of elections. He suggested Martin Macken, one of the party backroom team and later its general secretary. No one is entirely clear what the intention behind that phone call was, whether it was an overly nuanced attempt to alert Reynolds to what might happen and encourage him to withdraw or whether it was about

Mary and Martin at the time of the candidate selection

finding out whether he had some inkling already of what was in store. Albert Reynolds asked during that phone call whether he would have to make a speech. He was told by Bertie Ahern he would not, that his proposer and seconder would do so instead, as was procedure.

With five minutes to go before the selection meeting was to start in Leinster House, Fianna Fáil party chairman Rory O'Hanlon asked the McAleeses who their proposer and seconder would be. They had already asked Dick Roche was he proposing and he said he thought Mary O'Rourke was doing it. Now Rory O'Hanlon asked Dick Roche the same question and he said 'no'. He has said recently that, at that moment, he was then 'in such turmoil at the failure to have the proper nomination process arranged, but I understood Mary O'Rourke was to nominate Mary McAleese. I was opposed to that. I felt very strongly that it was wrong. Mary McAleese had no axe to grind with anyone in the party. She was not part of any cabal, group or faction.' The matter of proposer and seconder was quickly resolved however by Rory O'Hanlon when he secured agreement from the other two candidates to drop the procedure and instead invite each of them to speak for five minutes. It was decided to do so alphabetically, which meant Mary McAleese was first.

She had been up late into the early morning preparing a shorter, three-minute speech which she delivered without once looking at the page.

It began:

'Will this woman be the next President of Ireland? That decision is in your hands. This is the most important job interview I have ever attended. Before you ask who will be President it is critical to ask first what is the President? The answer to that question can be found in two important places. The first is in the 1937 Constitution and the second is in the hearts of the people who will on October 30th make their choice, in other words, it is in your hearts.

I sought the Presidential nomination because I have a dream for the eighth presidency of Ireland which I hope you will recognise as your dream too. It is a dream for a Presidency which will embrace the future with hope and confidence ...'

The speech continued with an exposition of Mary McAleese's vision of her Presidency, which is set out on p38 of this book, and also appeared in her campaign literature.

It ended: 'You know what you want for Ireland. When you come to decide who you want to be President I hope you will decide that you and I can embrace our future together.'

The speech had an electrifying effect. The applause was enthusiastic and long. For many of those present it was their first time to hear her speak. One description of the address afterwards was that 'It was a goose-pimply speech. People were in awe afterwards. She pushed all the right buttons.'

Michael O'Kennedy followed. 'Michael was Michael, hands all over the place,' was a description of his performance. And Albert Reynolds was the last speaker. Some felt he was at a disadvantage in that he didn't know he would be speaking which, it was said, was due 'more to a cock-up than a conspiracy.' Reynolds spoke mainly about the function of the President in promoting Irish industry. The strong response indicated that he, too, had a lot of support in the room.

As neither of the McAleeses was a member of the parliamentary party, they sat in a separate room after Mary McAleese spoke and awaited the outcome of the secret ballot. To gain the nomination a contender had to have half of the votes cast, plus one. There was shock, deep shock on the part of Albert Reynolds's supporters when it was announced that he had received 49 votes to Mary McAleese's 42 and Michael O'Kennedy's 21. The scale of what this implied where the party leadership was concerned was breathtaking in its audacity. Or betrayal, as some felt.

As the general secretary Pat Farrell stood to deal with a procedural matter before a second ballot could be taken, Albert Reynolds took his seat beside Bertie Ahern. As an observer recalled 'In that macho Fianna Fáil way, Bertie took his ballot paper and wrote Albert Reynolds name on it.' Then he placed it in the ballot box. That was when Albert Reynolds decided, regardless of the outcome of the second ballot, he was not going to be a candidate for the Presidency. He told the Taoiseach this. In fact, he realised then that he was finished.

In the second ballot, twenty of Michael O'Kennedy's votes went to Mary McAleese and Albert Reynolds dropped one when Senator Paddy McGowan had to leave for a medical appointment. The result was 62 to 48. It was a sensation. Albert Reynolds and his supporters were crushed and humiliated. There was shock and unspoken outrage at this treatment of Albert Reynolds on the part of his supporters and some family members present. One of the first things Mary McAleese did was to sympathise with him. She spoke to him about his enormous contribution to the peace process and towards bringing the Celtic Tiger Ireland into being. Graciously, and while admitting that it was 'a bitter blow', Albert Reynolds assured all that 'When we leave this room we leave as a united party.' It was, of course, the Fianna Fáil mantra, party *über alles*. Party above all! It was why he believed he should seek the nomination in the first place — for the party. A party in which loyalty used to be the supreme virtue.

Mary McAleese was taken from Leinster House to Buswell's Hotel across the road for a pre-arranged press conference, where the media was in a frenzy. It would become something of a template for what lay ahead.

Mary McAleese is presented to the press as the Fianna Fáil Presidential candidate, 1997

Nasty ...

It was an ugly campaign. First casualty was a political innocent – Adi Roche. Supported by the Labour Party, Democratic Left and the Greens, she was simply taken out. The first opinion poll of the presidential election campaign, an Irish Marketing Surveys' poll published in the *Sunday Independent* on 22 September, showed Roche in the lead, at 38 per cent to Mary McAleese's 35 per cent, Mary Banotti's 18 per cent and Dana on 9 per cent. Derek Nally had yet to enter the race. The following Sunday's newspapers carried stories alleging that Adi Roche was a bully when it came to running the Chernobyl Children's Project, which she had founded and for which she was primarily known up to then. The charity helped children who were suffering as a result of the 1986 meltdown at the Soviet nuclear reactor in Chernobyl. These stories were followed up by reports that her brother had been compulsorily retired from the army in 1969 for alleged republican sympathies. Her standing in polls simply went down, down, down after that. Fianna Fáil were blamed, but leader Bertie Ahern denied his party had anything to do with it.

He launched the Fianna Fáil candidate in the Shelbourne Hotel on 25 September. By then Mary McAleese had been transformed. The 'passionate amateurs', as they were referred to, who pushed her campaign for the Fianna Fáil nomination, had been replaced by the party machine. The hairdressers, make-up people and designer dressers had moved in. A slogan had been tested by market research and chosen – it was 'building bridges' and was based on her speech to the parliamentary party when she made her pitch for the

The Presidential candidates: Mary McAleese, Dana Rosemary Scallon, Adi Roche, Mary Banotti, Derek Nally

nomination. The chosen director of elections was Noel Dempsey, one of two men nominated by the party leadership because they were die-hard Albert Reynolds supporters and involvement by either in the presidential election campaign was a way of ensuring there was a united party behind her. The other man suggested was Brian Cowen. Brian Lenihan, who had been due to propose Michael O'Kennedy before proposers and seconders were dispensed with, was appointed election agent. Party general secretary Pat Farrell was appointed deputy director of elections. The campaign team included party press officer Martin Mackin, public relations consultant Eileen Gleeson, special events organiser Wally Young, as well as PJ Mara. PD Liz O'Donnell headed a team from that party, which also became involved in the campaign when it endorsed Mary McAleese's candidature.

Almost from the beginning it became clear that the candidate's relationship with the media and in particular with RTÉ would be fraught. 'The degree of antipathy towards her there [RTÉ] was poisonous,' one of the campaign team recalled. There was also tension between the candidate and reporters from the print media, particularly from among female reporters. 'The media attitude to her was that she was not a woman's woman,' said one campaign source. It became petty. One newspaper profile of her said she had been head girl at St Dominic's in Belfast. She had not, and she was perturbed that the girl who had been would think she was making such claims, and for ulterior purposes. The campaign team contacted the reporter concerned, to correct the error. The reporter refused to do so on the grounds that her sources were reliable. The error was never corrected.

An editorial in *The Irish Times* of 18 September 1997, the day after Mary McAleese won the Fianna Fáil nomination, referred to this media attitude. Observing that commentators had, in advance, written off her chances of securing the Fianna Fáil nomination, it said 'It is not the first time the Dublin media have misjudged the feisty Queen's University law professor and pro vice-chancellor. Her surprise appearance in the Catholic Hierarchy's delegation to the New Ireland Forum in 1984 has made her something of a *bête noire* for the Dublin media ever since. The distaste has often been mutual. Referring to her brief second career as an RTÉ presenter and reporter, she has said her presence beside the bishops meant she was perceived as "having broken ranks with the trendy image of the journalist into which I had been pigeon-holed by people who don't know me".'

The rest of that editorial is worth reproducing if only to dispel a view since purveyed that a reason Mary McAleese was treated so outrageously by media later in the campaign was because a caricature of her as a narrow, traditional, right-wing Northern Irish Catholic republican was believed to be the reality.

It continued, 'She is a devout Catholic who is able to talk unselfconsciously about her "spiritual and prayerful side". She says her religion enabled her to overcome the despair and anger of seeing her family put out of their home by loyalist gunmen and her deaf brother beaten senseless in a sectarian murder attempt.

Those experiences made her into that rare Northern phenomenon, a pacifist. However, in other respects, when she talks about Northern Catholics, she could be speaking about herself. "Mainly on account of people having suffered a great deal, their devotion is enhanced. But the world changes: openness on sexuality, women, the breakdown of the class structure, have all affected the way people look at the Church as well."

'That sentence should be a caution to anyone trying to caricature Prof McAleese as "the thinking person's Dana". Within the Church, she is known as a courageous critic of the injustices of a hierarchical power structure and a strong advocate of women priests. She is widely admired by Catholic women – and others – for her thoughtful and outspoken feminism.

'She is also a convinced ecumenist. A leading Protestant layman who worked with her on a ground-breaking inter-church report on sectarianism says, "She is no triumphalist Catholic wanting to stick people's noses in the dirt. She can be a tough cookie but she strikes me as the sort of person who would strive to be fair and understand other people's point of view, particularly those of Protestants."

'Her nationalism is similarly sophisticated. She remembers the New Ireland Forum as being the point when "nationalists started to get their voice back". Up to then they had been ground between the "revisionists saying nationalism is dead and gone" and "the Provos saying we are super-nationalists, the true voice and the only voice".

'The Forum planted the seeds of nationalist flexibility, she believes, allowing for the first discussion of joint sovereignty and leading to the historic developments of the Anglo-Irish Agreement, the Downing Street Declaration and the current peace process.

'As an outstanding and outspoken representative of the rising Northern nationalist middle-class, she arouses strong feelings among unionists. When she left her job as Reid professor of criminal law at Trinity College Dublin to become director of Queen's University's Institute of Professional Legal Studies, she ran into a storm of controversy. Questions in the Commons about her suitability were couched in language which only barely covered their sectarian undertone.

'Unionists are not the only people who don't like her. Southern liberals continue to view her as a conservative, anti-abortion Catholic. Many of her fellow Northern academics dislike her brashness and occasional abrasiveness. They resent her obvious ambition and "can-do" self-confidence. She is superbly articulate, the kind of Northern straight-talker who makes many Southerners feel uncomfortable. She is a fighter; when attacked, she defends herself with a mixture of the rapier and the bludgeon.

'If she does not allow her natural combativeness to be curbed by her Fianna Fáil handlers, her involvement in the presidential campaign will add greatly to its liveliness and will do much to raise its intellectual level.'

Her 'natural combativeness' was, however, to be mightily curbed by her Fianna Fáil handlers. In fact, at their very first meeting, campaign director Noel Dempsey made it clear that if he was to do the job it was he who must call the shots, even when she might feel his judgment call was wrong. She would be severely tested on that. At the same meeting she told him about her involvement with the Redemptorist Peace Ministry at Clonard and how, under no circumstances, could she talk about it.

Derek Nally had been asked by some of the voluntary organisations he had been involved with to be a candidate in the Presidential election campaign, to highlight the work of the voluntary sector in Irish society. A former Garda, he had been president of the Association of Garda Sergeants and Inspectors (AGSI) and was a founder of the Irish Association for Victim Support in the 1980s. Mary McAleese was then Reid Professor of Law at Trinity College and he invited her to be on its steering committee, an invitation she accepted. He took the Dana route to nomination – he sought the support of four County Councils. Five backed him: Clare, Carlow, Wexford, Kildare and South Dublin. On his nomination he was contacted by radio and TV producer John Caden, who he knew from appearances on RTÉ programmes such as Radio 1's 'The Gay Byrne Show' and 'The Late Late Show' which John Caden had produced. He admired Nally for two things in particular. 'He was always very strong on Northern terrorism and he stood up to Haughey. As President of the AGSI he challenged Haughey on interference with security issues.'

John Caden became Nally's director of publicity. Another man who approached Derek Nally to offer his support was Munster MEP Pat Cox. He and John Caden helped prepare his launch speech. Very early in the campaign Caden gave Derek Nally an envelope. It was a letter from Eoghan Harris explaining he had no time to get involved in the campaign, but giving some advice on appearance and what clothes to wear for television etc. He said he backed his candidacy and intended to vote for him.

Six days after Derek Nally launched his campaign, he was a guest on RTÉ's 'Questions and Answers'. The previous day, 12 October 1997, a report by Emily O'Reilly in the *Sunday Business Post* claimed that Mary McAleese was sympathetic to Sinn Féin. It was based on a leaked internal memo written by Department of Foreign Affairs first secretary Dympna Hayes following meetings she had with Mary McAleese in January and May 1997, when the IRA was not on ceasefire. The memo said 'She [Mary McAleese] was very pleased with Sinn Féin's performance in the general election and confident they will be able to perform better in the local elections: she expects Mick Murphy, the Sinn Féin candidate in Rostrevor, her own constituency, to pick up a seat this time.'

Derek Nally issued a statement which began, 'Sinn Féin poses people with moral as well as political problems. Like me, most Irish people would never vote for Sinn Féin, peace process or no peace process, because they have been carrying on a murder campaign for twenty-five years. One of their victims was

Garda Gerry McCabe. That is why they get 2 per cent of the vote in the Republic. Mary McAleese seems to work on a different set of moral assumptions. A story in the *Sunday Business Post* carries a report of her conversation with a civil servant in Foreign Affairs in which she clearly comes across as sympathetic to Sinn Féin at a time when they were still carrying on terrorist activities.'

His statement was picked up by the broadcast media and clearly would feature on 'Questions and Answers'. John Caden rang and asked to meet him at RTÉ. Caden had the four questions that were to be asked on the programme later. He wanted Nally to meet Eoghan Harris. Eoghan Harris told him there was only one of the questions he needed to bother about and that concerned Mary McAleese's moral agenda. 'He ranted and raved,' Nally recalls. 'He gave me a piece of paper and wrote one sentence on it and he said "pull this out of your pocket and read what's there [on "Questions and Answers"]".' Nally cannot remember what the sentence said. However it is believed to have been the line from the Dympna Hayes memo about Mary McAleese being 'very pleased with Sinn Féin's performance in the general election ...'.

On the programme Derek Nally did as advised, while also asking Mary McAleese what connection she had with Sinn Féin. She said she had none and disputed the accuracy of the Dympna Hayes memo. She said she had never voted for Sinn Féin and had always opposed violence. She did not recognise the comments she was supposed to have made to Dympna Hayes. Explaining the background to the two conversations involved, she said that after the breakdown of the first IRA ceasefire she had been asked in 1996 to join the Redemptorist Peace Ministry, headed up by Fr Alec Reid. The ministry had been involved in bringing about the first ceasefire, so she felt honoured to be asked and agreed to help, she said. Its work involved meetings with members of Sinn Féin and the SDLP, with a view to finding the ground on which a new ceasefire could be established. 'I never met Sinn Féin on my own and I only met them in the context of that peace initiative,' she said. She had also 'never, ever' met the IRA.

Derek Nally said the Foreign Affairs document had quoted her as saying she was 'very pleased with Sinn Féin's performance in the (UK) general election'. She was also quoted as saying she was not interested in 'running for politics' in the North unless there was a Sinn Féin–SDLP pact. She said that was 'untrue'. She remembered her two conversations with Dympna Hayes quite clearly. She had told her that they were working quite assiduously in the peace ministry to bring about the conditions for a ceasefire which, John Hume had made clear, were the conditions required for a Sinn Féin–SDLP pact. 'This particular official at no stage took notes, and let me be just be very clear about this, nor did she tell me that notes would be taken and made of the conversation,' she said. She also said she had never in her life taken the view that Sinn Féin was right not to condemn the deaths of gardaí. 'I do not believe that one single person should have shed one single drop of blood in this country for the things that they shed them for. I have always been strongly opposed to violence.'

It was an electrifying exchange and did not end there. Campaign colleagues said Mary McAleese was 'seething' at the time, mainly because she had calls from her children in Rostrevor to say they had heard radio reports that she supported the IRA. They were afraid. The RUC moved in to give them police protection. Her concern for her children was why the only reason she made any, even limited, reference to the Redemptorist peace ministry talks she had been involved in.

The following evening there was a debate in Trinity College in which both candidates participated. The motion was 'Is the next President going to be a clone of Mary Robinson?' Earlier that day, Sean Flynn of *The Irish Times* had contacted the Nally campaign seeking an opinion piece for the following day's edition, dealing with the leaked Foreign Affairs documents. 'He asked for an article by me about my involvement,' John Caden recalls. 'I said to Derek I didn't want to do it. The campaign was about him, the candidate, not about me. "No John, do it, do it, do it," he said to me. I advised him I shouldn't. He absolutely insisted.'

John Caden wrote the piece, albeit reluctantly, and it was approved by Derek Nally. It ended 'Derek Nally does not accept the McAleese denial. She has made too many denials and back-turns, about the relationship with Charles Haughey, about her views on the EU, about her views on Northern Ireland as an "archetypal police state", for her denials to be accepted at face value. What Derek Nally said on 'Questions and Answers' still stands. If she wants to clear her name she should sue.'

John Caden's prepared speech for Nally for the Trinity debate focused on young people and had no reference to Northern Ireland issues. But when he arrived for the debate at Trinity he heard Derek Nally deliver a very different speech. And at the end of the debate, Caden recalls, 'A female student stood up and asked him, "Do you withdraw what you said about Mary McAleese?" He said, "I do". There was mayhem. There had been no preparation for this.'

Then Mary McAleese approached John Caden. 'Are you going to withdraw the *Irish Times* article now,' she asked him. He cannot remember what he said to her, but was very surprised that she should be aware of the article in the first place. Nally, he recalls, 'was in conclave with his group of ex-Garda supporters. Everything had changed fundamentally, leaving me offside. The whole position had changed.' He also felt there was a certain aggression being directed at him by the Nally supporters. 'Derek didn't ask me to withdraw the article. "Whatever you think yourself, John", was what he said about it. It was total chaos. He was going in one direction. I was going in another over something that was so important to his platform.'

Derek Nally also remembers that night in Trinity College and the student asking the question. 'I'll never forget this. She said, "Derek Nally, do you believe Mary McAleese when she says she is not a supporter of Sinn Féin and has never supported them?" I replied, "Of course I do, in the absence of any evidence to the contrary. I based what I said on what was in the report from a Department of Foreign Affairs first secretary, which Mary McAleese addressed on 'Questions and Answers'. I do, of course I do. I have no evidence to the contrary." He believes the student who asked the question was planted by Fianna Fáil. At the end of the debate he was approached by Wally Young who had accompanied Mary McAleese. He told him she wanted to have a word, privately. As he went over to her, John Caden asked where he was headed and he said that Mary McAleese had asked for a private word. "No private chats," warned Caden, whereupon Nally turned on him and said he would talk to whoever he liked. 'She was very pleasant. I always found her very pleasant. As far as I was concerned the matter was dead by then.' She spoke to him about her concerns for the safety of her children.

Later that night Nally was on radio with Vincent Browne and 'sold me down the river', according to John Caden. 'At a principled level, he sold out. I was extremely annoyed.'

There was a phone call to the Nally campaign HQ in Naas that night. It was Eoghan Harris. Nally recalls it as 'one of the most outrageous calls I ever received. He called me "a cowardly f***er", "lily livered". There were six or seven of us at the table and I held the phone out.' One of his colleagues told him to hang up on Harris. 'I never heard such a tirade in all my life. It ended the whole affair.'

But not quite. Publication of John Caden's article in *The Irish Times* the following day was accompanied by a biting editorial headed 'An Apology Due, Mr Nally'. There was a similarly strong editorial in the *Irish Independent* that same day. The following Thursday morning John Caden told Nally he was standing back from the campaign. 'I knew I was damaged. No good could come of any of this. He was still the candidate. Let him run,' was his view.

Then Gerry Adams came on the Pat Kenny Show on RTÉ Radio 1 later that morning. Asked who he would vote for in the presidential election campaign, he said, 'Personally I would probably vote for Mary McAleese, if I had a vote.' His other preferences would be Adi Roche, Mary Banotti, and Dana, in that order. He would not vote for Derek Nally. It prompted Fine Gael leader John Bruton to issue a statement questioning the propriety of someone 'endorsed by Sinn Féin' being the Government candidate in the campaign. Which prompted Noel Dempsey to query whether Fine Gael had a hand in the leaked Foreign Affairs memo. He implied that the leaking had been hatched at a lunch in Dublin the previous week which was attended by John Bruton, Eoghan Harris, and Fine Gael advisor Ray Dooney. They had been seen by Brian Cowen, who was sitting at another table in the same restaurant. The alleged conspiracy was vehemently denied by John Bruton and has been since by Eoghan Harris. 'It was a celebration of something,' he says, but is not sure of what.

At lunchtime that Thursday, Eoghan Harris was interviewed on the 'News At One'. Mary McAleese would make a 'very dangerous and tribal President', he said. Derek Nally's attacks on her had been vindicated by 'Gerry Adams's endorsement of her'. 'Mary McAleese is clearly, as Chris McGimpsey said, an unreconstructed Northern nationalist who will drag all sorts of tribal baggage with her when she is elected President of Ireland,' he said. 'Nobody will be able to control Mary McAleese. She's arrogant and she's a self-sufficient candidate who is using the Southern election to advance her career. She is not a Sinn Féin-er, she's a me féin-er.' 'I don't believe it's a wise thing for the Republic of Ireland at this time to elect any kind of Northern nationalist, any extreme Northern nationalist, because it sends appalling signals to unionists at a sensitive time in the peace process, and every unionist I spoke to in Northern Ireland confirmed that. But Mary McAleese is a particularly extreme nationalist who's got a very soft ride from the media given that she is a protégé of Charles Haughey, and given that she defends him … And I believe Bertie Ahern will really regret this … that he picked somebody who is basically a tribal time-bomb.'

Earlier in the interview he explained that he had become involved in the Nally campaign [despite his earlier letter to Nally saying that he had no time to do so] and had written a campaign strategy. 'I wrote a three-page document called "Strategic Issues for the Presidential Campaign", which set out the fact that I believe this campaign … would want to return to a traditional Presidency and wouldn't be into huggy-wuggy, clap-happy stuff, and that Derek Nally is a man who is well poised to do well …'

'The reason I support him is that he is a candidate who is most opposed to Mary McAleese … I mean, let there be no huggy-muggy about it, my main reason for supporting Derek Nally is that he was the candidate likely to most point up Mary McAleese's weaknesses. I would vote for Donald Duck if they opposed Mary McAleese. I think she will make a very dangerous and tribal President.'

Later that day he said he felt he had achieved his main aim, which was to damage the McAleese candidacy. He expected that the controversy over her dealings with Sinn Féin could knock three to five points off her opinion poll rating in favour of the Fine Gael candidate, Mary Banotti.

The following night the five candidates were on 'The Late Late Show'. All was sweetness and light. However, asked about the involvement of Eoghan Harris in his campaign, Derek Nally said 'Harris wasn't on my campaign. He was one of the backroom cloaked people who was pulling the strings. What's important was I got rid of them early.'

John Caden believes that what Derek Nally did on that programme was 'appalling. He said he was duped. I was extremely disappointed in him for having done so. It was absolutely appalling. If we duped him so did Pat Cox. Pat Cox is a very shrewd operator.'

Pat Cox, who remained with the Nally campaign, forcefully denied that Derek Nally had been duped by John Caden or Eoghan Harris. What still rankles with John Caden from the entire episode is the suggestion by Derek Nally that he had been somehow dishonest with him. 'He knew right from the start where I was coming from and that Eoghan would be involved. I told him that I was going to ask Eoghan for his support. Every document we prepared he had long sight of it. Then at some stage he changed his mind, which he was entitled to do. He went about it the way he did. But he shouldn't have said the things he did.'

After 'The Late Late Show' there followed a brief period of calm in the campaign.

Gerry Adams has no regrets about endorsing Mary McAleese for the presidency on 'The Pat Kenny Show'. 'I said in that radio interview that if I

A family photo in St Stephen's Green, Dublin, in 1997, during the election campaign

had a vote I would vote for her, and of course that was seized on. She is a Northern Catholic who has experienced sectarianism first hand. She grew up in Belfast at a time of great turbulence and so I would have been very, very conscious of that. One thing I like about her is her common touch. Whether lecturing on theology or law she can also engage comfortably with the women she had lived beside all her life. It is one of her great qualities – to be so rooted. That she has come out of all of this doesn't mean she was in any way supportive of physical force. She kept well away from that. Mary McAleese was never an IRA or Sinn Féin sympathiser, not at all. For her the IRA were as John Hume saw them – neighbours' children with whom he disagreed but knew where they were coming from.'

Gerry Adams didn't really know Mary McAleese while she was growing up in Belfast but he knew her father, Paddy Leneghan. His Long Bar was not far from the Adams' family home on Abercorn Street North. When Gerry Adams was in his early twenties he didn't drink much, but he used to attend GAA and republican meetings held in the Long Bar. All sorts of local groups used the pub as a meeting place. His first memory of hearing about Mary McAleese was when he was told she had been an advisor to the Catholic bishops at their 1984 appearance at the New Ireland Forum in Dublin Castle. 'My first recollection of meeting her was at Clonard monastery. Fr Alec was trying to widen out support for the [Hume/Adams] talks. Part of his thrust was to get the Catholic Church involved. He and Fr Des Wilson tried to get various bishops engaged, but it was futile. Fr Des lost patience. The talks were quite far on when she became involved so it hadn't any real effect on the context or the process. It did bring a sense that others out there were supportive. John Hume was in considerable trouble with elements in his own party. I was not privy to the details of what they [Mary McAleese and Jim Fitzpatrick] did but it was very useful to have someone there who was supportive.

'Criticism of the *Irish News* by Brid Rodgers was indicative of a kickback element in the SDLP who thought I was colonising John Hume. Then that might have been due to his leadership style — that he wasn't keeping the others informed. Brid Rodgers complained about Mary McAleese, Fr Reid and what was going on, in an Irish Government briefing. Jim Fitzpatrick was also trying to broaden out [support]. He became involved, with very good intentions. It was not a defining contribution in terms of the detailed discussions between myself and John Hume, but it was another strand of opinion. Jim Fitzpatrick did good work with the loyalists, as have Mary and Martin since. They were not involved in the detail of the talks. From Fr Alec's point of view there was a need for an alternative ... he saw the role of the Church as being to provide an alternative beyond condemnation. I had not as much faith in that institution as Fr Reid. Mary and Jim were active lay Catholics. He may have dealt with them in great detail but I did not attend many meetings with them. There were a couple with myself and John Hume. From Fr Reid's perspective he had been charged by me to come forward with an alternative. Jim and Mary would have sown the seed. They were useful from my point of view in that they gave their opinions and brought into the process points of view which reflected their perspective, especially Mary, coming from her academic and Irish Government circles and she knew opinion makers and opinion formers. They were not spectators, but they were not writing drafts [of Hume–Adams documents]. Mary was also able to give an insight, strange as it may seem, into middle-class Unionist impressions and points of view. By then, ten years had passed since we started the first talks. It was a long ten years. Fr Alec spent five or six years trying to get meetings with Haughey, Cahal Daly, Seamus Mallon. On receipt of his letter John Hume wrote back. It struck me as stupid that we had not gone to him in the first place. But it was because we had thought that Seamus Mallon was the nationalist in the SDLP.

'Where the Presidency is concerned it was hugely important to have a Northerner in that position and hugely important it was a woman. It is good, too, that it is a woman from Ardoyne, though why they play 'The Star of the County Down' when she comes into a room instead of 'The Glens of Antrim' I will never know. It is good to know that a wee girl from Ardoyne can go to the Áras and be Head of State. Martin and herself have done some great work "building bridges", bringing busloads from unionist townlands and villages [to Áras an Uachtaráin]. All quiet nation building.'

He was 'delighted she stood for a second term'. It was also 'exactly the right time' to have a bridge builder in such a position. He complimented the President on her 'very open engagement with unionism'. He commended her bravery in visiting the 'even dangerous' loyalist Village area of Belfast. 'It is really important that her outreach to working class unionists and loyalists is seen to be on an ongoing basis.' He recalled how at the height of the Holy Cross situation, when Catholic schoolchildren were barracked by their loyalist neighbours on their way to school, he got a call from the Áras asking, 'Can we help?' It led to 'a brilliant week' with busloads of children, some of them teenagers from the Short Strand, going to Dublin, visiting the Áras for lunch, Croke Park and other places in Dublin. 'You can thank Siobhan O'Hanlon for that. Both [unionist and nationalist visits to the Áras] were just two recent examples of quiet and very practical intervention.'

But he feels that for the President to host a visit by Queen Elizabeth of Britain to the Republic 'would be deeply provocative. We have to put up with it here. There is very little we can do about it. But we would object to her visiting the Republic.'

… and Brutish

The comparative serenity of the five Presidential candidates, particularly Mary McAleese, on that Friday night's 'Late Late Show' was dissipated within twenty-four hours. Early editions of the *Sunday Business Post* the following evening had further reports by Emily O'Reilly of more details from the Dympna Hayes Foreign Affairs memos about her meetings earlier that year with Mary McAleese. There was also a third explosive memo of a conversation Ms Hayes had with SDLP deputy leader Brid Rodgers. Reading the content, people began to wonder whether Eoghan Harris may have been correct after all.

The Hayes memo of her conversation with Brid Rodgers on 3 April 1997 included the following: 'Ms Rodgers is concerned with the poor coverage available to the SDLP in the *Irish News* of late. She put this down to the fact that the editor-in-chief of the *Irish News*, Mr Jim Fitzpatrick, has recently formed an unofficial alliance with Father Alec Reid and Mary McAleese of QUB. Referring to this group as the "triumvirate", Ms Rodgers described their main object as promoting a new nationalist consensus which owes more to Sinn Féin than the SDLP. All three are in regular touch with the Sinn Féin leadership and are in reality pushing the Sinn Féin agenda.'

The memo of Ms Hayes's 28 January meeting with Mary McAleese said, 'Ms McAleese is in regular contact with both John Hume and Gerry Adams. She has recently tried to convince Mr Adams that his interpretation of Hume's *Sunday Independent* article is too narrow, particularly regarding the reference to Sinn Féin's policy of abstention.' And that 'on a personal level Ms McAleese has no interest in participating in the upcoming elections in "any shape or form" in the absence of an SDLP-Sinn Féin joint election platform. She expects that the elections will return the status quo in terms of overall community representation. The most interesting angle will be the direction of the nationalist vote. Ms McAleese is of the view that Sinn Féin will gain a lot of ground from the SDLP. Most nationalists equate the SDLP with John Hume and John Hume is now firmly attached to the Hume-Adams process in the nationalist psyche. Now for the first time many middle-class voters, especially first generation middle-class nationalists like herself, will be able to countenance voting for Sinn Féin as continuing to support John Hume while, at the same time, landing a more direct swipe at the British government.'

Hayes's memo of her 26 May 1997 meeting with Mary McAleese included: 'The new Labour government had produced a great boost for Sinn Féin's election prospects by arranging the meeting between Sinn Féin and the NIO [Northern Ireland Office] officials on the same day as the local elections. A lot of new voters in the nationalist community came out and voted for Sinn Féin in the general election (she did accept the point that a lot of those voters had also supported the SDLP even if that support didn't translate into seats).

'Ms McAleese feels that a lot of the "new" Sinn Féin support has come from the young middle-aged and upwardly mobile nationalists rather than first-time voters, and that they see Sinn Féin as far more likely to deliver on the political front than the SDLP. She attributed the SDLP's failure to pick up either of the Mid-Ulster or West Tyrone [seats] in part to their poor PR. The same tired old faces continue to front for the SDLP while Sinn Féin publicise a range of candidates who all look young and fresh by comparison.'

It was damning, but there was more. That same memo included the following paragraph: 'She has not had much contact with Adams since the election although she returned from London last Monday evening on the same flight as Adams and McGuinness. Both of them were in great form and had thoroughly enjoyed their visit to Westminster! (A well-known and highly successful consultant from Touche Ross whom Ms McAleese had known for many years was seated beside her on the plane and proceeded to ignore her for the rest of the journey after hearing her exchange with the Sinn Féin leaders.)'

The content of the three memos demanded a response. But Noel Dempsey insisted that Mary McAleese would not respond to media queries on the memos or anything else throughout that long Sunday. He pointed out that she had not wanted details of the Clonard talks to come out. She was to stay quiet. It would be the most trying day of her campaign. It was the annual Fianna Fáil Bodenstown Wolfe Tone Commemoration Sunday, which she was scheduled to attend. The media was there in force. She would not answer questions. They sensed blood. She was furious. They were furious. But worse was to come. A press conference had been arranged for the Skeffington Arms Hotel on Galway's Eyre Square for 7.30 that evening, in advance of a Fianna Fáil/Progressive Democrat rally in the Great Southern Hotel across the Square. It was decided that the press conference would not go ahead and that she would arrive too late for it. They knew this would drive an already angry media into a rage. But Noel Dempsey's rationale, as explained since, was, 'I knew that any denial of the allegations would be much stronger coming from somebody else other than Mary ... I needed to make space to allow that happen. We didn't know what else would be released in the papers, and we couldn't spend the campaign answering allegations and commenting on other people's opinions of her. It was a gamble, but all my political instincts told me it was a gamble that would pay off.'

But it was more than that. It was a glorious opportunity. Even at that late stage in the campaign, even if Mary McAleese was leading in the polls, support for her among Fianna Fáil's core voters remained low. Further, it was proving difficult to motivate party activists to get out there and canvass for her. This was as much due to the fact that the presidential election followed so closely on the June general election, but there was also a level of resentment among many in the party at the way Albert Reynolds had been treated. And Mary McAleese was still something of an unknown quantity where many Fianna Fáilers were concerned. But that was about to change dramatically. Nothing was quite as likely to stir the green heart of core Fianna Fáilers as the image suggested of this broth of an Irish girl with a hint of sulphur, as portrayed in Dympna Hayes's memos. And nothing was quite as likely to motivate them in her defence as to see her – their candidate – harassed by the hated media. This strategy, too, was a gamble, but it paid off in spades. She would top all news bulletins and grace all front pages the following day. The only people in Ireland who didn't know about Mary McAleese after this would be in graveyards.

But back to Galway. When Mary McAleese arrived at the Great Southern in the city shortly before 8.30 that evening, she was led from her car by a piper through a phalanx of minders on each side of her keeping off a scrum of reporters shouting questions and thrusting microphones at the candidate all the way to the hotel entrance. It was bedlam.

This was how Catherine Cleary reported it in the following day's *Irish Times*. 'It is not often you see a Government Minister take a lunge at someone. But last night the Minister for the Environment and Rural Development, Mr Dempsey, got carried away with the bluster of it all. Launching himself across the lobby of the Great Southern in Galway he grabbed RTÉ's Jim Fahy and tried to drag him away from the Fianna Fáil and Progressive Democrat presidential candidate, Prof Mary McAleese. It was great television but not great public relations. Why are you acting like this, reporters asked Prof McAleese and the team of media handlers-turned-rugby-forwards who surrounded her. She did not answer. Mr Dempsey accused us of launching an assault on the presidential candidate. Reporters who had been shoved out of the candidate's way as she smiled grimly into the television camera wondered what the former journalist thought of the heavy-gang tactics.

'It had all been going so well until then. Another set piece with a grassroots rally for the popular presidential candidate. A piper waited to play 'O'Neill's March' as she made her triumphant way into a ballroom full of supporters. A press conference had been scheduled but this was to be left until after the rally. When she arrived 'O'Neill's March' was lost in the din of McAleese's Charge. They manhandled her through the press pack and into an ante room. And while the candidate composed herself, outside they straightened their clothes and glowered. In the ballroom she stood between the PDs' Bobby Molloy and Fianna Fáil's Éamon Ó Cuív, a picture of happiness, supported literally by both Government parties. She smiled serenely at the display of Irish dancing to taped accordion music, while the bard read a poem of welcome. Bobby Molloy gave a fire and brimstone speech against the "evil-minded people" who were trying to blacken the candidate's name. He spoke darkly about feeling as a PD member that there were "people amongst us" who supported other candidates and were sinking to underhand tactics. A Minister of State, Mr Noel Treacy, added his thunder: "There are those with blatant agendas with hidden schemes to try and destroy the opportunity for Ireland that is Mary McAleese."

There was standing room only and the crowd loved it. Mr Ó Cuív spoke of the "people who take risks" as the "easy targets". "Prof McAleese took risks. She took risks for peace. If we're going to criticise people who worked behind the scenes building bridges then I think this country has gone wrong." The candidate gave her usual hustings speech, telling the audience that she had saved that speech for them. Another local anecdote was pulled, Haughey-like, from a hat and the honeyed speech about the modern phenomenon that is Ireland flowed. When she finally spoke to the media, Prof McAleese suggested we all sit down and watch her on 'The Late Late Show' if we wanted answers to the questions. "Absolutely comprehensively," was how she had dealt with the issue she said, repeating the phrase. "I've explained it comprehensively and I've no intention of explaining it any further." With the word comprehensively used as comprehensively as she could, her tones relaxed again when she spoke of the "warm welcome" in the city of tribes. Asked why she refused to speak to the media before the rally, she said: "I wasn't at all unwilling to speak to you on the way in. You know perfectly well what happened on the way in. We were late, extremely late, and I had a lot of people here to whom I had to give priority." The media tribe tried for another question but the handlers said enough was enough. There was flesh to be pressed, flowers to be accepted and smiling photo opportunities to be given.'

Sitting at home in Navan, watching the events outside the Great Southern run as item number one on the RTÉ Nine O'Clock News, Harry Casey was fit to be tied. He rang Fr Brendan Callanan, the Redemptorists' provincial in Ireland, to say he was amazed he was being silent while all of this went on. He was the man who, along with Fr Reid, had invited Mary McAleese to join the Clonard Peace Ministry. The priest explained that he had faxed a statement to RTÉ earlier that evening in time for the Nine O'Clock News explaining the Peace Ministry, how it abhorred violence in all its forms and how it was deplorable that those involved should be slighted in any way. RTÉ had received the statement, he said, 'we checked after sending it'. Harry Casey rang RTÉ to see why they hadn't used the statement. 'What statement?' was the response. He explained and said it had been faxed in earlier that evening. Someone went off to check the fax machine and came back to say 'Yeah, it's here.' They had missed it because no one was watching the fax machine. Fr Callanan's statement was published in the papers the next day, as was a statement from Jim Fitzpatrick which said Mary McAleese was 'an honourable and trusting individual who is totally committed to peace'.

There wasn't a peep out of anyone in the SDLP.

The Irish Times was unhappy. Its editorial that Monday was headed 'McAleese must give frank explanation of views.' It began, 'Prof Mary McAleese now has a serious problem in her bid for the Presidency. It demands nothing less than the frankest explanation of her views on Northern Ireland policy, the SDLP, Sinn Féin and the peace process for confidence in her ability to be a truly representative head of state to be restored. The problem has been created for her not only by the circumstances surrounding Mr Gerry Adams's endorsement of her candidacy but by any objective assessment of the opinions offered by her, and about her, in the three information-gathering reports for the Department of Foreign Affairs in January, April and May of this year.'

And it concluded, 'If the Department of Foreign Affairs assessments are credible, the Mary McAleese revealed by them is, as former Progressive Democrats TD, Mr Michael McDowell, has said, a "very dark shade of green". There is nothing wrong with that. There would be no peace process if people did not speak to Sinn Féin. There is even a certain legitimacy in hoping that the Sinn Féin vote would increase, if only to give the doves sway over the IRA hawks. What has gone wrong for Mary McAleese is that it would appear that she is concealing her real political self from the voters in the presidential election.'

The Alliance Party leader in the North, John Alderdice, said she should withdraw from the election. Instead, she visited the Aran islands. Reports were being received by the campaign team that the candidate was beginning to be seen as arrogant in continuing to refuse to answer media questions and that the initial sympathy inspired by the media frenzy was wearing off. It was decided that there should be a press conference. Some on her campaign team were amazed at the coverage of the Hayes memos, not so much for their content, as the fact that not one journalist had bothered to check Mary McAleese's track record down the decades where peace was concerned, and then attempt to square that with the person portrayed in the Dympna Hayes memos. It simply didn't add up. If anything, there seemed, in media coverage, to be a leaning to Ms Hayes's understanding rather than to Mary McAleese's deeds or track record.

The press conference was in the heritage centre on Inis Mór. All sides were tense, and local people were deeply hostile to the media. She denied allegations that she was 'pushing a Sinn Féin agenda' and said she has no intention of stepping down as a candidate. She said the discussions 'involved very well-known members of Sinn Féin and very, very well-known members of the SDLP'. Asked to clarify her relationship with Gerry Adams, she said to the reporter, 'I'm on speaking terms with you because you've followed me now for a while. I think I've probably met you more times now than I've ever met Gerry Adams. I don't know what you want to insinuate by that …' She added, 'I go into meetings, very formal meetings, and these were very formal meetings. He's not a personal friend. He's not a person I go out with at night. He's not a person that I converse with in the normal course of events. I think what I was trying to indicate is, very clearly, that I'm not a member of Sinn Féin. I'm not a supporter of Sinn Féin and to the extent that you or anybody else has tried to indicate that I am and that there is some mystery here, let me absolutely reassure you, for probably I don't know how many times now, that there is not.' She 'barely' knew the deputy SDLP leader, Brid Rodgers. 'That was the very first time I met her; was in that context.' She said she had 'no intention of opening up for the curiosity of journalists, and only really to feed the curiosity of journalists, everything that was said in those meetings.' Asked to respond to the new documents, she said it was 'exactly the same story' that related to 'comments allegedly made by Brid Rodgers and allegedly transcribed so I don't know how accurate those are ... If they were as inaccurate and as mischievously spun out as those that were made in relation to me, then, frankly, I've nothing to fear from them, because if they're that inaccurate, I don't see why I should have to deal with them at all.'

An indication of what relations were like between the candidate and the media at the time can also be gleaned from the following in a report by Catherine Cleary of *The Irish Times*. 'Then someone asked if she could read upside down as she read while a reporter scribbled. No, she said, she was just making sure she was speaking at the right speed. This *Irish Times* reporter had noted this foible on a previous occasion, she [Mary McAleese] said, and had put a "nasty gloss" on it without checking her motivation. Suddenly there was a nip in the air again.'

On that Monday the SDLP at last overcame its shyness. John Hume described as 'absolutely false' and 'an absolute outrage' the allegations surrounding Mary McAleese's role in the peace process. And Brid Rodgers said she wished to 'refute the unworthy implications from some quarters' being ascribed to Mary McAleese's role in the peace process. Seamus Mallon and Joe Hendron also spoke in her defence. Sinn Féin's Martin McGuinness said he had always believed she was an SDLP supporter. Eddie McGrady went so far as to breach an SDLP rule not to intervene in southern elections by actually endorsing her candidacy.

Statements in support of her as a woman of peace also came from Protestant clergymen in Northern Ireland such as Rev. Ken Newell, Sam Burch, and Tim Kinahan, also from Presbyterian Dr David Stevens of the Irish Council of Churches.

However there was an RTÉ interview to do, for 'Prime Time'. It was conducted by Eamon Lawlor in Limerick on that Tuesday and it outraged her campaign team, her supporters; even the neutrals were taken aback at its intensity. She was tense and he was aggressive, asking her at one point if she was 'intimate' with Gerry Adams. Harry Casey said he 'felt very sorry for her that night'. He described the interview as 'psychological rape by television. It was a savage assault'. He spoke of the pressure it had put on the McAleese family in Rostrevor where the grandparents 'were trying to distract the children from watching and Emma was crying her eyes out, asking "why are they doing this to Mum?"'

It was another low point, but almost the last of them. Support from Northern Ireland continued and probably the most extraordinary and unexpected intervention came from John Taylor, deputy leader of the UUP. Speaking on RTÉ's 'This Week' programme the following Sunday, he said, he never considered Mary McAleese to be a supporter of Sinn Féin. He said Brid Rodgers's views [of Mary McAleese] were not supported by most SDLP supporters in the North. He said he was surprised to see some members of the SDLP accusing her of supporting Sinn Féin. 'But I do not believe that those members of the SDLP are representative of the SDLP throughout Northern Ireland. I think they are a minority.' Mary McAleese was totally different from the majority of people in the North. 'She is an out-and-out nationalist, very, very green nationalist and promotes her Catholicism too much. She overdoes it. But having said that, and pointing out how different she is from me, as a Protestant and a British citizen here in Northern Ireland, she was a most able person. She steered the new campus in Armagh in an excellent and efficient way and although we disagree in politics and religion I found her quite easy to work with.'

Speaking about this intervention in recent times, John Taylor says that, on her election, President McAleese had sent him 'a beautiful, handwritten letter' to thank him for what he had said then. He and his wife had also been invited to visit Áras an Uachtaráin for lunch, which they have yet to do.

With days left to polling, Mary McAleese's lead in the polls was holding. An IMS/*Irish Independent* poll published on Tuesday 28 October, two days before the vote, showed she had 49 per cent support, to Mary Banotti's 32 per cent. None of the other candidates had more than 7 per cent. There was one last media duty, an appearance on 'Prime Time' with Miriam O'Callaghan in which all candidates took part. Deliberately she sat to one side as the other candidates bickered. She was now hot favourite to win the election.

There was a 47 per cent turnout, one of the lowest for a presidential election, which would probably have been lower but for the Galway 'debacle'. However, Mary McAleese's was the biggest victory by any presidential election candidate in the history of the State. She beat her nearest rival, Mary Banotti, by 202,422 votes on the first count and by 308,743 votes on the second, easily breaking the 120,467 margin recorded by Eamon de Valera over Sean MacEoin in 1959. She had won 45.2 per cent of the vote to Mary Banotti's 29.3 per cent.

She had been elected eighth President of Ireland. 'The campaign is now over,' she told a packed St Patrick's Hall in Dublin when she was declared elected. 'I will be a President, I believe, as I want to be, for all the people — for those who voted for me, for those who voted for my fellow candidates and for those who didn't vote at all.'

Bertie Ahern, Mary McAleese, Noel Dempsey and Pat Farrell (in shadow) arriving at the count centre in Dublin Castle on the evening she was declared elected

Nothing Personal

Eoghan Harris feels that Mary McAleese, when she came to Dublin first in 1975, was 'probably unaware that being anti-Provo was the dominant ideology of southern Ireland, that the Provisionals were seen as immoral. Revisionism was the dominant ideology. Conor Cruise O'Brien won the intellectual war of the 1970s.'

At that time, too, management in RTÉ was more concerned about infiltration by the Provos rather than by the Workers' Party. Harris, the guru of much revisionist thinking at RTÉ and a member of the Workers' Party at the time, was a producer on current affairs programmes, including 'Féach' where Joe Mulholland had also worked. He says, 'I never felt marginalised in my beliefs in RTÉ, though there were some hard-line nationalists in the news room. Being anti-Provo was what the Coalition believed in.' Mary McAleese 'must have found it [RTÉ] as alien as Mars'. In the newspapers of the day you had journalists like 'John Feeney, Kevin Marron, Kevin Myers, Hugh Leonard, Benedict Kiely, John B Keane – nearly all journalists with the *Irish Press* – who were all strongly anti-Provo.' Being sympathetic to the Provisionals had become 'quite socially unacceptable. It was like a de-Nazification. It was socially and morally unacceptable to be pro-Provo. It was like being a Nazi in 1948/49.' Those who were seen as 'pro-Provo' he had deemed 'hush puppies' at the time. 'It was a comical phrase, but the fact they had to "hush" was significant.'

'Mary McAleese arrived with all the ambivalence of a Northern nationalist,' he says. By then Joe Mulholland 'had fought hard for ten years against such ambivalence. 'RTÉ was a mirror of Irish society. It was very representative of

Irish society.' And a majority at the station were not against Section 31. 'Mary McAleese was perceived to be somewhere between the Provisionals and the very green end of the SDLP at the time.' He was on leave when she worked on 'Today Tonight', but he heard others speak of her 'in disbelief, with derision, and a certain grudging respect, as a throwback'. 'Why is she so concerned about those guys jailed in the H-Blocks. If they wanted to kill themselves, let them at it,' was the view. She was seen as 'an extreme nationalist and as an extreme Catholic. While Ireland was struggling [with its conscience] she was seen as having a pre-historic nationalist attitude and also where religion was concerned, while a majority of the working class were fighting for divorce.'

After the 1986 divorce referendum had failed, Sean MacMathúna had written in the *Irish Press* of the many people for whom it meant they could never be sexually happy. In the South at the time there was an ongoing 'huge struggle for the development of a modern Catholicism'. The new Irish middle class was liberal Catholic. Once during those years Harris saw Mary McAleese on television in a pub in Skibbereen. 'I remember staring at her on the TV screen, the hard Belfast accent, the fanatical edge to that hard voice, it sent out the wrong cultural signals. The slightly frumpy, conservative dress. Out of touch with the more subtle social, sexual mores [of the South]. Probably judgemental.'

Many years later it struck him how, from her Northern point of view, Dublin then must have seemed 'an effete, soft society, where to hear Conor Cruise O'Brien, who was demonised [among nationalists], spoken of warmly … it must've been shocking.' She was 'a fish out of water, a northern pike'. 'Arriving in the promised land, carrying the huge grievances of those who lived in a marginalised society and then finding yourself among people who acted like neo-Unionists, she must have felt betrayed, abandoned, surrounded by hostile forces and by people who didn't like any of her beliefs, or her personally.'

She was 'very good-looking. Everyone thought that, too. A very attractive woman, but like a young old fogey. Like a young Tory. Like that former Tory party leader William Hague, spouting green nationalist, traditional Catholic nonsense.' She had arrived in a society which was repudiating republicanism, with difficulty. She had been catapulted into a revolutionary society, from a military revolution into a real revolution. 'Her every word would make people uneasy, her very presence … it was not an easy subtext to discover that the Republic was a foreign language to her as she was a foreign language to us. How bereft she must have felt.'

Harris says, 'Her particular misfortune was that her boss was a man from Donegal [Joe Mulholland] whose hardest struggle of all was to free himself from nationalism. It is easy to blame the Workers' Party, Conor Cruise O'Brien, Garret FitzGerald, Des O'Malley. I had to set my face like flint, such was the struggle within myself, from entertaining any soft thoughts about nationalism. I am sorry about her emotional suffering. I am very glad to be made up with her. She is very like me. She has an ideological mind and if she changes her mind it is a full conversion, very like me. Fish, fowl, or good red herring, there is nothing neutral about her. She is not a hurler on the ditch. She is true to herself.'

He got involved with Derek Nally's bid for the presidency in 1997 because at the time 'the general view was that Mary McAleese was a hardline Northern nationalist. The leaks [Dympna Hayes's notes of her meetings with Mary McAleese and Brid Rodgers in 1997] confirmed all my horrors. She was regarded as the Provos' candidate and had the normal ambivalence of a Northern nationalist at the time. She was too close to Sinn Féin for comfort. When she dropped the mask, Gerry Adams would be walking all over the Áras in a week. I didn't think she could be beaten. She was a very attractive candidate, very good looking, a good manner. I felt it was going to be a total walkover.'

Mary Banotti, he felt, came from 'the well-heeled, articulate wing of Fine Gael. There was a certain class smugness about her … I knew she was on a hiding to nothing.'

He believed Derek Nally 'had a fantastic anti-Provo record at the Association of Garda Sergeants and Inspectors. I told him he couldn't win but that he could run Mary Banotti close. He could become the centre of the election. He was very happy with that. John Caden was happy to work for him. So I predicted what would happen, that all of Fianna Fáil would be on his head and that all he had to do was stick it out, persist. They would come down on him like a ton of bricks. His number twos would go to Mary Banotti. His job was to flush out Mary McAleese's real politics and increase the anti-McAleese vote. The media mob came down on him like a ton of bricks. All Nally had to do was hold tough. But she met Nally. She was so sore, so upset. Derek was a "decent man manipulated by anti-national forces", she said. He was "the good cop versus the anti-Provos" '.

He believes that the *Irish Times* article written by John Caden was 'crucially important' to his strategy. 'There is always a hinge to a campaign, according to Napoleon. The hinge in that campaign was Nally's querying her association with Sinn Féin, her being ambivalent about Sinn Féin. But Nally cracked. He had to press relentlessly. It had to be Nally equals the security of the State versus McAleese ambivalent about the security of the State, dodgy on the Provos.'

His comment about her being a 'tribal timebomb' wasn't personal. 'To me it was just business ... I felt that a very rough campaign would be a savage education for her about southern politics. I was educating her in the hardest way. She got a glimpse of how hard it could be. I believed she would win anyway. If Nally had stood the line she would have had to give real ground in distance from the Provos. She became very shrewd and conducted a pluralist campaign.'

'Mary McAleese learned a lot in that election. She was a changed woman within a year. Within a year she knew exactly what the Irish people wanted – a society which was pluralist enough, Catholic without being à la carte; it had done with anti-clericalism. It was anti-republican but ready to talk to Sinn Féin, without disturbing the pluralist agenda.' Referring to her opening of the Island of Ireland Peace Park in Flanders, he says, 'She took World War I as a metaphor. The genius of it was that it also involved the North. That was a measure of her political genius.'

He had 'taken the hit' after the Nally campaign, but she had not made a meal of what had happened. 'She didn't dance on my grave at the time.' She had even invited him to the Áras for RTÉ's 75th anniversary celebrations in 2001 and he was 'very touched' by that.

He believes she went into the 1997 presidential election campaign 'an unreconstructed Northern nationalist but, because of what the Nally campaign put her through, without doubt she has become a great President. A lot of Northern Unionists who supported Nally seem very pleased and very supportive of her. They also think Martin McAleese is a wonderful man. Both women Presidents have been very lucky in their consorts.'

Mary McAleese and himself are now 'beyond ideology'. Hers has been 'a very successful presidency'. He says that 'the more unionists are exposed to Mary McAleese, the more likely they are to like her.' He hopes that when she leaves office she might set up a Healing Foundation, headed by herself and run with Martin, which would help victims of the Troubles. It could be 'a super version of the Ireland Fund and independent of the Belfast Agreement.'

And of the 1997 presidential election campaign he says, 'It is one election I am glad I lost'.

Beginning the Beginning

The most unexpected thing for her family on the election of Mary McAleese was the sudden presence of gardaí everywhere. It seems it felt a bit like a secular version of 'The Breastplate of St Patrick' "... gardaí before me, gardaí behind me ... gardaí on my right, gardaí on my left ... gardaí where I sit down ... gardaí where I arise."' The McAleeses could no longer use their own car. And they now had a garda driver and gardaí travelling in a car behind, wherever they went.

Fianna Fáil had based the family at the Portmarnock Hotel in north County Dublin for the last three weeks of the election campaign. It was there that probably the most Chaplinesque episode surrounding this sudden and unexpected garda presence in their lives was played out. The story goes that when the President-elect and Martin left Dublin Castle after the count, with their new garda driver and new garda escort, they were taken to the hotel. Arriving there they got out of the car, thanked the gardaí, shook their hands, said goodnight and went inside. The gardaí followed. Arriving at the lift, the McAleeses realised the gardaí were still with them. So they thanked them again, shook their hands again, said good night again, and got into the lift. The gardaí got into the lift, too. And then followed them from the lift to the door of the suite where they were staying. They all arrived at the suite door. But there was no thanking them this time, no shaking hands, no goodnight. Rather, there was an apparently firm question from the President-elect as to whether the gardaí intended accompanying her and her husband to their bedroom. The men in blue assured the First Citizen and her husband they

The 1949 Rolls Royce Silver Wraith that has been the official car of every President since Seán T Ó Ceallaigh

did not intend accompanying them any further. So the ritual was repeated again. The McAleeses thanked the gardaí, shook their hands, said goodnight. The McAleese children, who had witnessed the latter part of this episode from the room door and who, unlike their parents, had instantly realised what was going on, thought it was all absolutely hilarious. They cracked up.

However, they weren't nearly as perky when it came to the move to Dublin a week later. They had been in Dublin on their Hallowe'en break during the election and count period, but had then returned to attend their St Louis Grammar school in Kilkeel. Security advice in Northern Ireland was that they should be moved to Dublin quickly, in the continuing anxiety for their safety following the Foreign Affairs leak during the election campaign. Martin collected them from school on the Friday before the inauguration, on his way home from work. It was trauma all around. The whole school gathered to say goodbye and give them presents. Martin read a message from the President-elect thanking everyone at the school. And suddenly everyone was crying. Emma (then fifteen) and the twins Sara and Justin (then twelve) had been very happy there. They used to be picked up by bus in Rostrevor every morning, practically at their front door, and were dropped off again every evening. When they got off the bus their two grandads were usually waiting for them, to accompany them up the avenue to their house. They knew everyone

The President-elect gets ready for the big day. The McAleese family in the Portmarnock Hotel on the morning of the inauguration, 11 November, 1997

188

The President waving from the Rolls Royce as she departs the Portmarnock Hotel for the Áras on the morning of her inauguration

in Rostrevor and they couldn't walk a yard of road without bumping into an aunt, an uncle, a grandparent, or a cousin. Now they were leaving all that behind for the maybe-not-so-great unknown. It all happened so fast and they cried all the way there.

To top it all, Justin's Tamagotchi died on the way. As Martin McAleese explained to Gay Byrne on 'The Late Late Show' that night, where he and the President-elect were guests, the electronic 'virtual pet', about the size of a mobile phone and popular with children at the time, had to be looked after or it would 'cry' and eventually 'die'. Whether through neglect arising from Justin's distracted state or a willed decision that anything was better than Dublin, Justin's Tamagotchi 'died' as they crossed the bridge in Drogheda. Justin knew where the blame lay, 'Sara has just killed my Tamagotchi!' he said. A hastily decided-upon decision by Martin to go to McDonalds in that town was of little consolation to the now doubly troubled Justin.

The family did not move into Áras an Uachtaráin until the night of the inauguration, on 11 November 1997. Between the election count and then they had been there for an informal look at its living quarters. The President's father-in-law, Charlie McAleese, came with them. The two girls began school at Loreto on Stephen's Green, where they were soon well settled-in, and Justin was at Belvedere College. A short time later he moved to Kings Hospital School. It was co-ed and he preferred that. He would later be head boy there. To her consternation, Emma found that she had walked straight into

Continuing a tradition begun
by President Mary Robinson,
the light in the window of the
Áras is now a lantern given to
the McAleese children by the
late folklorist Davy
Hammond.

Junior Cert year, but she just got down to it. And Justin began to treat Áras an Uachtaráin and its surrounds as if it was Rostrevor. Touring on his bicycle, he soon knew everyone who worked there and everything about them, including the gardaí. And he found a running companion for his father in Garda Micheál Ferry, a Donegal man who used to run marathons. He and Martin McAleese ran together every day until Garda Ferry retired. They still have the occasional run.

The President-elect was presented with the parchment containing the official result of the election on Saturday, 1 November at Dublin Castle by Lieut Col Des Johnston. With some pomp and ceremony he took a step forward and confirmed, *as Gaeilge*, that Mary McAleese had been elected President. He passed her the parchment and took one step back. '*Go raibh maith agat*,' she responded. Some photographers missed the moment. 'Can you do it again?' asked one. 'You can't re-create history,' an official said, but the President-elect posed as the officer pretended to hand over the document again, re-enacting very recently made history. There were some questions from the media. How did Mrs McAleese feel this morning? She was in 'very, very good form, thank you very much'. She had 'a very good night's sleep'. She was 'very relaxed and very much looking forward to the inauguration.' And to the following seven years. 'Was she absolutely sure that the document she held confirmed that she was the eighth President?' 'I'm fairly certain, yes,' the President-elect laughed. 'My Irish is good enough to be able to understand that very well.' She would also, she confirmed, be continuing Mary Robinson's tradition of the light in the window at Áras an Uachtaráin. But she would use a lantern given to her children by folklorist Davy Hammond, a friend 'from the other side of the traditional divide', who has since died. Such sweetness, in the main. And light at the end! The media has always loved a winner.

The following day was 'home is the hero' time in Rostrevor when the entire village turned out to greet her, also St Joseph's Pipe Band from Longstone, and a mass of media. Father Colm Wright, moved to hyperbole by the currents of goodwill assailing him from his congregation, announced in St Bronagh's Catholic Church that 'the people of Ireland now have an angel watching over them and had no need to feel afraid.' Across the street at the Church of Ireland church, Rev. Jim Simms was, as is the wont of such clergymen, more reserved, if also prescient. He said, 'If Mary McAleese can take from the village of Rostrevor the kind of ecumenical goodwill that exists in this part of south Down into the rest of Ireland, then her time as President of Ireland will be richly blessed.' And in the more 'spiritful' part of the village, celebration was just as intense. One elderly man, having a pint in the Corner House Bar which Paddy Leneghan once owned, was heard to say, 'Imagine, the President of Ireland used to serve me behind this bar'. While, in the Old Killowen Inn, folk singer Tommy Sands retitled a song he had written as 'Mary on the Misty Mourne Shore' which he sang and rededicated to his soon-to-be former neighbour.

Where the President-elect herself was concerned, her preoccupation was with preparations for the inauguration on 11 November and her address to it. She decided that over 800 schoolchildren from all over the thirty-two counties on the island would be among the invited attendance. They would gather in the Yard at Dublin Castle as she passed through to the inauguration ceremony in St Patrick's Hall, and she would meet them as the new President.

She also requested that 'while acknowledging the traditions and customs of the day' guests should dress informally. She asked that people be invited who represented twenty-five strands of Irish life, including a unionist from Northern Ireland, a farmer, a garda, a nurse, a journalist, an islander, a dancer, a politician, an entrepreneur, an unemployed person, a Down's Syndrome person, a peacekeeping soldier, a waitress, an elderly person and a child. They would sit in the front rows at St Patrick's Hall and as soon as she

Taoiseach Bertie Ahern, Tánaiste Mary Harney, members of the Government and the judiciary, along with former Presidents Robinson and Hillery and former Taoisigh Bruton and Cosgrave applaud the new President after her inauguration on 11 November 1997.

received her seal of office she would walk down to the group and greet them. And as she did so, uileann piper Liam Óg Ó Floinn would play a specially commissioned piece he had written called '*An Droichead*', ('The Bridge'), 'to emphasise the theme of inclusiveness and bridge building'. That is what the inauguration ceremony itself reflected.

The formal ceremony in St Patrick's Hall started with a prayer service led by leaders of the five main Christian Churches and the Chief Rabbi. The Declaration of Office was read in Irish by Chief Justice Liam Hamilton and repeated by the President, when she undertook to maintain the Constitution and uphold the laws of the State. Among the formal presence were Taoiseach Bertie Ahern, Government Ministers and Council of State members, including former Presidents Paddy Hillery and Mary Robinson, as well as four former Taoisigh. The first Irish President to be born in Northern Ireland, it was fitting that key players in the peace process were also there: the then Northern Secretary Mo Mowlam, SDLP leader John Hume, Sinn Féin president Gerry Adams, Alliance Party leader John Alderdice, and former US Senator George Mitchell, chairman of the multi-party talks in Northern Ireland.

Then she descended from the top platform to shake hands with the people from various strands of Irish life who had been invited to the ceremony, who included Northern Ireland unionist councillor Harvey Bicker.

In her inaugural address, President McAleese said it was her 'special privilege and delight to be the first President from Ulster.' She quoted Cearbhall Ó Dálaigh, Ireland's fifth president, who said at his inauguration in 1974, 'Presidents, under the Irish Constitution don't have policies. But … a President can have a theme.' She said the theme of her Presidency 'is Building Bridges. These bridges require no engineering skills, but they will demand patience, imagination and courage for Ireland's pace of change is now bewilderingly fast. We grow more complex by the day.' She wanted 'to see Ireland grow ever more comfortable and at ease with the flowering diversity that is now all around us. To quote a Belfast poet, Louis McNeice "a single purpose can be founded on a jumble of opposites".' But she felt that 'to speak of reconciliation is to raise a nervous query in the hearts of some north of the border, in the place of my birth. There is no more appropriate place to address that query than here in Dublin Castle, a place where the complex history of these two neighbouring and now very neighbourly islands has seen many chapters written. It is fortuitous too that the timing of today's inauguration coincides with the commemoration of those who died so tragically and heroically in two world wars. I think of nationalist and unionist, who fought and died together in those wars, the differences which separated them at home fading into insignificance as the bond of their common humanity forged friendships as intense as love can make them.

In Ireland, we know only too well the cruelty and capriciousness of violent conflict. Our own history has been hard on lives young and old. Too hard. Hard on those who died and those left behind with only shattered dreams and poignant memories. We hope and pray, indeed we insist, that we have seen the last of violence. We demand the right to solve our problems by dialogue and the noble pursuit of consensus. We hope to see that consensus pursued without the language of hatred and contempt and we wish all those engaged in that endeavour, well.'

It could be done, she said. 'We need look no further than our own European continent where once bitter enemies now work conscientiously with each other and for each other as friends and partners.'

She spoke of Gordon Wilson 'who faced his unbearable sorrow ten years ago at the horror that was Enniskillen [where his daughter, Marie, was killed]. His words of love and forgiveness shocked us as if we were hearing them for the very first time, as if they had not been uttered first two thousand years ago. His work, and the work of so many peacemakers who have risen above the awesome pain of loss to find a bridge to the other side, is work I want to help in every way I can. No side has a monopoly on pain. Each has suffered intensely.'

But she knew 'the distrusts go deep and the challenge is awesome. Across this island, North, South, East and West, there are people of such greatness of heart that I know with their help it can be done. I invite them to work in partnership with me to dedicate ourselves to the task of creating a wonderful millennium gift to the Child of Bethlehem whose two thousandth birthday we will soon celebrate — the gift of an island where difference is celebrated with joyful curiosity and generous respect and where in the words of John Hewitt "each may grasp his neighbour's hand as friend". There will be those who are wary of such invitations, afraid that they are being invited to the edge of a precipice. To them I have dedicated a poem, written by the English poet, Christopher Logue, himself a veteran of the Second World War:

Come to the edge.
We might fall
Come to the edge.
It's too high!
Come to the edge
And they came,
and he pushed
and they flew'

She continued, 'No one will be pushing, just gently inviting, but I hope that if ever and whenever you decide to walk over that edge, there will be no need to fly, you will find there a firm and steady bridge across which we will walk together both ways.

'Ireland sits tantalisingly ready to embrace a golden age of affluence, self-assurance, tolerance and peace. It will be my most profound privilege to be President of this beautiful, intriguing country.'

She asked 'Those of faith, whatever that faith may be, to pray for me and for our country that we will use these seven years well, to create a future where in the words of William Butler Yeats, "Everything we look upon is blest".'

It was a setting out of the stall, the value system and the theme for her presidency.

Christopher Logue was surprised to receive her phone call for permission to use his poem in her inauguration speech, but he felt honoured that she would do so. And there was another story behind her choice of 'Come to the Edge'. Mary McConnell, a librarian in Ballynahinch, County Down, had been a friend of Mary McAleese going back some time. Both shared a love of poetry. At the nadir of her campaign for the presidency, as the Foreign Affairs leaks controversy continued to explode, as though she had entered a minefield, with the media in hot pursuit, Mary McConnell sent her friend that poem. It was written in 1968 as a tribute to the French poet Apollinaire. Having been to that bitter edge, over which she then flew, the new President was calling out to those on another edge, in the belief that they too could fly.

And then, as she emerged after her inauguration, formality was abandoned and the assembled children greeted her like a pop star, with chants of 'Mary, Mary'. She spent the best part of half an hour shaking their hands and talking to them before leaving for Áras an Uachtaráin.

'Sham'substantiation?

It was audacious and so soon into her presidency. Mary McAleese was inaugurated on 11 November 1997 but by then she had already called on the GAA to remove rule 21 which banned members of the RUC or British army from joining, having described the rule as 'sectarian', and she had also attended Remembrance Day ceremonies in St Patrick's Cathedral, Dublin. On 5 December she paid her first official visit to Northern Ireland. The reception in Newry was attended by former chairman of Newry and Mourne Council, Danny Kennedy of the Ulster Unionist Party. He says, 'While we were glad to acknowledge her presence here, equally she knows we don't give her our allegiance, but that does not mean we cannot be gracious.' Continuing on to Belfast, she visited her old school, St Dominic's, on the Falls Road, where she met and shook hands with Sinn Féin president Gerry Adams. She was greeted in north Belfast by Ann McVicar of the Shankill Women's Centre, and her final function that night was in Queen's University as guest of honour at the twentieth anniversary dinner of the Institute of Professional Legal Studies of which she had been a director.

The President told reporters she was very moved by the 'sheer warmth' of her welcome in Northern Ireland. Speaking at the cross-community Flax Centre, beside her native Ardoyne, she said, 'It was important for me to come back here reasonably quickly after my inauguration to get my spiritual batteries recharged in this space where I was born, where I was reared, where so many happy days were lived.' She told the large gathering that one of the highlights of her day was being greeted in Irish at Belfast Airport by the deputy Lord Lieutenant for Belfast, Col Charles Hogg. She was moved by his effort to learn the '*cúpla focal*'. 'It was not a small gesture. It was a very, very big step across a bridge and I hope there will be many more of them. I thank him for his generosity of heart.'

Just weeks in the job, she was already laying the template for her presidency, and at a pace.

Two days after that first official visit to Northern Ireland, where unionists, who might have been expected to be otherwise, had been gracious and welcoming, she was to do something which provoked a reaction that was not at all gracious and from an unexpected quarter, at least where the general public was concerned. On Sunday, 7 December she attended a Eucharist service at Dublin's Christ Church Cathedral. As she stood in the pews, singing the Credo in Latin from Schubert's 'Mass in G' along with the splendid cathedral choir, it is doubtful whether she could have anticipated the furore to come. In a typically warm address, the Church of Ireland Archbishop of Dublin, the Most Rev. Walton Empey, commended Mrs McAleese's plan to make bridge-building the theme of her presidency, while in his sermon the former Beirut hostage Terry Waite spoke of bridge-building between the peoples of these islands. The Warrington Male Voice Choir had come along to show that all this talk had more substance than

The President takes Communion in Christ Church Cathedral, Dublin, 7 December, 1997

aspiration to it. In March 1993 two boys, three-year-old Johnathan Ball and twelve-year-old Tim Parry, were killed when an IRA bomb exploded in Warrington.

The President had asked to attend the Eucharist as part of her plan to visit services of all the main Christian denominations and faiths early in her Presidency. She was accompanied by her husband, Martin, and her two daughters, Emma and Sara. This took the Christ Church authorities by surprise. They had reserved places for the President and her husband only, with the result that a chair had to be found for the President's aide-de-camp, Col Bernard Howard.

When it came to Communion, the President rose from her pew, followed by her daughters and her husband, and all took Communion. Across the centre aisle the Lord Mayor of Dublin, Cllr John Stafford, proceeded to do the same. A report in *The Irish Times* next day noted that, 'The President, Mrs McAleese, broke new ecumenical ground yesterday when she took communion during the 11am sung Eucharist at Christ Church Cathedral in Dublin. In an unexpected move, which Church of Ireland sources believe may be the first for an Irish President from the Roman Catholic tradition, Mrs McAleese took bread from Canon Desmond Harman, rector of Sandford and Milltown, and wine from Canon Stanley Baird, of Swords. The Lord Mayor of Dublin, Mr John Stafford, also took communion during yesterday's Christ Church service.'

It would lead to one of the few controversies of her presidency, but it was also an event which all these years later still resonates deeply and positively with Ireland's Protestants, whether north or south of the border. Through that one action she shattered their stereotypical image of her. But among some Catholic clergy it reinforced another stereotypical image of her as being arrogant and independent where Church authority was concerned. First out of the traps the following day was Dungannon priest, the late Monsignor Denis Faul. He said that no Catholic can receive Communion in a Protestant church, and that the law applies in the same way to 'the Pope in Rome and President Mary McAleese as much as it does to Paddy and Biddy Murphy'. Catholics believed 'the living, risen, and glorious Body of Christ was really truly and substantially present in the Eucharist under the guise of bread and wine, and offered in the sacrifice of the Mass.' The Eucharist was central to the unity of the Catholic Church. 'It is why there is still just one Catholic Church, and about 500 Protestant churches.' He accused President McAleese of breaching the Catholic Church's code of canon law on an 'absolutely vital' issue. 'Eucharistic intercommunion' with Protestant churches was not possible, he said.

The following Friday, 11 December, Fr James McEvoy, Professor of Philosophy at St Patrick's College Maynooth, had a letter published in the *Irish News*. He did not restrain himself. He would find it 'repugnant if she [President McAleese] should ever again abuse the august office which she occupies, in a way which would once more embarrass the Catholic Church, by giving scandal to its members.' Even then the word 'scandal', especially when applied to laity, was disappearing from the clerical vocabulary. Not so with Rev. Professor McEvoy. Few at the time could remember such a full frontal attack on a serving president since Paddy Donegan, then Minister for Defence, criticised President Cearbhall Ó Dálaigh as 'a thundering disgrace' in October 1976. It led to the latter's resignation. Then there was Fr Ray Hannon, a curate in the Finglas area of Dublin, who told Pat Kenny on his RTÉ Radio I show that what President McAleese had done was a further indication of 'little flaws there in her character'. He had first detected these flaws when she said she would, as President, sign abortion legislation should it be presented to her. He was also surprised she did not have a Mass said at her inauguration, and he objected to her description in the past of the 'atican's views on women priests as 'Pope's cant'. He had 'very strong views on Mary Robinson and her liberal agenda'. But over the past couple of weeks he had not liked what Mrs McAleese had been doing either. 'I think she'll end up a candyfloss President,' he said.

Some more liberal Catholic priests, such as Fr Gabriel Daly, Fr Austin Flannery, Fr Sean Fagan and Fr Walter Forde, spoke out in defence of the President, bolstering their arguments with the relevant theology. Not so the Catholic bishops. On 16 December their standing committee had been meeting in Maynooth, and their spokesman, Fr Martin Clarke, said of the controversy that they did not wish 'to censure or embarrass' the President, but 'it is hoped the issue will not arise again'. Her action 'took everyone by surprise'.

The following day it emerged that this was not the first time Communion had become an issue where an Irish President was concerned. Erskine Childers, President of Ireland from 1973 until his death in November 1974, was 'always very distressed' that he was not allowed to receive Communion at Catholic services, and that his wife, Rita, a Catholic, could not take Communion with him at Church of Ireland services. President Childers was a member of the Church of Ireland. In newspaper reports and recalling conversations with him about the matter, the Very Rev. Victor Griffin, former dean of St Patrick's Cathedral in Dublin, said Erskine Childers could not understand why ecclesiastical regulations should prohibit individuals who wanted to, from receiving Communion. The late President believed Christians should never forget that it was the Lord's service and the Lord's table, and that the invitation to take Communion came from the Lord and not from ministers or priests of any denomination. Dean Griffin said it was 'the height of presumption' on the part of any priest or minister to judge who should receive. It was a matter for the individual to decide who should come forward. That was the Anglican position, he said. In his book *The Mark of Protest*, Dean Griffin recalled how at his inauguration in 1973 President Childers was anxious that there should be a Eucharist at St Patrick's to mark the occasion. It was 'a source of great sadness' to the President that he had to take Communion on his own, the Dean said.

On 16 December the Catholic Archbishop of Dublin, now Cardinal Desmond Connell, did a radio interview with broadcaster Eamon Dunphy. He said it was 'a sham' for a Catholic to take Communion in a Protestant church and he took issue with comments by the then Church of Ireland Archdeacon of Dublin, the Venerable Gordon Linney, who had said that a Catholic may take Communion from a Protestant in exceptional circumstances. 'Under no circumstances is that possible,' the Archbishop said. A Catholic priest 'might give the Eucharist to a Protestant in exceptional

Cardinals Desmond Connell, Sean Brady and Cahal B Daly

circumstances, provided the Protestant expresses a faith that is identical with the Catholic Eucharistic faith', he said. If a Catholic wanted to be truly courteous in attending a Church of Ireland service, 'you will not engage in the deception that is involved in taking Communion.' He continued that participating in the Eucharist was the most profound expression of one's faith. Catholics celebrated the Eucharist in the light of their apostolic faith. 'You cannot at the same time celebrate the Eucharist professing that apostolic faith, as we would maintain it, and professing a faith that is other than the apostolic faith, that is incompatible with it ... though people do not seem to appreciate it.' If Catholics took Communion in a Protestant church, 'they have their own Catholic faith and they profess that, and what they are in fact doing in partaking of the Eucharist in a Protestant church, is a sham.' Therefore it seemed to him 'profoundly insulting to the Church of Ireland or to any other Protestant church' to do so.

There was uproar, and all down to his use of that word 'sham'. Though it was not what he said, some began to assume that what Archbishop Connell really meant was that the Protestant Eucharist was 'a sham'. As the debate unfolded, and when it became clear to a wider public that the Catholic Church does not recognise orders [the ministry/priesthood] in the Reformed churches as valid, and that it believes that the bread and wine is totally transformed into the body and blood of Christ [transubstantiation], it did indeed seem possible that it was the Church of Ireland Eucharist itself which Archbishop Connell was really describing as 'a sham'. This was particularly the feeling within the Church of Ireland. The Protestant churches' beliefs about Communion range from consubstantiation – where it is held that the substance of bread and wine remain alongside the substance of the body and blood of Christ, which would be the view of most in the Church of Ireland – to a belief that the bread and wine are just symbols of the body and blood of Christ.

And to think that just one week prior to President McAleese's attendance at that Christ Church service, it had all been so different. On 30 November she attended Mass at St Andrew's Church on Dublin's Westland Row to mark the beginning of her term of office. Archbishop Connell concelebrated it. In his homily that first Sunday in Advent he said that the President's presence was a source of special joy. He wished to express delight at the opportunity they had to tell her of their admiration and support. 'We thank her for the inspiring words of her address on the day of her inauguration, when she spoke with such eloquent conviction of the spirit of the people of Ireland. She

The President and Martin McAleese host a reception in Rome to mark the elevation of Cardinal Seán Brady

is proud of us, of our history, of our achievements, of our ethos of generous sharing. She will be a builder of bridges in a spirit of reconciliation and love,' he said. True, but not as he expected. He continued that the President had evoked in the hearts of all a ready response to the unforgettable words in which she invited them to work in partnership with her 'to dedicate ourselves to the task of creating a wonderful millennium gift to the child of Bethlehem, whose two thousandth birthday we will soon celebrate.'

Following that 'sham' interview, the then Church of Ireland Primate Archbishop Robin Eames expressed regret that something 'as sacred as the Eucharist or Holy Communion' should become the source of remarks or speculation which could be divisive '... the perception that remarks, even if taken out of context, were derogatory of either tradition,' was also to be regretted. And everyone knew to whom he was referring. The then Church of Ireland Archbishop of Dublin, Most Rev. Walton Empey, said that the Church of Ireland was confident 'of its Catholicity, its Apostolicity and its understanding and discipline concerning the Holy Eucharist.' The growing controversy over inter-church Communion 'deeply saddened' him, but it was 'essentially a problem for another Christian Communion [the Catholic Church].'

On the Sunday following Archbishop's Connell's 'sham' interview, the controversy threatened to go international as one of America's leading Catholic families felt the need to act. The US ambassador to Ireland, Jean

Kennedy Smith, took Communion at Christ Church Cathedral in Dublin. She attended the 11am Eucharist service alone and unannounced. Afterwards she said she was there as a private citizen, not as a representative of any government. She had attended Christ Church the previous Christmas Day with her son Stephen, and had also taken Communion then, she said. She intended to go there again on Christmas Day 1997. She regularly took communion at the Episcopalian [Anglican] church near her home in New York.

On 22 December Archbishop Connell said, 'I'm very sorry for the offence … I blame that offence very much on the way *The Irish Times* put its headline: "Taking Church of Ireland Communion a sham, says archbishop". That was very bad. I am very sorry that people have been offended. I wouldn't offend people deliberately. I was present in Christ Church, I have been involved in the ecumenical movement.'

In a feisty editorial the following day, *The Irish Times* said of the headline, 'As an exercise in sub-editing, it was in fact, exemplary of that rather exacting craft. It reflected fairly and with a proper sense of priority that which was newsworthy in his remarks.' And it concluded that the journalists involved 'should not have anyone's finger pointed at them when they have done their jobs with competence and professionalism.'

The principal of the Church of Ireland Theological College in Dublin, Canon John Bartlett, welcomed Dr Connell's apology. He was happy to accept it and said that, for his own part, he had not been personally offended. But he could understand why offence might have been taken by others. He felt some sympathy for Dr Connell, who he believed was a very caring person.

Hostilities ceased for Christmas, though the debate raged on for most of the following month.

By taking Communion in Christ Church that morning Mary McAleese signalled that she was not going to be a President just for the majority population of Catholic nationalists on the island. She had begun and would continue to reach out to the growing number of minorities in what was becoming an increasingly diverse Ireland. It was not her first time to take Communion in a Reformed Church, nor would it be the last.

What the event highlighted was her very independent approach to her religion. A devout person whose faith is central to her life, she adheres very much to Catholic teaching where fractious issues such as contraception, divorce and abortion are concerned. But she had been very critical of Church structures, particularly where the issue of women priests is concerned. Her impatience with those structures has been forcefully expressed, most famously in an article she wrote for Britain's Catholic weekly *The Tablet*, published in March 1997.

Titled 'It Won't Wash With Women', she wrote that 'most intelligent men and women can recognise sexist cant, no matter how nobly dressed up, no matter how elevated the speaker, from miles away. So when the Holy Father admits the Church just might have been a teensie-weensie bit sexist at times, we wait for the next obvious statement, that the Church is going to take a long, hard, scholarly look at itself. It is going to try to understand how its own thinking, its very own understanding of God, has been skewed and damaged by 2,000 years of shameful codology dressed up as theology and,

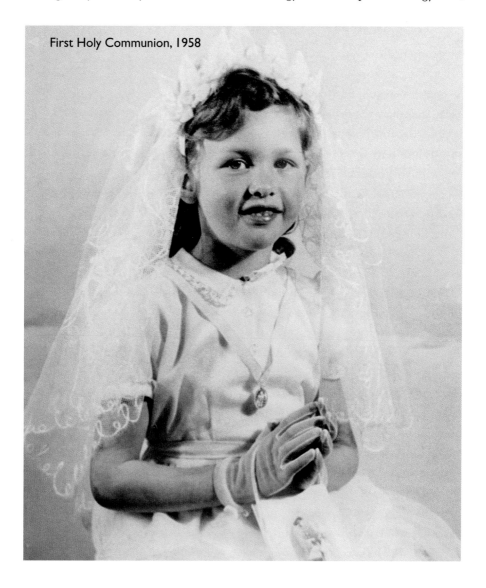

First Holy Communion, 1958

worse still, God's will. But the statement does not come. Instead the big gun, the howitzer of Infallibility, is armed and aimed. Do the faithful lie down and take it? Do they humbly submit to an edict which purports to bind in perpetuity? Not in Ireland, they don't. Nowadays, they argue back, armed with the insights of fresh, modern scholarship which puts conservative dogmatic theologians under a harsh and unforgiving spotlight. Nowadays, women of profound faith can be heard to say that they feel called to the priesthood. They speak with a new-found confidence and are listened to with a new-found respect.'

Defenders of the Vatican line, she said, 'who sound more and more like Communist Party apparatchiks hawking redundant clichés, have often in the past characterised Ireland as Catholicism's heartland, the one place where the faith would never waver, where a sure witness to fidelity could be always found. Curiously, I believe they are right, but for the wrong reasons. Few hierarchies face as tough a battle to maintain credibility and relevance as the Irish hierarchy. They need allies, in particular among women of faith. Those women are willing to forge new alliances, but today the women talk a language many of these men simply do not understand and have difficulty relating to. It is the language of tomorrow's world, not the language of yesterday's seminary. That old language has yet to be unlearnt. It is rapidly becoming a badge of irrelevance and long past its sell-by date.'

This is not the language of a humble daughter of the Church but of a confident, theologically literate woman assailing Christianity's most male citadel. In a speech she delivered in January 1998 at the Catholic Independent Schools' Conference at the well-known English Benedictine College, Ampleforth, she touched on the same subject. 'I was twenty years away from school when I read Aquinas in full for the first time, and realised to what extent he was unknown to me. Woman was "defective and misbegotten", I read. The intellectual colossus started to list ever so slightly. By the time I had finished hearing that I had been created as a helper for man solely in the realm of childbearing, since I was not much use for anything else, I began to realise that there was a lot less to this business of being a saint than a life of unreproachable saintliness ... In my study I have a collection of fifty-four books, bought several years ago, entitled *The Great Ideas*. They cover the hierarchy of contributors to Western thought, from Sophocles to Kepler, from Montaigne to Freud. Not a single one among them was written by a woman. Since I bought them, six new volumes have been added. But you have to get to volume fifty-nine before a tentative reference is made to the twentieth-century American writer, Willa Cather, who's hardly a household name. Not until volume sixty is a substantial female contribution to any ideas, let alone great ones, acknowledged. Virginia Woolf shares her volume with ten other writers, including Lawrence, Eliot and Beckett. Aquinas, by contrast, gets two volumes to himself.'

In that same address she spoke in very humorous terms of how her faith was formed. 'I was raised in Belfast, my physical landscape dominated by the Passionist Monastery in which God was male, Irish and Catholic, his mother having presumably emigrated to Nazareth from Ireland after the Famine. My Protestant friends who lived in the same street but went different ways on Sunday, and practised their music in the Orange Hall, understood God to be male also, but, of course, Protestant and British. I believed the Pope was Peter's God-ordained successor. They believed the Pope was an anti-Christ. Reared between these two parochial Gods who carried their crosses like lances in a jousting tournament, we were both introduced to the Ya-boo school of theology, the my-God-is-bigger-than-your-God school of theological bully boys.

'Ours was a devout Catholic home; a prayerful home pervaded by an ethos of faith, it was also the home in which I learnt that I was Irish not British, that I had a language, an identity, a history and a culture which was quite different from that of many of the Protestant friends with whom I played, for the streets I grew up in were predominantly Protestant ... the poet Tom Paulin, who was born into Northern Ireland's Protestant tradition writes, "I was nurtured in a puritan anti-aesthetic, told to be suspicious of what's rhetorical or ornate..." I, by contrast, was nurtured with the rhetoric of the doctrine of transubstantiation; the smell of incense; the plaster statues.

'In that same world I learnt of the Plantation, the Reformation, the Penal Laws, the Famine and the occasional rebellion against the Crown, including the rebellion of 1916. The versions I learnt were intended to and indeed succeeded in reflecting little credit on the Crown. The terms in which my ancestors had been brutally oppressed burnt into my consciousness, and cried out for vindication. It seemed to me, that every right-thinking person, knowing these facts, would be on our side. But of course, on the other side — to quote the late Scottish author David Thompson, who understood Ireland so well — English schoolbooks glossed over the atrocities of the Penal Laws, the Famine was played down, the retaliation visited upon the Protestants of Ulster by Catholics in 1641 rounded up, so that, in the twentieth century, when both sides faced each other over barricades, it was with a certainty that both were victims and martyrs, both were in the right, and both had God exclusively on their side. We lived, not just in ignorance of each others' pain, but with an inherited gaping wound, inflicted, we believed, by the other side. We each waited in vain for the other to apologise, and to acknowledge the pain they had inflicted.'

She reflected that 'some time ago, walking past the Presbyterian church in my village, my son, then aged five or six, asked me – "Mammy, do you know Catholics and Protestants – which ones are we, I forget". Yet, it seems essential to remember. We aren't permitted to forget.'

In her book *Reconciled Being, Love in Chaos*, published in December 1997, a month after her inauguration, Mary McAleese explored further her own faith formation. The book's contents were first presented by her to the John Main Seminar held in Dublin earlier in 1997. It was named after Dom John Main, a former professor of law at Trinity College Dublin, who became a Benedictine monk and who inspired the President with his devotion to prayer and meditation.

In it she recalled how 'In the [Passionist] monastery there were over forty men who, dressed in their flowing black habits, dominated the thinking and spiritual landscape of my childhood. I was taken aback to hear my daughter ask me some years ago if monks were examples of cross-dressers. Strange how a new vocabulary can shake your perspective!' She continued, 'I owe those prayerful men a lot, for their love of God was palpable, but there was also a deficit. It was not deliberate or mal-intended but there was a deficit nonetheless. On the day I spoke out loud my desire to be a lawyer, the first to say, "You can't because you are a woman; you can't because no one belonging to you is in the law", was the Dublin-born parish priest who weekly shared a whiskey or three with my father. It was said with the kind of dismissive authority which is intended to silence protest or debate. The owner of superior knowledge, of real certitude had spoken, and that was that. The same priest, incidentally, kept a double-entry scorebook of the indignities heaped upon Catholics by the Protestant government at Stormont, many of which ironically involved keeping Catholics out of jobs for no reason other than the fact that they were Catholics. The irony of the similar group exclusion of women was unfortunately lost on him. My mother had inculcated into us a respect for the priesthood bordering on awe. I watched therefore in amazement as the chair was pulled out from under the cleric and he was propelled to the front door before the bottle of baby Powers had been uncorked. "You – out," she roared at him. "And you," she said to me, "ignore him." That was the only advice I ever received from either parent on the subject of career choice.'

She has also said that her own track record on meditation has been 'less than inspiring, according to my daughter Emma'. She recounts the story of how 'some years ago when she was four or five I used to disappear into my study regularly for this mysterious thing called meditation. Asked to explain what I did there I simply told her I talked to God. One day she asked me if she could come too and would I teach her how to meditate ... I told her, "Close your eyes lightly and repeat the word Maranatha over and over in absolute silence." I did the same. Five minutes into my meditation the little voice interrupted me. "Excuse me, Mammy, but is God talking to you?" Ignoring everything John Main had ever said about meditation, I rashly answered "Yes". "Right," she said, "Will you please tell him that when he is finished with you I am still waiting?"'

The person who had most influence on Mary McAleese's spiritual life was Fr Justin Coyne. A Mullingar man, he was one of the occupants of the Passionist monastery near where she was born. He was the 'children's priest' and from the age of thirteen to almost her eighteenth birthday — he died five days beforehand from cancer — he became her

The picture of Father Justin Coyne that sits on the President's desk.

spiritual guide. She named her son after him and keeps a photographs of the priest, regarded as a saint when alive, on her desk. She has described him as her *anam chara*, her 'soul friend'. It was he who reminded her frequently that the most important commandment was to love unconditionally. At the height of the 'leaks' controversy during the Presidential election campaign she received a parcel from Sister Gemma Coyne, a sister of Fr Justin's. Although living in England, she'd been following events at home and was concerned. The parcel she sent contained Fr Justin's cross. Ordinarily it would have meant a lot to the President. Then it was like divine intervention.

Mary McAleese's interest in ecumenism probably goes back to her first year at Queen's University where she saw a sign inviting people in for a cup of tea at the Church of Ireland Chaplaincy. She went in and met Rev. Cecil Kerr, who became a lifelong friend. A Fermanagh man, he founded the Christian Renewal Centre at Rostrevor, County Down, where he still lives. A noted ecumenist, he received an ESB/People of the Year Award in 1986 in Dublin for his work in the area. She also took part in the inter-Church Ballymascanlon talks from 1983 and co-chaired a working group it set up to prepare a paper on sectarianism, which began its work in February 1991 and produced its paper over two years later. However it was her decision to appear with the Catholic bishops at the New Ireland Forum in 1984 which was to make the most public impact where her religion-related activities were concerned.

Cardinal Cahal Daly says, 'She seemed an obvious person to involve in the bishops' delegation. She was being talked about at the time in connection with law and was concerned about right-to-life issues.' He recalls that 'she performed well and, in the preparations, was very helpful.' He believed she also 'made an important contribution' at the Forum. She continued to be an advisor to the bishops on pro-life issues and the presentation of their case. In general, where the Bishops were concerned, 'her opinions were always listened to with respect' and she was consulted by them 'quite often'. But he was not aware of her being consulted by the Bishops on issues other than abortion. Cardinal Daly used to teach Scholastic Philosophy at Queen's University before his appointment as Bishop of Ardagh and Clonmacnoise in 1967. He wasn't at Queen's when Mary McAleese attended as a student. He remembers meeting her when she was Director of the Institute for Professional Legal Studies and her remark that Queen's University had been 'a cold house for Catholics'. It was the first time he had heard the phrase. He would not have been as aware of that even while teaching at Queen's, he said, as many of his own students were Catholic, many of them seminarians. Of course all changed with the influx of Catholic students thanks to the Butler (Education) Act when those such as John Hume and Seamus Heaney began to attend the university in the late 60s, early 70s. There had been 'very significant change' at the university, where 'quite a number of the academics are Catholic now'.

He and the President meet at events. They don't meet regularly or have exceptional personal contact but would be 'good friends'. He feels that her election as a Northern Catholic to the Presidency was significant 'particularly later when she made reconciliation in Northern Ireland a specific part of her mission.' She as 'now accepted, broadly speaking, within the unionist community as a welcome figure.' Visits to Northern Ireland had become 'a very characteristic part of her sense of being President of Ireland' and had made 'a major contribution to reconciliation. It has not been without its difficulties but those have been handled very well. She has very good communications skills.' Incidents such as those at Coleraine in June 2008, when loyalists protested at her visit, had upset local unionists. 'They were very upset as it gave the impression she was not welcome. It was quite clear the protesters were totally unrepresentative of unionists in the area. She remained calm, not unduly disturbed and was made feel very welcome on the whole. She was there at the invitation of the local Protestant, unionist community.'

Where Northern Catholics and nationalists were concerned 'she has been treated very much as "our President". Her election, one of our own, as President of Ireland – at least where the nationalist community was concerned – was a very significant boost to the self confidence of the Catholics and nationalists in Northern Ireland. It indirectly helped create the climate in which a growing confidence on the part of the Northern nationalist community was to have an important role. It lessened the sense of being an oppressed minority and increased the willingness to share power with unionists, without the sense of oppression, discrimination, and the denial of civil and human rights. It underscored a readiness for peace and the growing sense that violence, which was always rejected by the great majority of the nationalist community, was totally futile and retarded progress.'

Cardinal Desmond Connell's birthday falls on 24 March, which is also Martin McAleese's birthday. Early in 2001, Archbishop Connell received an invitation to share a joint birthday with Martin McAleese at Áras an Uachtaráin. He accepted and a very pleasant evening was had by all. No one made reference to the elephant in the room and everyone averted their gaze so he wasn't noticed all that evening. For his part, he kept mercifully quiet.

In Her Footsteps

Roscommon is a traditional county, described as 'the heart of Ireland' in a book of the same name by Fr Patrick Sharkey, published in 1927. It is a place where to be Irish was unquestioningly, unconsciously, to be Catholic and nationalist/republican. The most rural county in Ireland is also one of the most homogenous. According to the 2006 census, of its 58,768 population just 1,287 are Protestant (including Church of Ireland, Methodist and Presbyterian). It was a place where to be seen openly to commemorate anyone or anything associated with the British army was unthinkable. And that included those sons of Roscommon who were slaughtered in its ranks.

But, on Monday, 18 February 2008, at Messines near Ypres in Flanders (Belgium), a cross-party delegation from Roscommon County Council laid a wreath in memory of the young men from the county who were killed in World War I. As a blood-red sun set over those green fields which will be forever darkened by death and the memory of war, the delegation of County Councillors and Council staff, led by the Mayor of Roscommon, Cllr John Kelly, placed a poppy wreath at the Irish Peace Tower in the Island of Ireland Peace Park to commemorate the 330 men from the county who had died in that bloody conflict. A card attached to the wreath read, 'Thank you for your efforts and sacrifice. You have helped to shape the Ireland, the Europe and the freedom that we enjoy today. From the people of County Roscommon.'

The delegation were following in the footsteps of President McAleese whose words spoken at Messines, less than ten years earlier, had set them on that road to commemorate and bring back to history those young men their previous generations had sought to forget.

On Armistice Day, 11 November 1998, President McAleese opened the Island of Ireland Peace Park, accompanied by Queen Elizabeth II of Britain and King Albert II of Belgium. It was created in memory of the 69,947 young men from both main traditions on the island of Ireland who were killed, wounded or went missing (presumed dead) in World War I. The most conservative figure for the number of those young men confirmed dead is 35,000 (not including those from the island of Ireland who enlisted in England, Scotland and Wales), while at the Irish National War Memorial Gardens in Dublin's Islandbridge the figure given is 49,400. Over 140,500 men from the island volunteered to serve in World War I. That was in addition to the 58,000 already serving. In both instances the great majority, as with the island's population, was from the Catholic, nationalist tradition.

The Island of Ireland Peace Park at Messines was the brainchild of former Fine Gael TD for Donegal, Paddy Harte, and Derry community leader and former UDA political adviser, Glen Barr, together with the cross-Border Journey of Reconciliation Trust. The Peace Tower, a round tower about 110ft high, was built with stone from a former British army barracks in Tipperary and from a workhouse near Mullingar in Westmeath. It houses bronze cubicles containing record books listing the known dead from Ireland in World War I. The tower design is such that it allows the sun to illuminate its interior only on the eleventh hour of the eleventh day of the eleventh month

The Island of Ireland
Peace Park and Round
Tower, Messines Ridge,
Belgium

each year, the anniversary of the armistice which ended the war. Three pillars in the Peace Park give figures for those killed, wounded, and missing (presumed dead) in World War I of three divisions from Ireland: the 10th (Irish) Division: 9,363 (at Gallipoli, Salonika, Palestine); the 16th (Irish) Division: 28,398 (in Flanders and France); the 36th (Ulster) Division: 32,186 (in Flanders and France). It was at Messines that the 36th Ulster Division, drawn from the pre-war Ulster Volunteer Force, and the 16th Irish Division, largely drawn from the Irish National Volunteers, fought side by side in June 1917 to win a major victory.

That day at Messines, in one of the most significant speeches of her presidency, President McAleese, also Supreme Commander of the Irish Defence Forces, said the event 'was not just another journey down a well-travelled path. For much of the past eighty years, the very idea of such a ceremony would probably have been unthinkable. Those whom we commemorate here were doubly tragic. They fell victim to a war against oppression in Europe. Their memory too fell victim to a war for independence at home in Ireland.

'In the history of conflict which has blighted my homeland for generations respect for the memory of one set of heroes was often at the expense of respect for the memory of the other. As former Taoiseach Sean Lemass, himself a protagonist in the Irish people's fight for independence, said thirty years ago, "In later years it was common – and I was also guilty in this respect – to question the motives of those who joined the new British armies at the outbreak of the war, but it must, in their honour and in fairness to their memory, be said that they were motivated by the highest purpose."'

She continued, 'Today we are keenly aware that if we are to build the culture of consensus promised by the Good Friday Agreement then we need to create mutually respectful space for differing traditions, differing loyalties, for all our heroes and heroines. The men of the 36th Ulster Division and the 16th Irish Division died here.

A bowl carved from a tree from the site of the Battle of the Boyne, presented to the President by Taoiseach Berie Ahern. A similar bowl was presented to Dr Ian Paisley by An Taoiseach

They came from every corner of Ireland. Among them were Protestants, Catholics, unionists and nationalists, their differences transcended by a common commitment not to flag but to freedom. Today we seek to put their memory at the service of another common cause expressed so well by Professor Tom Kettle, an Irish nationalist and proud soldier who died at the Somme: "Used with the wisdom which is sown in tears and blood, this tragedy of Europe may be and must be the prologue to the two reconciliations of which all statesmen have dreamed, the reconciliation of Protestant Ulster with Ireland and the reconciliation of Ireland with Great Britain."

'I do not think that it is too bold to suggest that this day has been a day of historic significance. The problems we face in building a culture of consensus are difficult but not impossible. We can draw strength from the collegial partnerships built in Europe this past forty years between once bitter enemies and the enormous goodwill towards Ireland from our friends around the world, not least here in Belgium. None of us has the power to change what is past but we do have the power to use today well to shape a better future. The Peace Park does not invite us to forget the past but to remember it differently. We are asked to look with sorrow and respect on the memory of our countrymen who died with such courage far from the common homeland they loved deeply. Their vitality, genius, youth and commitment were lost to Ireland. In this generation we redeem their memory, acknowledging their

President McAleese lays a wreath during the 91st Easter 1916 Commemoration Ceremony at the GPO, O'Connell Street, Dublin

sacrifice and the pain of those who loved them. We pray that just as this Park has changed the landscape of Belgium, so too it will help to change the landscape of our memory. These too are Ireland's children as those who fought for her independence are her children, and those who fought against each other in our country's civil war – and of course the dead of recent decades – their children's children – who have not known the peace for which they yearned. To each let us give his or her acknowledged place among our island's cherished dead.

'In the Irish language I wish God's blessing on their souls:
Ar dheis Dé go raibh a n–anamacha uasal.

'We hope that the goal of peace promised by the Good Friday Agreement will be our gift to the next generation ...'

A bronze tablet inside the entrance to the Peace Park has the following inscription, under the heading 'Peace Pledge': From the crest of this ridge, which was the scene of terrific carnage in the First World War on which we have built a Peace Park and Round Tower to commemorate the thousands of young men from all parts of Ireland who fought a common enemy, defended democracy and the rights of all nations, whose graves are in shockingly uncountable numbers and those who have no graves, we condemn war and the futility of war. We repudiate and denounce violence, aggression, intimidation, threats and unfriendly behaviour.

As Protestants and Catholics, we apologise for the terrible deeds we have done to each other and ask forgiveness. From this sacred shrine of remembrance, where soldiers of all nationalities, creeds and political allegiances were united in death, we appeal to all people in Ireland to help build a peaceful and tolerant society. Let us remember the solidarity and trust that developed between Protestant and Catholic soldiers when they served together in these trenches.

As we jointly thank the armistice of 11 November 1918 – when the guns fell silent along this western front – we affirm that a fitting tribute to the principles for which men and women from the island of Ireland died in both World Wars would be permanent peace.'

Prior to arriving in Messines that February evening, the Roscommon delegation had seen evidence of the conditions under which their county men had fought and died. It began at the Passchendaele Museum in Zonnebeke which commemorates the Third Battle of Ypres leading to the final capture of Passchendaele (Valley of Suffering) in early November 1917.

The President at the National Day of Commemoration Ceremony, 2006 in The Royal Hospital Kilmainham

Zonnebeke and Passendale (the modern Dutch name) are two small villages close to Ypres. During the British attack of 1917, there were 500,000 casualties in 100 days for a territorial gain of just five miles. There, in the museum, they saw a recreation of how the soldiers had to live underground in cramped, rat-infested dug-outs which were swamped with water and mud. Maybe to give themselves some comfort, some feeling of home, young soldiers began to give names to their area of dug-out. Such as one intersection they called 'Birr Cross Roads'. Probably named by young lads from Offaly.

And they saw the Essex Farm cemetery, with its row upon row of white headstones and Irish names. The scene was the same at Artillery Wood cemetery where poet Francis Ledwidge is buried. 'F E Ledwidge, Royal Inniskilling Fus.' is on his headstone, and the date of his death, 31st July 1917. A member of the delegation, Sean Kilbride, recited the opening lines of Ledwidge's 'Lament for Thomas McDonagh', a poem Ledwidge wrote in tribute to his friend, the executed 1916 leader:

'He shall not hear the bittern cry
In the wild sky where he is lain ...'

Buried in the rows alongside Francis Ledwidge are an Orr, a Conroy, a Regan, an O'Grady, a Jordan, a Curran, and two unidentified soldiers 'Known unto God'.

The Roscommon delegation visited the German cemetery at Langemark where 44,294 men are buried, most of them young students, and 25,000 — not far off half the population of Roscommon — are buried in a mass grave little more than the size of a decent suburban lawn. Only 17,000 of the soldier buried there were identified. And there was the Tyne Cott cemetery where 11,952 Commonwealth soldiers are buried, 8,365 unidentified. It is the largest cemetery containing Commonwealth dead in the world. On the wall of its interpretative centre the delegation read the words of Britain's King George V from May 1922: 'We can truly say that the whole circuit of the earth is girdled with the graves of our dead.' And they passed the spot in the Flanders countryside where Tom Kettle wrote his poem 'The Gift of Love' for his baby daughter Betty, who he had not seen. Two days later he was killed. They saw the place where he died.

Most poignant of all for them was the grave of Martin O'Callaghan from Cloonbonniffe near Castlerea, County Roscommon, in the White House cemetery near Ieper [Ypres] in West Flanders where he rests with 1,400 others, 300 unknown. A young man in his twenties, he was killed on 22 October 1917. His white gravestone is simple, as all are there. He is identified as 'Private M Callaghan of the King's Own Yorkshire LI' (Light Infantry), 'Born at Conniffe, Castlerea'. Beneath is written 'Heart of Jesus Have Mercy on Him. Mother'. Relatives were allowed chose words to be inscribed on the gravestone. There was a charge per word. The delegation reflected on his poor mother and what it was likely she could afford then. An entry in the cemetery memorial book records a visit by O'Callaghan's grand-niece, Anne O'Callaghan, in 2007. She wrote 'Martin, never forgotten by your family in Ireland.'

But Martin was not the only one of that family to die in Belgium. Ten months later, on 28 August 1918, Martin's brother John died in Flanders from wounds received while serving with the Royal Irish Regiment. Both brothers were working at the O'Connor Don Clonalis House near Castlerea when they were encouraged to enlist and fight for 'poor little Catholic Belgium'.

Back in Ireland, yet another O'Callaghan brother was involved in conflict. Micheál O'Callaghan was interned at the Curragh in 1921 when a receipt with his name on it was found on the body of IRA man Sean Bergin after he was shot dead by Black and Tans in Loughglynn, County Roscommon that April. He was released when the Truce was signed in the summer of 1921. He was the father of the late Micheál O'Callaghan, who had been editor of the *Roscommon Herald*. In 1964 he published *For Ireland and Freedom*, his account of Roscommon's contribution to the fight for independence. Micheál O'Callaghan would have been well-known to most of the Roscommon delegation but he was not nearly as well known as John's son, the highly regarded 'Doc' Callaghan who was a Fianna Fáil County Councillor in Castlerea for many years. Not many knew before the visit to Flanders that Doc's father and uncle had died there in the First World War.

You might say the story of the O'Callaghan brothers is an illustration of the tragic history of Ireland in the twentieth century as it played out in one Roscommon family. Two went to war for the freedom of small nations and to save 'poor little Catholic Belgium', as encouraged by their political and Church leaders. They fought and died with thousands of other young innocents from this island similarly encouraged to enlist. They had no funerals and, in the new southern State, their families could not even grieve

With members of the Government at the 90th Anniversary Commemoration of the Battle of The Somme in The War Memorial Park Islandbridge, 2006

for them, while the brother who did his bit for 'the cause' was celebrated.

At Messines that evening, after the delegation had laid the wreath at the Peace Tower, Mayor Kelly spoke for all when he said, 'Few of us understood what went on out here, the horrendous conditions endured by soldiers from our county and what their families suffered at home, as we saw in letters we read today.' He was referring to letters from young soldiers sent to their families in Ireland and which are on exhibition at the Passchendaele Memorial Museum. 'I did history at secondary school. These things were not taught at school.' He suggested that anyone who might be tempted to criticise their visit to Flanders should go there themselves and 'visit the graves of the young men we visited today. It was very emotional.' For his part he was 'proud as Mayor of Roscommon to be here on behalf of the people of Roscommon, to honour our deceased.'

The Roscommon County Manager John Tiernan gave an address.

'Today has been a day filled with emotion and reverence. What we have seen in this theatre of war were scenes of mass killings such as at Tyne Cot where there are the graves of almost 12,000 young men. One million young men lost their lives here ... who were cajoled, persuaded, or decided for reasons unknown to us. Some did so for high-minded reasons – out of a sense of duty, for the good or mankind. Sure there was adventure and travel, and money too. Hugged by their mothers, they left County Roscommon never to come back again. Perhaps never to be found again ...

'It is fitting that we should be here to honour our own among those dead. The twenty or so of our countymen and women – its first citizen, the Mayor of Roscommon, and elected members, have come out here to bring their memory back to life and to pay our respects. We as a nation are going through a process of growing up and maturing where our past is concerned. We were part of the British Empire and we should be proud of that and not deny it. There are many reasons why we could continue to harbour resentment – the disaster/catastrophe of what happened to our own Irish 16th Division out here, for one. But we have to move on. We're looking to a new era – a new maturity.

'So to the 330 or so Roscommon men who fell in these battles – we have come to say "Thank you for your efforts and sacrifice. You have helped shape the Europe and the Ireland and the freedom we enjoy today."'

He concluded by quoting Tom Kettle's poem 'The Gift of Love', written just days before his death, to his baby daughter:

'In wiser days, my darling rosebud, blown
To beauty proud as was your mother's prime –
In that desired, delayed incredible time
You'll ask why I abandoned you, my own,
And the dear breast that was your baby's throne
To dice with death, and, oh! They'll give you rhyme
And reason; one will call the thing sublime,
And one decry it in a knowing tone.
So here, while the mad guns curse overhead,
And tired men sigh, with mud for couch and floor,
Know that we fools, now with the foolish dead,
Died not for Flag, nor King, nor Emperor,
But for a dream, born in a herdsman's shed,
And for the Secret Scripture of the poor.'

From Messines, the Roscommon delegation went to the Menin Gate Memorial in Ypres town where at 8 o'clock every evening, buglers from Ypres Fire Brigade play the Last Post, its sound echoing through the evening air around the great arch which commemorates those 54,896 World War I soldiers whose remains were never found, including those who were Irish or of Irish extraction. The names of a further 34,984 of the missing are recorded on carved panels at Tyne Cot cemetery. In one of the more poignant tributes paid that day on behalf of the people of Roscommon, Mayor Kelly stood at the centre of the gate, as is the protocol for representatives coming to pay tribute, and read Laurence Binyan's 'For The Fallen'.

'They shall grow not old, as we that are left grow old,
Age shall not weary them, nor the years condemn.
At the going down of the sun and in the morning
We will remember them'.

The President and
Dr Ian Paisley at
the Somme Heritage
Centre, Newtownards,
2007

Through Orange Eyes

Dromore in County Down belongs very much to the old unionist ascendancy Ulster. It was a market town in its heyday and its most famous son was Henry Ferguson who invented the modern, lightweight tractor. Many of its almost 5,000 residents now work elsewhere, notably Belfast for which it has become something of a commuter town. Bearing witness to its continuing allegiance are the offices around the square of Basil McCrea, UUP MLA, 'New Face. New Thinking' and of Jeffrey Donaldson, DUP MP and MLA. A statue of a soldier on the square commemorates the dead of the 1914-18 war. It is surrounded on all sides by poppy wreaths. Its Gospel Hall proclaims, 'What shall it profit a man, if he gains the whole world and loses his soul. Matthew 8:36'. And a sign at Cross Lane reads, 'The wages of sin is death but the gift of God is eternal life through Jesus Christ. Romans 6:23.'

Drew Nelson's solicitors' office is opposite that sign, between The House Bakery shop and The Razor's Edge barbers. He is Grand Secretary of the Grand Orange Lodge of Ireland. A certificate in the waiting area confirms that he completed a 'Managing Change in a Diverse Society' workshop at the John Fitzgerald Kennedy School of Government in Harvard University. He attended Queen's University between 1975 and 1978, after which he worked with Bill Craig for many years. He was also a part-time member of the UDR and a UUP councillor on Banbridge District Council for nine years.

Nelson says that Dromore is 90 per cent unionist. He recalls that the first approach to the Orange Order from Áras an Uachtaráin came in 2005 through solicitor Denis Moloney, whose name keeps cropping up when it comes to contact between the Presidency and the majority community in Northern Ireland. An unofficial 'Ambassador for the President', as one unionist has described him, by all accounts Mr Moloney has a persuasive style, though shy of the media.

By the time of his initial approach on behalf of the Áras, the Orange Order was already in discussions with the Department of Foreign Affairs in Dublin and had prepared a document, at its request, which addressed four things the Order would like to see done in the Republic. These were: (i) development of the Boyne site with signage there in Ulster-Scots as well as English and Irish; (ii) funding for Orange halls in the Republic, particularly in border areas where Protestants had said they felt discriminated against in such matters; (iii) a memorial to Protestants murdered during the War of Independence; and (iv) the restoration of an obelisk erected at the Boyne site in 1740 to commemorate the Battle of the Boyne and destroyed around 1922.

With regard to the memorial request, Nelson explains that 'a high percentage' of the Protestants now involved in Northern Ireland politics are descended from people originally from the south but who were forced out in the War of Independence period. He instances Traditional Unionist Jim Allister as an example. The Northern Ireland census of 1926 recorded that 24,000 'southerners', nearly all Protestant, had moved there. 'You go into any decent-sized town in the Republic and you won't see one memorial to Protestants killed there, but you will see plenty to those who murdered them,' he says. The obelisk at the Boyne had been erected 'by the aristocracy, and rumours now suggested it was dynamited by Free State soldiers, whether drunk or semi-official we don't know ... Its base is still there, on the northern side of the river.' It had been thought until recently that it was the IRA who had destroyed it.

Nelson is very appreciative of the role that Martin McAleese played at meetings with Department of Foreign Affairs officials. 'I cannot emphasise enough how helpful Martin McAleese has been. He encouraged meetings between the [Orange Order] County Grand Masters in the Republic and the county managers. In my opinion he did more for that section of the Orange community there than anyone since 1921. The feedback from the County Grand Masters has been extremely positive where the county managers are concerned. I cannot over-emphasise the importance of the legitimacy that kind of official contact bestowed – in Cavan, Monaghan, Donegal, Leitrim.'

Drew Nelson has relatives in Cork. 'Speaking as an outsider, all my life I've been going down to Cork. My relatives there just keep their heads down. It is how they survived. They are not prepared to put their heads above the parapet, even though they complain privately that they are not being treated fairly.' He also has strong connections with the Border counties through the

Order for the past twenty-five years. He has noticed how in those areas over that period 'things have almost completely changed and have moved on from that attitude of keep your head down to the situation now where they are prepared to more openly ask for their fair share of the cake if they believe they are not getting it.'

He was present at a 'seminal event which changed the attitude of the authorities in the Republic two years ago in Áras an Uachtaráin when Martin hosted a meeting between Grand Lodge officers and County Grand Masters in the Republic with senior government officials from a number of Departments. During the meeting the County Grand Master from Donegal complained that the county council had been asked a number of times to provide facilities for the 12th of July parade at Rossnowlagh but had been let down each time. A senior civil servant promised that something would be done about this and asked the County Grand Master why he had not complained about this beforehand. He replied that he was afraid. That struck a deep chord with the civil servant – that one of his fellow citizens was afraid to complain to the county council. It marked a turning point for both sides. The Protestants were willing to say what they wanted for the first time and the senior civil servant was hearing it for the first time. Since then things have continuously improved.'

In April 2007 he met Martin McAleese at the Four Seasons Hotel in Monaghan and presented him with a submission on what could be done to help Orange Order members in the border counties. It detailed incidents of intimidation and attacks on Orange halls in those counties and the need for the creation of three development officer posts to help rebuild community infrastructure. It pointed out that it was 'important that aspects of Protestant culture are recognised as important to the "living heritage" of the State, in the same way as many buildings, landmarks and sites are protected under government legislation.'

He believes that there has been an increased sense of confidence among those Protestants who are members of the Order in the southern counties. s In late 2007 he became aware of a report which was prepared for the Special European Programme Board (SEUPB) on the border Protestant community in the Republic and the allocation of EU Peace Programme monies where they were concerned. The report concluded that the money was not accruing to them because of 'residual sectarianism'.

It said, 'The border Protestant community is an indigenous religious minority whose identity and culture has been threatened by falling numbers and a lack of recognition. It has felt ignored, tolerated or resented by the majority community. It did not feel appreciated or valued. The people and their property have been subjected to personal and physical attack down the years and there remains a residual sectarianism. The Protestants in the southern border counties, as Channel Research (a previous and similar evaluation report) found, "feel that they were abandoned by both the Irish Government and by northern Protestants". Many of the problems facing the minority Protestant community derive from the lack of pluralist thinking in society. Hence the feelings of alienation repeatedly recounted by the border Protestant community in the course of this research and the misunderstandings experienced by the majority community. Funding cross-community projects, especially on a cross-border basis, should be prioritised to support both communities together in the building of a genuinely pluralist and shared society.'

According to Drew Nelson, an effect of the report was that 'it concentrated the minds of officials in the Republic and helped them to recognise that there was a problem, which had been under government radar up to then. It allowed for general social exclusion and the vandalising of Protestant properties. I believe that report really opened the door to the funding which has now become available, with more to be announced.'

In February 2008 Éamon Ó Cuív, the Republic's Minister for Community, Rural and Gaeltacht Affairs, gave approval for funding of almost €250,000 to a company that has been set up by the Orange lodges based along the Border. The money was allotted for a two-year period. The company, Cadelmo Ltd, will operate on a community-based initiative in Cavan, Donegal, Leitrim and Monaghan. The funding is intended to support the work of a development officer who will cater for the needs of Orange lodges and other groups that meet in Orange halls in the counties. Making the announcement, Minister Ó Cuív pointed out that his department had already been involved in supporting the refurbishment of a number of Orange halls in the Cavan/Monaghan area under local grant schemes. He also deplored the recent attacks on Orange halls. In November 2007 a small Orange hall in Drummartin, County Cavan, was burned to the ground, the third of the eight Orange halls in the county to be completely destroyed. An Orange hall in County Monaghan was vandalised with republican and sectarian graffiti in January 2007.

In the Republic the Orange Order has lodges in Leitrim, Cavan, Monaghan, Donegal, Dublin, Wicklow and west Cork but the only Orange parade now held in the Republic is at Rossnowlagh, County Donegal, each summer. The 12th July parade was once a regular feature in Dublin but none has taken place there for more than seventy years.

Drew Nelson says that the announcement by Minister Ó Cuív will eventually help attitudes change and provide a much better outlook for the Protestant community in the border counties. For his own part he is actively engaged in encouraging the border Protestant community to engage and integrate into the life of the Republic. 'All the above could have happened without Martin McAleese, but it would've taken years longer. And it may not have happened in the way it did through giving sufficient recognition to the problems faced by the Protestant community in the Republic.'

Recalling the visit of the Grand Lodge officers to Áras an Uachtaráin, he says it was to be a private lunch. The Grand Master, Robert Saulters, the Grand Treasurer, Mervyn Bishop, and himself were on the way to Dublin on the train when they received a phone call from the media. A Dublin paper – he thinks it may have been the *Evening Herald* – had a report about their impending visit. 'It was difficult. We were not prepared for that.' And when they arrived at the Áras there was a photographer there. He wanted to take a picture. Drew Nelson asked 'what for?' The photographer said it was 'for private use'. He told the photographer that details of the visit were already in a Dublin paper and the photographer withdrew. They group had met the President by then.

'The visit was to meet Martin. She "happened" to be there. She was not on the programme. But it wasn't a big problem,' he says. 'The meeting took place and we did media interviews, including with a UTV crew who only became aware we were there from the Dublin news report. It had gone around like wildfire.' He had words about the matter with the President. He was annoyed and says he spoke forcefully,

A knitted Orangeman given to the President by her friend Patricia Montgomery but cannot remember what he said to her.

He has 'difficulties' with the President in some areas: how 'she continually describes herself as the President of Ireland [on visits to Northern Ireland]. It drives our people round the bend. The Orange Order regards "Ireland" as the island of Ireland. The vast majority believe she is making a political point – a throwback to Article 3 of the Constitution. That it is a surreptitious way of keeping the constitutional claim alive.' Also 'there is the issue about the President being so free and easy with her visits [to Northern Ireland] as Head of State of the Republic while the Queen, our Head of State, does not appear to be welcome in the Republic.' He feels it would be helpful if on her visits to Northern Ireland Mrs McAleese described herself as 'President of the Republic of Ireland'.

As regards the January 2005 'Nazi' remark [set out in detail in the chapter 'She Mentioned the War'] he 'can't understand why she said that. It was repeated by Fr Alec Reid in an outburst following decommissioning. [In October 2005 Fr Reid said that for 60 years unionists had treated Catholics in Northern Ireland in the same way as the Nazis treated the Jews. He later apologised for the remark]. Following on that the SDLP's Alisdair McDonnell said the [loyalist] people on the Donegall Road were behaving like Nazis when they attacked immigrants. It was a gut reaction on her part, part of the raw Mary McAleese,' Nelson feels.

Denis Moloney 'began dropping hints about inviting her to visit Grand Lodge headquarters' in 2005. 'It became an outright request but the time was not right. In my view someone had a definite agenda to get her an official invitation to Orange Order headquarters so she could make amends for the Nazi remarks. That was probably Denis's agenda. It would be far more appropriate for her to visit Orange halls in the Republic. If they had been getting their fair share of funding before this she could have been at the opening of the halls.'

But he recognised 'her courage and her willingness to show solidarity with the Protestant community by taking Communion in Christ Church. I admired her for doing that and have said so at meetings. I have admired much she has done. She is a complex character. Taking that Communion was a public act of solidarity. Inevitably in the context of the Republic and Northern Ireland, and our shared and contested history, she has attempted to walk a tightrope in her unusually high number of visits to Northern Ireland. Perhaps President McAleese is trying too hard by being up here far too often. Less is more.'

The Orange Order 'would very much welcome a visit by the Queen to the Republic. It is one of the last remaining pieces of the normality jigsaw to be fitted in.' Besides, he suspects that 'the number of people who describe themselves as British in the Republic is very high and that a very substantial number of traditional Republicans value their British heritage.'

Rev. Brian Kennaway is a former convenor of the education committee of the Grand Orange Lodge of Ireland and author of *The Orange Order: A Tradition Betrayed*. He has been one of the Order's most trenchant internal critics and a consistent force for its modernisation and reform. He saw Mary McAleese being interviewed on television 'in the early to mid 1990s' when she spoke of Orange parades in her youth which passed a Catholic Church, playing 'God Save the Queen'. 'That was factually incorrect as they only played the national anthem at the end of the sessions which followed the parades,' he says. 'It coloured my opinion of her.' He remembers Eoghan Harris saying during her presidential election campaign that "someone from her bitter nationalist background would not be good for Ireland". Then she was elected and began building bridges.'

He has attended a number of the 12th of July celebrations at Áras an Uachtaráin. 'It worked. There was a good mix, a wide-open network, with singing and Irish dancing. There was never anything specifically Orange about it. Something which she might do before she leaves office is invite the Dublin and Wicklow Lodge to parade in the grounds of the Áras.'

He was also part of a delegation of mostly unionist councillors and Orange Order officers who took part in a trip to Dublin prior to the December 2000 visit of US President Bill Clinton. They had dinner at the US ambassador's residence in the Phoenix Park and later had tea at Áras an Uachtaráin.

'A large section of the unionist community do not trust her while another section believe she is just naïve and that she sometimes just doesn't understand the protocol of the job and inadvertently gets herself caught up in trouble. The visit of the Queen is a political issue. She shouldn't mention politics. The Queen wouldn't do so. As Head of State she overstepped her role. Maurice Hayes was right.' This was a reference to the former Northern Ireland Ombudsman who, in his *Irish Independent* column following President McAleese's comments on when the Queen could visit Ireland, had described them as 'gauche'. However, Rev. Kennaway believes 'her presidency has made a significant contribution to understanding between North and South'. He feels it is difficult to measure the President's achievements. 'All are little links in the chain of building bridges. Her speech last year [at the 12th of July 2007 celebrations] was very positive, very encouraging from the perspective of balance and understanding. I wrote to her afterwards to commend her on it. I think that over her whole reign she has improved. There have been blips ... she apologised. Let's get on with it. In my view when you make an apology that's an end to it. And I'm sure it was a sincere apology. It's a pity she was not more sensitive before her election, but on balance her presidency has been very positive and very encouraging from my Unionist, Protestant, Orange perspective. Her own understanding has grown and developed and she has made good use of the opportunities her office has offered. She has an agenda but not the one I thought she had. I believe now it is about promoting peace and understanding. Before I used to feel her agenda was to undermine the unionist community and to present a hard-nosed nationalist perspective. I do think that has changed. It is possible she was being political then, to get votes. Only she can answer that. I don't think it is her agenda now.'

A Republican Unionist

The President and Martin McAleese may be the architects of those
bridges being built towards the majority community in Northern
Ireland, but most certainly one of their chief engineers on that
project is the remarkable Harvey Bicker. Harvey Bicker OBE, MBE, retired
British Army Colonel who served with the Royal Ulster Rifles from the early
1960s [it became the Royal Irish Rangers in 1968], who transferred to the
Ulster Defence Regiment in 1972, and who retired in 1993 at the age of fifty-
five. And also Ulster Unionist Party (UUP) councillor, who became involved
in community associations in Ballynahinch, County Down and ended up
being co-opted onto Down District Council as a UUP councillor. Since

Members of the Vincentian Refugee Centre, St Peter's Church, Phibsborough,
Dublin passing a painting of the First Meeting of the Council of State during a
visit to Áras an Uachtaráin

229

2004 the same Harvey Bicker has been a member of the President's Council of State in the Republic of Ireland and, since February 2008, a member of Fianna Fáil, the republican party. That is some journey!

His first contact with Mary McAleese was after she won the Fianna Fáil nomination for the presidency in September 1997. Then a UUP councillor, he rang her to offer his support. They had never met, but his long-time solicitor was Nicholas Fenton whose wife Anne had been assistant director at the Institute of Professional Legal Studies at Queen's when Mary McAleese was director and who succeeded her in that position when she left. During the campaign, when she was under most pressure over the Foreign Affairs leaks saga, Harvey went public in support of her, saying she was 'the best person for the job and the best person to lead Ireland and represent Ireland abroad into the next century.'

He explains his reason for supporting Mary McAleese. 'When Mary Robinson became President my [unionist] community tried hard to find a point of contact with her. The fact that Nick Robinson's father was an officer in the British army was enough. If Albert Reynolds was elected, my community would have looked on him as just another foreigner. But if Mary McAleese became President, my community would look on her as a fellow Northerner and one of their own. The "Building Bridges" campaign slogan struck a chord with me. Only a Northern President would have been in the position to build the bridges that she later did. I wanted to be on that journey with her and I didn't mind being a lonely figure because I knew I would not be lonely for long.'

But Harvey Bicker had form in building such bridges. Before being co-opted onto Down District Council in 1997 he had 'never been in a political party in my life, but my father was a strong unionist and an Orangeman, and he was Mayor of Lisburn once.' He was co-opted because of the level of his involvement and effectiveness with local community groups and associations where, by then too, he had already been active in cross-community projects. There was a pretty even balance between both communities in Down District and this was reflected in their local authority representatives who tended to allocate places on committees proportionate to their number. It meant there was 'no animosity and you could get away with things you wouldn't have a chance of doing in Ballymena, for instance,' he says. What the councillors did was concentrate on dealing with local needs rather than on their own differences. He found himself co-operating with nationalist local representatives and their electorates on an increasing number of projects, which was also something he encouraged. Then he was appointed to the East Border Region, a cross-border economic development body, which also included councillors from Monaghan and Louth in the Republic.

He asked to be put on it. His unionist colleagues wanted to know why he would do such a thing. 'Because it is the right thing to do,' he said. He was the first unionist to sit on that body. He attended Local Authority Members' Association (which represented local authority councillors in the Republic) conferences in the South 'and I got to know people all over Ireland'. He also, of course, attended conferences of the Northern Ireland Local Government Association, which meant his network of councillors expanded there, too. All of which would prove very useful in the years ahead. There was no pressure from his unionist colleagues about all of this cross-border and cross community activity, though 'there were some murmurings but no threats. David Trimble used say I was the best republican unionist he ever had.'

He had no problem with the description. The Bickers were Dutch mercenaries who came to Ireland in 1688 with the Williamite army and were given land in Louth. Direct lineal ancestors feature in Rembrandt paintings in Amsterdam's Rijksmuseum. In 1642 Rembrandt painted the Amsterdam burgomaster Andries Bicker and his wife and son, and in 1643 he completed a great portrait group, 'The Company of Captain Roelof Bicker and Lieutenant Blaeuw'. It is in the same group of paintings as Rembrandt's 'Nightwatch.' An ancestor of Andries Bicker was one of the signatories to the Dutch declaration of independence against the Spanish in 1581. It cleared the way for the Dutch Republic. This was how he could say to Gerry Adams in more recent years, 'You needn't talk to me about republicanism. You're over 400 years too late!'

He has always had an Irish passport, 'since I was seventeen. Because my grandfather had one.' His grandfather, William, who had businesses in Newry and Dundalk at the time, was also friendly with Frank Aiken, later Fianna Fáil Tánaiste and Minister for External Affairs. When Aiken was an IRA man on the run during the Civil War period he was hidden in Harvey's grandfather's house at Ravensdale, County Louth. When his grandfather died, Frank Aiken was at the United Nations in New York. He flew home for the funeral. Harvey's grandfather is buried in the Presbyterian graveyard in Poyntzpass. He thinks that sort of background is a reason why he finds it easy to mix and talk to anybody. 'My grandfather was very open.' Harvey was raised with his grandfather in Poyntzpass, County Armagh, rather than with his parents in Lisburn because this was during the Second World War years and they felt he would be safer in a more rural area.

Of the Ulster Defence Regiment he says, 'It did what the military does in any conflict, it kept things going, water, electricity. It held the infrastructure together; otherwise Northern Ireland would have been another Lebanon. The army also needed additional manpower to do this, and that helped prevent many young men from joining the paramilitaries. But then, when you have 13,000 involved you can't control them all.' He helped oversee the transformation of the Ulster Defence Regiment into the Royal Irish Regiment in 1992, for which he received the MBE.

He didn't take much part in Mary McAleese's election campaign but did attend a few fundraising lunches. At one he was sitting beside her when someone said, 'Surely it's not true that anyone in the unionist community is supporting the campaign?' He recalls, 'Mary kicked me under the table and I said, "I am a unionist and I am sitting beside Professor McAleese. Not only that, I am an elected unionist councillor. Not only that, but I am a British army officer." He [the questioner] couldn't believe it.'

He was at the count in Dublin Castle which saw her elected. The first thing he did afterwards was talk to her about meeting with all sections of the unionist community. In the period before the inauguration he brought her to meet members of the Royal British Legion (Republic of Ireland) to which he belonged. They met at the old Hibernian Club in Dublin. The following Sunday she attended the Remembrance Day service in St Patrick's Cathedral, Dublin, in a private capacity. It was the Sunday before her inauguration. 'She hasn't missed one since,' he says.

He, along with Martin McAleese, Denis Moloney and others have been very hands-on in the Building Bridges project in those areas where it just was not possible for the office of President to be so. But all such activity has taken place under her supervision and all of it involved her husband, Martin. It is all done on a voluntary basis. And whatever is and has been done is with the knowledge of both the Irish and British governments. Both are kept quietly informed.

After the 1997 election it was very difficult for the McAleeses to engage with the broad unionist community because of the controversies during that election campaign. There was a lot of suspicion among leading unionists about Mary McAleese, but they continued with the outreach. Their strategy was to address the broad unionist community in segments, with the professional and middle classes the first segment. 'We outreached to them. Mary and Martin had a lot of unionists friends themselves and through them we made contact with their friends. Denis Moloney and I helped there as well, as did other nationalist friends.'

Speaking of this outreach, Martin McAleese has said, 'We had to be very careful that there would be no surprises down the line. That we didn't expose ourselves to criticism from some members of the establishment, either North or South. The whole purpose of the outreach was to bring people from the unionist tradition into contact with this House (Áras an Uachtaráin), to bring them here to meet Mary, to have lunch or breakfast and to have them well-received, generously received.'

Then there were the business, farming, fishing, political, military communities – and the Orange Order.

They accessed unionists who were interested in golf. They selected twenty or twenty-five Northern Ireland golfers and matched them up with a similar number from the Republic. All would go to Áras an Uachtaráin for breakfast or lunch, depending on the time of year, and from there they would be taken down to the K Club, Mount Juliet or Druids Glen for a game of golf, followed by dinner and prizes.

They were also careful who they matched the visitors with in the Republic. They wanted to expose them to all types of civic society in the South. So,

President and Dr Martin McAleese at a Twelfth of July celebration in the grounds of the Áras listen to a 17th-century barber-surgeon explain his trade

233

ministers Charlie McCreevy, Noel Dempsey, Frank Fahey, the late Seamus Brennan were all involved at times, and, on the Fine Gael side, Enda Kenny, Phil Hogan, Sean Barrett. The president of the High Court, Fred Morris, was also active, as well as the late President Paddy Hillery, Garda Commissioner Pat Byrne, members of the diplomatic corps, British ambassador Ivor Roberts – 'a great golfer, he was heavily involved in this,' American Ambassador Michael Sullivan, sports people such as former Tipperary hurling manager Babs Keating, broadcasters Pat Kenny and Des Cahill. So the visitors were meeting prominent people. At dinner afterwards the guest list was often extended to include people who didn't play golf, such as broadcaster Gay Byrne and entrepreneur Martin Naughton.

When they were invited in turn to Northern Ireland, among the people who joined them there for dinner were then RUC Chief Constable Ronnie Flanagan, John Hume's wife Pat, David Trimble's wife Daphne, and many others. Nothing was forced. There was no agenda other than making contact. Things were just encouraged. It was remarkable the good that came of it.

Then the McAleeses went on to the business community. They decided to bring business people from the Protestant tradition into contact with the Irish operation in Brussels. The message was that if you really wanted to do business there was not much point in going through London and Belfast. They wanted to show them how the Republic operated in Brussels. At that time there were approximately 800 Irish people working in the Belgian capital, between the Commission, the Parliament and other organisations. The first trip involved Martin McAleese taking twelve to fourteen people from the business community in Northern Ireland to Brussels for a two-day visit on 29-30 March 2001.

They met Irish MEPs and Irish Commissioner David Byrne, had briefings from EU and Irish officials. They visited EU institutions, had lunches and dinners. The trip was so successful that it was intended to do it again, but increased security after 9/11 changed that. It turned out to be a blessing in disguise. Rather than going to Brussels, they decided to bring Brussels to Dublin. So, for the following two years, they organised business seminars, with 120 people at each of them. The Irish Ambassador to the EU and the current Irish Commissioner came over from Brussels, as did Pat Cox, then President of the Parliament, and Irish MEPs. Over the two days of the seminars, opportunities available within the EU, as well as opportunities as a result of enlargement, were highlighted. They brought along people from the 'new' countries. Those from Poland told how they had set up businesses, the difficulties involved and how they overcame those difficulties. Eugene McCague, from Arthur Cox solicitors, talked about legal difficulties in doing business in some EU countries. RTÉ's Tommie Gorman was MC on both occasions. And afterwards everyone would go to Áras an Uachtaráin for a reception and a chat.

Where farming was concerned, they organised ten to twelve separate days, each involving a group of fifty farmers. A busload would come down from Northern Ireland to An Bord Bia. There would be a reception, a lunch and a meeting with the Minister, at the time, Joe Walsh, and subsequently Mary Coughlan. Three presentations on topics of interest to the Northern farmers were given by Department of Agriculture officials. Martin McAleese would have gone through the topics in advance with the Northerners, gauging what they wanted to hear. Each presentation was be followed by a question-and-answer session. Then, Martin McAleese would say a few words, wrap it up and all would go back to Áras an Uachtaráin to meet the President.

The Northern Ireland fishing community was also involved. Dermot Ahern hosted a day for them at Farmleigh, with a formula similar to that used for the farmers.

Then there was the political community. Initially the McAleeses concentrated on district councillors from the UUP, the Alliance, some SDLP and some Independents. Later, representatives from the DUP came to the Áras, especially those from the City of Derry. Before Bill Clinton's last visit to Ireland as President of the US in December 2000 they hit on the idea of inviting some members of the Councils to come to Dublin, over a period of time, to have lunch with the US Ambassador Michael Sullivan. That would give the unionist councillors a chance to tell the ambassador the kind of things they would like Bill Clinton to say in his speeches. They jumped at it. Each delegation met Ambassador Sullivan. Martin McAleese also attended the lunches. All the hard political talk was at the lunches. Then they would go across to the Áras for tea and coffee, and to meet the President. The delegations were able to go back and tell their people that they had put their case to the US Ambassador and that he would talk to the State Department about their concerns.

The military community was Harvey Bicker's specialty. He is on the Military Heritage of Ireland Trust, and the trust with responsibility for the Irish National War Memorial at Islandbridge in Dublin. He feels deeply about the common military heritage of all the people of this island down the centuries. He is a soldiers' soldier, regardless of who that soldier served. The First World

Celebrating 'The Twelfth' has become an annual event at Áras an Uachtaráin during Mary McAleese's Presidency

War has a personal resonance for him. His uncle, Bertie Bicker, was killed while fighting with the Dublin Fusiliers at the Battle of St Quentin in Picardy [France] on 23 March 1918. His remains were never found.

The McAleeses brought down non-serving military from Northern Ireland to visit McKee barracks in Dublin. Included were representatives of the Somme Association, the Irish Regimental Historical Society, QUB [Queen's University Belfast] Officers training corps, civilian administration officers from the territorial army, the Ulster Aviation Society, the Reserves Forces and Cadets Association, the Queen's Services club, the regimental associations of the Royal Irish Fusiliers, the Royal Enniskilling Fusiliers and more. About fifty to sixty representatives in all.

Martin McAleese explains, 'This was tied into the commemoration of those Irishmen who fought and died in the First World War and which I think will be Mary's greatest legacy. Opening the Peace Park at Messines with Queen Elizabeth of Britain and King Albert of the Belgians in 1998; going every year to St Patrick's Cathedral on Remembrance Day to lay a wreath – the impact of these actions within the unionist community in the North we can never measure.'

Lieutenant General Colm Mangan, then the Irish Defence Forces chief of staff, welcomed everybody. There were three demonstrations in the square of McKee barracks: artillery, carriers, rangers. There was lunch and lectures. And then back to the Áras to meet the President. All of these military organisations live and breathe the First World War. What was remarkable after the President visited Messines was the feedback throughout the Republic from so many staunch nationalists who talked for the first time about their great-grandfather, or an uncle, or a grandfather who fought or died in that war. So many people feel safe to talk about those relatives now. They had kept it bottled up for generations. It was like a huge burden had been taken off their shoulders.

Outreach to the Orange Order is ongoing. Martin McAleese has met them in Belfast many times. As already explained by the Order's Grand Secretary, Drew Nelson in an earlier chapter, they came down to Áras an Uachtaráin for lunch over two years ago, where an attempt was made to work out an agenda to help build relationships. Senior people from the Grand Lodge in Belfast, Grand Master Robert Saulters, Drew Nelson, Grand Treasurer Mervyn Bishop and representatives from all the lodges in the Republic were there. So were representatives from the Department of the Taoiseach, from Foreign Affairs, the International Fund for Ireland and from the Equality Authority. They looked at issues surrounding the Order's interests in the Republic. Robert Saulters and his colleagues were brought to the Boyne and shown the plans for the interpretative centre. And the National Roads Authority produced a map of what was happening on the Aughrim battle site [in County Galway].

More recently, Martin McAleese, with the support of the President, has been involved in local issues regarding Orange Lodges in the four border counties of Donegal, Cavan, Monaghan and Leitrim. Some of their Orange Halls had been vandalised over the years and the members there were very reluctant to kick up a fuss. At Martin McAleese's instigation, the Áras team recruited the four relevant county managers, the Equality Authority, the Gardaí and the International Fund for Ireland. All were brought together over a series of meetings. The end result was that funds from the International Fund for Ireland and the Department of the Gaeltacht and Community Affairs were made available to address the repair of the damaged Orange Halls.

Surveys were done – the number of halls, the damage, the plans. When the information was all there, the Department agreed to fund a full-time development officer. Money has since been released for repair of the damaged Orange Halls, while more grant applications are up for approval.

All this happened as a result of the engagement between Áras an Uachtaráin and the members of the Orange Order.

Afterwards there was a lunch arranged at the Áras for members of the Order in the border counties. 'That was a very emotional day,' Martin McAleese says. 'Mary spoke very, very well to them. It was a lovely occasion. It took eighteen months, but we got very tangible results.'

President McAleese's desire is that everybody on these Northern delegations who comes through Áras an Uachtaráin leaves there as an ambassador. Everybody invited there has been invited back, and has also been asked to bring along three or four of their closest friends, preferably people who have never crossed the border before and/or people who would have difficulty going there because of where it is. And, in order to make sure things are not just a once off, as well as keeping the contacts up, the President sends Christmas cards to every single person who has come on those visits. Sometimes St Patrick's Day and birthday cards, too.

Another part of the Áras outreach, the North-South Round Table Group, is an economic business group, set up five or six years ago. It was initially intended as a support for the work of Intertrade Ireland and to encourage development of the conditions that would help fluency in the island economy. It would look at the obstacles that could prevent that from happening. Then they would pull in expertise to analyse problems and suggest solutions. The group is made up of private sector people from North and South, and of both traditions. There are also some civil servants involved, as well as public and trade union representatives. But it is essentially a private sector driven lobby, using their own expertise to pull people together to sort out a solution. They would go to both Governments at the one time. They approached the first Executive in Northern Ireland to say, 'Look, we are private sector North and South, of both persuasions. We have identified these problems. Here are some solutions.' They had a steering group jointly chaired by Laurence Crowley, former governor of the Bank of Ireland, and Stephen Kingon, currently chairman of Invest Northern Ireland.

They chaired monthly or six-weekly steering group meetings, and they organised two plenary sessions every year with a raft of sub-groups. The bottom line was to make people comfortable with the island economy. The reason was simple. Martin McAleese says, 'I believe that the island economy is the next stage of the Celtic Tiger economy, despite the current downturn, and that this will produce huge benefits, North and South. It will drive the Northern Ireland economy. To get people comfortable with the idea of an island economy was difficult at first as a lot of unionists were very nervous about such talk. Although there are no constitutional or political elements to it, some of them felt that it was not too far away from economic, or even political unity. So the talk tended to be about an island economy or a two-jurisdiction economy, or a collaborative island economy, or the third economy.' There has been good engagement and by now the McAleeses feel they have got to the point where everyone is comfortable with the idea. Now the phrase 'the island economy' has become common currency. That has taken a huge amount of work.

But there remain areas of instability. There are a lot of loyalists and republicans who feel, ten years on, 'What does this peace process mean? We don't see any evidence of it.' And there are the so-called 'peace walls'. The McAleeses are trying to initiate the building of networks across the walls between those communities. When the walls come down, as hopefully they will, at least there will be something to replace them and fill the vacuum. It won't be bricks and mortar; it will be a network of human energy. That is the intention. To build relationships of trust across those walls and at their interface which will enable the networks to facilitate the smooth reconciliation of two sides into one living organism of relationships. It is a difficult task.

The other area of Áras outreach has to do with victims' groups. There is a tendency to say, 'This peace process is moving on, you cannot hold it back. For God's sake get over it and move on like the rest of us.' Where Protestant groups are concerned, the role of the Irish Presidency in this context may be superficial. As the figurehead of nationalism, Mary McAleese can, by having people visit Áras an Uachtaráin, tell them their hurt is recognised and express a desire to share the journey with them. But ultimately that cannot really be done. What happened, happened. But what help can be provided from the Áras will be provided. There are counselling and other on-hand services available. But sometimes simply the acknowledgement is enough.

Martin McAleese says that 'while people today are living in a state of relative calm in Northern Ireland, there is still potential instability there, still a potential for things to spiral out of control. People have lived apart, causing communities to drift away from each other, creating ignorance of each other and generating many ill-informed misperceptions of the other. Ultimately, this lack of engagement seedbeds sectarianism which has polluted and

The Peace Bell at Áras an Uachtaráin
commemorating the 10th Anniversary of
The Good Friday Agreement

dehumanised the landscape of Northern Ireland for so long. Our challenge now is to decommission sectarianism.'

The thinking behind reaching out to loyalism particularly has to do with the realisation that if real peace is ever going to prevail on this island there has to be reconciliation. Both Martin and Mary McAleese would describe themselves as Irish Catholic nationalists. Their constitutional ambition is to live in a secular united Ireland brought about by democratic politics and persuasion. No violence, no duress. Loyalists want to defend and maintain the constitutional link with the UK. They want to defend Northern Ireland from interference, and most particularly from interference by the Irish Government. They also want to defend what they see as the Protestant ethos against the Catholic Church. Those two positions are different and diametrically opposed. The challenge for the McAleeses was to establish a reconciliation between both. To establish a happy co-existence.

All in all, to date in this presidency over 13,000 people from the various groups mentioned above have visited Áras an Uachtaráin.

'We're all getting jangled [mixed together],' says Harvey Bicker, while making observations about 'the changing streams in Irish society North and South'. You might say he is the personification of this himself: a man who once swore loyalty to the Queen as a serving British army officer and now serving on President Mary McAleese's Council of State. He sees no contradiction. 'I've retired from the British army,' he points out. And joining Fianna Fáil was 'an obvious thing to do for anyone with the island's business and farming interests at heart.' He doesn't know where all this 'jangled' business is leading but he knows one thing: 'it is in the right direction'.

About the President he says, 'It has been nothing but an honour for me to serve her in any way I can. She is a spiritual person. I'm not, but it is something I deeply admire in her. And there is no doubt in my mind that we got two for the price of one when you include Martin. Absolutely no doubt about it ... I know we Northerners are slightly raw-edged, even abrasive, compared to Dublin sophisticates and can be hard to handle. She has got over that and advanced beyond it.' In general he says, 'I can't but admire what she has done.'

The President has visited Northern Ireland officially on ninety-seven occasions since assuming office. Undoubtedly the most powerful of those visits, in terms of its impact on her, was to Omagh following the bombing there on 15 August 1998, which killed twenty-eight people. She was clearly shocked, angry, but above all grief-stricken. She knew the town and its people through her academic outreach programmes from her days at Queen's University. She was described in The Irish Times as having been 'an ever-present and visible symbol of the unequivocal grief and concern of the people of the Republic' in Omagh that week. On 20 August, the Northern Ireland First Minister, David Trimble, attended the funerals of three children killed at Omagh, Oran Doherty (8), Shaun McLaughlin (12) and James Barker (12), 'two Catholic and two Protestant'. The same newspaper observed that 'in a normal society, to make such an observation would seem bizarre and uncalled-for but in a deeply-divided community that kind of balance is important.

'His [David Trimble's] visit to Buncrana, where he was warmly greeted by his former academic sparring partner, Mrs Mary McAleese, was another indication that Mr Trimble understands the difference between being First Minister and just another party leader.'

It was the first time Ireland's new President had met David Trimble in public since her election. In fact, though invited, he never did visit Áras an Uachtaráin while Northern Ireland's First Minister. 'I did receive invitations to Áras an Uachtaráin but I didn't take them up. I didn't particularly want to. It was nothing personal. There were more pressing political priorities and I was already fighting [politically] on many fronts.' He agrees that when they met that time in Buncrana their greeting was 'wholehearted. Why not? It's not as if we were unknown to each other.' He observes that, while the Robinson presidency had been the cause of 'a little controversy' among unionists where visits to Northern Ireland were concerned, 'that has not been the case with Mary McAleese. She has handled matters more sensitively, rather better.' He describes Northern Ireland reaction at the time of her election in 1997: 'Nationalist reaction was enthusiastic, but in the unionist community there was some concern she would be more forceful politically than Mary Robinson. But that was soon dissipated'.

'From a Northern point of view her presidency has been a positive one. There have been a couple of blips, one unfortunate Nazi one. She was not the only one from a nationalist background to have said that. I scratched my head and said "where did that come from?" It's so far from the reality. But, apart from those, there has been sensitivity. And the blips were slight.' On the outreach by her Presidency to loyalists he says there was 'a very negative attitude to the loyalist leadership among unionists', but the reaching out to them by the McAleeses was 'not a cause of discomfort to mainstream unionists. I cannot say it is regarded with opprobrium. There is a political need to try to wean them off the way they conduct themselves and to get them behind the political dispensation.'

At one time Trimble was a frequent visitor to the Leneghan pub in Rostrevor. 'In 1975/76 I was taking out a young lady [now his wife, Daphne] from Warrenpoint and two pubs in Rostrevor were owned by parents of former pupils of mine. Hers was one. We used to visit both.'

The Belfast Agreement document, with the signatures of George Mitchell, Tony Blair, Bertie Ahern, Martin McGuinness, Joe Hendron, Liz O'Donnell, David Trimble, Mo Mowlam, John Hume, Gerry Adams, Billy Hutchinson, among others.

A Most Unexpected Friendship

No one needs Google Earth to find Sandy Row. There it is right beside Day's Hotel, 'Northern Ireland's largest hotel with 250 *en suite* bedrooms ... located right in the heart of Belfast City'. A huge mural shows the way. 'You Are Now Entering Loyalist Sandy Row, Heartland of South Belfast Ulster Freedom Fighters, *Quis Separabit*', it says, with its two red hands and its two red fists. As you traverse the heartland you will come across further murals. One of 'George Best 1940 to 2005'. Another of Robert Dougan, 'Murdered by enemies 10th February 1998. In proud memory of our fallen comrade. Gone but not forgotten. Quis Separabit.' The letters UDA and UFF are inscribed alongside.

None of this prepares you for the sight at the top of the stairs as you enter the McMichael Centre in the very centre of this loyalist heartland. For there you will see a collage of photographs of President Mary McAleese and her husband Martin with what turns out to be residents of the area on their visits to Áras an Uachtaráin. There is even one taken in the Council of State room posed in front of probably the most famous painting in Áras an Uachtaráin. By Simon Coleman RHA, it is of the first meeting of a Council of State, the President's advisory body, presided over by President Douglas Hyde in 1940.

Jackie McDonald is friendliness itself. It seems abrupt to start with the obvious question, but it must be done. 'Are you Brigadier of the UDA?' To which he replies 'allegedly'. He is candid about his past. 'I got ten years for blackmail, extortion and threats to kill, providing money for the UDA war chest. I went in, in 1989 and was out in 1994.' He now works full-time as an organiser at the McMichael centre, catering mainly for ex-prisoners and doing community work with the Prisoners Enterprise Project and the Community Foundation, Northern Ireland. The centre is named after John McMichael, a leading figure in the UDA, who stood unsuccessfully for the Ulster Loyalist Democratic Party in a south Belfast by-election in 1981 and remained leader of the party until his death. He was killed in a car bomb in what was believed to have been a UDA inside job in 1987. His son, Gary, then tried to build up the party as the political wing of the UDA, but following its collapse he dropped out of politics.

Jackie McDonald's first contact with President Mary and Martin McAleese was organised through his solicitor of thirty years, Denis Moloney, who is a long-time friend of the McAleeses and a member of the current Council of State in the Republic. It was December 2002. 'I was going to Scotland to a Rangers match with friends and called to see Denis on the way to the boat when Denis asked me whether I would like to have a chat with Martin. He sorted it out there and then. He called Martin and passed the phone to me and we started talking as if we'd known each other forever.' They agreed to keep in contact.

There was a major internal loyalist feud going on at the time, involving the Johnny Adair faction. On 5 June 2003 a body found in a shallow grave on the outskirts of north Belfast was believed to be that of loyalist and close Adair associate Alan McCullough (21). He had been missing since the Wednesday of the previous week after he returned to Belfast from England, believing UDA leaders had granted him a reprieve after his siding with Adair in the feud. The BBC received a call from the UDA claiming that it had killed McCullough after linking him with the murder of John Gregg, one of the UDA's most senior figures and the so-called brigadier of the organisation in south-east Antrim. Gregg was killed at Belfast docks in February 2003, after returning from a Rangers game in Glasgow, by Adair's 'C-company' of which Alan McCullough was a senior member. His (Alan McCullough's) body had been found in the command area of murdered John Gregg, giving weight to reports that he was handed over by UDA elements in the Shankill to Gregg's local associates. Alan McCullough's father, UDA man William 'Bucky' McCullough, was murdered in 1981. He was shot dead by the INLA, but is believed to have been set up by another UDA leader, Jim Craig, who in turn was murdered by his own organisation in 1988. Craig was blamed for setting up UDA leader John McMichael for murder.

The events leading to Alan McCullough's death began after the killing of Gregg in February 2003. He then fled to Britain with Adair's wife, Gina, and about twenty other loyalists who sided with Adair. Though Adair was already back in prison at that stage, taken by police in January during the height of the murderous dispute between the lower Shankill 'C-company' of the UDA and the UDA leadership, nonetheless, the UDA was convinced that

The President is greeted by Jackie McDonald on her visit to Taughmonagh Primary School, Belfast in 2005

Adair had orchestrated Gregg's murder. Alan McCullough hated life in England and made several overtures to the UDA to be allowed to return to Belfast. It was reported that as part of a deal he switched sides and gave the UDA information about where Adair's associates were living. This is believed also to have led to a drive-by shooting on a house in Brighton where Gina Adair was staying.

That is the world into which Martin McAleese made an entrance on 23 February 2003.

He met Jackie McDonald at the Taughmonagh social club in south Belfast, believed to be the headquarters of the UDA in that area. 'It was very brave of him in the circumstances. We were all under threat,' comments Jackie McDonald. Martin was accompanied by his driver 'and the PSNI were hanging about the place because of the threats.' There would be no PSNI presence at any future meetings involving Martin McAleese, Jackie McDonald and his associates. Martin McAleese requested this, as a gesture of trust. He and Jackie McDonald went into the back room at the social club that first time they met, and they talked. It was the beginning of an extraordinary friendship. Martin said that if there was going to be a new future for the island of Ireland every part of every single community had to be involved, or at least must be invited to take part, and that this included loyalists as well. They must take risks on each other, he said, and that if you want to make a change, you must be in an uncomfortable place. You must have the odd sleepless night; otherwise you are not making progress. When Jackie commented on the risk he [Martin] was taking, Martin responded that Jackie and his associates were taking an even bigger risk. That they could be accused of betrayal or fraternising with the enemy, and in a paramilitary environment where the consequences could be brutal.

They talked about the future and the future of their children. Martin McAleese promised to do whatever he could to help.

At their second meeting, in the Stormont Hotel, on 8 April, 'I talked to him about facilities which were needed at the local Dunmurray Young Men's Football Club. He agreed to talk to his friends and see what he could do.' They arranged to meet again to discuss bringing people from the area on a visit to Áras an Uachtaráin as a way of breaking the ice.

There was a visa problem when Jackie McDonald wanted to attend another Rangers match at Easter 2003. So it was arranged that he could have an Irish passport. He needed it in a rush, so southern intermediaries had to collect his application form in Belfast and bring it to Dublin for speedy processing.

President McAleese with then Secretary of State for Northern Ireland, Mo Mowlam, at Lansdowne Road, 1999

On 28 April 2003 Jackie McDonald came to Dublin with sixty people from loyalist Belfast. There were two busloads, one big, one small. 'I brought Mary a bunch of flowers, champagne, a box of chocolates, an Ulster flag and a Rangers scarf. It was for her father. It was a wind-up because her father is a Celtic man.' By all accounts, the President was very emotional about the gesture. The scarf was subsequently given to her father. A strong nationalist republican, that Rangers scarf is said to be one of his most cherished possessions.

They were treated to lunch in Áras an Uachtaráin. 'Martin and Mary entertained everyone. We were a bit apprehensive going down but on the way back it was "when are we going down again?"' he says. From the Áras they were taken to Farmleigh House and it was there that Martin presented him with his Irish passport. It was there too that it was agreed that Martin would meet with Jackie McDonald's associates.

They met at the Stormont Hotel on 21 May: Martin McAleese, Denis Moloney, Jackie McDonald and his associates. It was tense at the beginning. There was no small talk and Jackie's associates were not friendly. But they sat down and Martin McAleese spoke about his own background in the city and the President's background there, too. He was very open and frank. He emphasised that there was no pressure on anyone, that his and the President's only interest, in the context, was in the place where they were born and came from. They wanted to do something to help change things for the future. He was also very frank about being a Catholic and a nationalist and about where they came from, politically and religion-wise.

He talked about trust and memories. How trust was a hugely important thing. How all were working towards a shared future but that before you could get there there had to be shared memories. There were very few shared memories in their pasts because the past had been built in such a way that there was just one single identity. The one exception to that were the men of the First World War. The recovery of their memory on the Catholic nationalist side had been a great kick-start for all towards a shared future, he said. But that it would probably not be enough. They would have to build in the present the shared memories that would give all a shared future.

He talked about the difference between the Protestant and Catholic outlook. How the Protestant regards words as precise and direct. In negotiations, very often find the Protestant opening line is the bottom line. On the other hand, the Catholic is less precise, more elastic, subtle. A Protestant and a Catholic arriving at an agreement can interpret it differently. So Catholics, looking at the Protestant, might say he or she is just intransigent, while the Protestant looking at the Catholic would say he or she is just devious. Understanding where the two are coming from makes it easier to cope.

And the men talked about lack of education in Loyalist communities. One man spoke of a young lad in his community who was the first in living memory to get the 11 plus. The youngster and his parents were so ashamed of it that they didn't talk about it. It just went to show the lack of education in those areas. That young man would have been the butt of ridicule – the pansy, the softie – where his peers or the paramilitaries were concerned.

That meeting went on for over two and a half hours. It was agreed that there would be a follow-up. Before the meeting ended Jackie McDonald said, 'Martin, there is talk about whether Mary will stand again next year. Tell her from us, we want her to stand.' Martin McAleese, apparently, was completely taken aback.

Soon afterwards a golf outing was arranged at the K Club in Kildare with Martin McAleese, some of his business friends, and Jackie McDonald. At a meal afterwards he was presented with a cheque for £19,641 for the Dunmurray Football Club. It has been used to update its training facilities. Martin McAleese's friends also raised money for other clubs in Belfast, and in republican areas as well. 'They are very, very friendly people,' he says. Jackie has met them many times since. He explained how people in his community couldn't accept money from the Irish Government, that 'it is too sensitive'. Which was why 'we very, very much appreciate what Martin has done for so many loyalist areas in Northern Ireland through organising some sort of sponsorship. Martin is a frequent visitor. He helped introduce us to Bertie, who was very helpful. Martin has made it easier for others to talk to us simply by extending the hand of friendship.'

And busloads of loyalists have been to Dublin again. In June 2003 a group attended a workshop in the House of Lords arts centre in Foster Place, hosted by Laurence Crowley, then governor of the Bank of Ireland.

Most bizarre of all was the occasion when a busload of loyalists and republicans from Belfast were escorted through the Dublin traffic to Áras an Uachtaráin by police outriders. 'The republicans and loyalists were hanging

British Prime Minister Tony Blair signs the visitor's book at Áras an Uachtaráin

out the windows with their mobile phone,' he says. 'It was the first time that republicans and loyalists were together that the sirens sounded and no one ran!'

'Martin extended the hand of friendship. He said "a hand up is not a hand out". He stayed with us when things were bad and so did the President. They were very, very helpful. They have encouraged us when we needed it and they explained different angles. That's why we hoped she would go forward again. It would've fallen flat if Mary hadn't carried on. We told Mary that we hoped she would go for a second term. And when she did and I was invited to the inauguration I said I didn't want to get her into bother. But she said "You're coming to the inauguration. You are my friend." At the inauguration lunch in the Áras, Martin asked, "Do you have any preference where you sit?" I hadn't, so he brought me over as his guest to the same table as Denis Moloney, Martin McGuinness, Dermot Ahern (then Minister for Foreign Affairs) and Fr Alec Reid. I had a good conversation with Dermot. He was going to Yasser Arafat's funeral. And later on Bertie was standing on his own and he said, "Hello Jackie". His whole approach was friendly. He was not stand-offish in any way. He understood where the loyalists were coming from [over decommissioning] and how they were under pressure, too. The contact helped. A lot up here are very wary of supporting people like myself, but because of Bertie and the President, it has made it easier for others to talk to me.'

He recalls how the President visited the primary school in Taughmonagh, a 100 per cent loyalist area, in September 2005, and when it was suggested they take down a Union Jack there she said, "Not at all".' She was greeted by school principal Janet Douds and Jackie McDonald. She toured the classes and sat and chatted with the children, who also sang for her. Ms Douds said that of the 177 pupils at the school only one was prevented by her parents from meeting the President. 'I have been here over fifteen years and I never ever dreamed that we would have the Irish President in the midst of Taughmonagh Primary School. It has been wonderful for the children,' she said. Jackie McDonald said that the President's presence was a 'morale-booster' for the Taughmonagh estate and the school, which was in the middle of a rebuilding programme and needed funds for computers and a library. There were a lot of mobile classrooms at the school at the time, but since the visit contracts have been signed for a new school. 'Mary heightened its profile,' he says. 'A new school will be built and I believe Mary's visit made it happen. It was all down to Mary and Martin. Because both are from Northern Ireland, people could identify with them more readily. They understood our problems and extended the hand of friendship. After thirty-five years there's a lot of hatred and anger here. We had to break the mould, to move on.'

There had been some resentment among the businessmen he met in the Republic. 'One said he was wary about being asked to the dinner [to which Jackie McDonald had been invited]. He said he still had time to get out but that he realised I hadn't two heads. I told him neither had he. He said, "If Ireland was playing England, who would you support?" I said, "England, of course". He asked me if a car with a southern registration was parked in Belfast what would happen to it and I said that in some areas it would be wrecked.'

'Mary and Martin have tried hard, worked hard as ambassadors. They reached out to an isolated people when others were afraid to do so. They were afraid to make us respectable, electable. They don't want to divide the [unionist/loyalist] vote. The folks on the hill [Stormont] won't talk to me. The people on Sandy Row can't understand that. Most politicians are middle class. They don't know what it's like where decommissioning is concerned. They won't come down to our level. This is not a normal society. Our people are excluded. Dyslexia, depression, no future etc., we encounter that every day.

'They think that if they get the guns that's the end of it, but there is a criminal element out there and people have been dependent on the paramilitaries [for protection] for thirty-five years. They feel that if we give up the guns we will have deserted them, like Paisley deserted them. Hopefully [Peter] Robinson will deal with these issues. There's a feeling of isolation, neglect and apathy in loyalist areas. No one bothers at all. We are treated like dirt when we have guns. What would it be like if we hadn't? Yes, there is a criminal element out there and they are not tolerated in loyalist areas. They are making fortunes out of drugs. If the UDA decommission, the people are vulnerable. That's what happened in west Belfast. We don't want it to happen here. It's all about community.

The war with Sinn Féin/IRA is over. Now it's a war against criminals. Paramilitaries have been involved in drugs. They went from being saviours to being criminals. Most of those are now gone. It was a very, very tough struggle. If there is one criminal left in the UDA, it is one too many. But if there is a problem now we are told to go to the PSNI. Unfortunately, they are not dealing with the situation, so people go back to the paramilitaries. Everyone has to get together to get the moral fibre back. How can you tell a young fella who is stealing a video that it is wrong, if his father is in jail for murder? The whole moral code is gone. We have to rebuild it. It is easier to convince an ex-prisoner of this than the young macho culture. They [the young] don't look at the downside. People won't forgive. They want hatred and bigotry.'

He was at the Ireland versus England rugby match in February 2007 in Croke Park. Martin McAleese arranged the tickets for him and three friends. After the playing of 'God Save the Queen' a fellow recognised him and tapped him on the shoulder and said, "Jackie, the words are coming up [on a screen] to help you with the next one [the Irish national anthem]." He saw an Orangeman there who he knew and he was wrapped in a tricolour. It was all 'very, very friendly'.

He recalls a conversation with Martin McAleese in Áras an Uachtaráin when he said, 'Jackie, you and I have an opportunity to try to change things, and we agreed to go for it.' He remembers that on his second visit to the Áras he brought a rose bush for the President. He bought two at the Taughmonagh garden centre locally and planted one 'at Taughmonagh and I took the other one to Mary. I said I hope it blossoms like our friendship'. The third time he visited he brought 'a crystal clock engraved to Martin and Mary with the words "a united notion". I made sure the engraver got the spelling right.'

One person who was part of a trip to the Áras was James Watson, the man who shot Bernadette McAliskey. 'They didn't have a problem. He served twelve years of a life sentence. A typical ex-lifer. He was a spark [electrician] at Shortts, a hard-working, decent fellow who just got involved because of the Troubles.' A photograph of Jackie, Martin McAleese, and former IRA man 'Spike' Murray had appeared in the *Irish News* and James Watson said to him, 'I bet that's the nearest you've been to a Provo without a gun in your hand.'

Jackie McDonald just wants 'a better future for the kids. They are good kids. Others just want to hate people. I hope they are in a minority and I'd say they are.' He also believes very much in devolved government for Northern Ireland. 'People say Jackie helped Paisley by saying such things.' He met journalist Barry White at a function who said to him, 'Jackie, you made all this possible. Paisley knew he didn't have the loyalist paramilitaries on his back.' There had been a reception for community workers after the new executive was established at Stormont and he was there. So too were Ian Paisley and Martin McGuinness. 'We were thanked for our brave leadership and told it would not have been possible without us. And as soon as McGuinness finished, Paisley disappeared. McGuinness, Gerry Kelly, Alex

Maskey walked around shaking hands.' He told the *Belfast Telegraph* at the time that Ian Paisley 'didn't want to be photographed with us. I wish Paisley the best, but he, Craig and Molyneux used [to] tell the paramilitaries what to do, block roads, strikes etc. Once John McMichael decided the UDA would decide its own destiny, Paisley did not talk [to the UDA leadership] for thirty years.'

But now 'everyone has to work together. Peace is not going to come about in bits and pieces.' For his own part, he hopes his friendship with the McAleeses 'will go on even after Mary and Martin leave office. I hope we will remain friends then. I hope we will be friends forever. They are fantastic.'

The President presents the gold torc to poet Seamus Heaney on his election as Saoi of Aosdána

She Mentioned the War

On 19 March 2008, four generations of one family waited to see Queen Elizabeth of Britain, their Queen, when she arrived to visit the East Belfast (Methodist) Mission. Elizabeth Fisher (89), her daughter Yvonne, her grand-daughter Wendy and her great grand-daughter Amy ('I'm 8') were among the crowds of people who had gathered in the heart of loyalist east Belfast to catch a glimpse of the Queen and Prince Philip. 'We must be the most loyal part of the UK,' said Yvonne, 'we even play the national anthem when the pubs close.'

'You see there,' Yvonne pointed to a shop building with 'Stepping Stone Project' written over its entrance, 'Prince Charles opened that.' It is a social/community centre which gives people employment advice. Elizabeth Fisher recalls, 'He said to me, "you look very nice" and I said to him "Son, you made my day". My legs were shaking.' Union Jacks were being handed out for people to wave and a policeman passed by. 'NIPS I call them, Northern Ireland Police Service. I'd stick to the old name [RUC] any day,' said Yvonne. 'So would I,' said the passing policeman.

The East Belfast Mission was founded in 1985 to help with community development in that part of Belfast which contains two of the ten most deprived electoral areas in all of Northern Ireland. The Mission is run by the dynamic minister Rev. Gary Mason who was awarded an MBE for his work there. Methodists have been worshipping at the same site in east Belfast since 1826. But in 1941, as Nazi bombers were heading towards the nearby shipyards during World War II, they dropped their bombs prematurely and

The President and Queen Elizabeth arrive at Crosby Hall for the Co-operation Ireland Dinner, 2005

the Methodist church was demolished. It was rebuilt in 1952. Two cranes dominate the local skyline. Nicknamed Samson and Goliath, they are among what remains of the Belfast shipyard. In the early 1960s, 30,000 people were employed there, right on the church's doorstep. Today it employs 100 people. The sectarian conflict has also ripped the economic heart out of the community.

President McAleese and Rev. Gary Mason are old acquaintances and both worked on the committee that produced the 1993 document on sectarianism for the Ballymascanlon inter-church meeting. Both would have been among the more radical voices on that committee. The President visited the East Belfast Mission in September 2004. In May 2004 Rev. Mason had taken seven local paramilitary loyalists to Auschwitz 'to see where bigotry and prejudice led'. He believes that trip was a success and is planning a further one.

In January 2005 President McAleese herself visited Auschwitz to attend a ceremony marking the Red Army's arrival, in January 1945, at the camp where the Nazis slaughtered more than a million Jews. She joined dozens of other heads of state in paying tribute to survivors of the camp and to Red Army veterans.

Speaking on RTÉ's 'Morning Ireland' programme before she attended the remembrance service, she said, 'The Nazis didn't invent anti-semitism, but they used it and built upon it. Anti-semitism was for centuries an element for many who on the surface lived very good lives and would have regarded themselves as very good Christians. But they gave to their children an irrational hatred of Jews in the same way that people in Northern Ireland transmitted to their children an irrational hatred, for example, of Catholics ... in the same way that people give to their children an outrageous and irrational hatred of those who are of different colour and all of those things ... All of those hatreds that can, in the wrong circumstances, outcrop, like for instance, on a street in Dublin in a young girl from Somalia being pelted by eggs. It can outcrop in a knife being used in a fight and a man from Eastern Europe being stabbed to death. It is a toxin, it's a poison that starts in a weak and diluted form, but when concentrated you get Auschwitz, you get Birkenau, you get Rwanda and you get Darfur. That is what you get if you don't stop that toxin.'

Her remarks sparked outrage among unionists. The UUP's Michael McGimpsey described them as deep-seated sectarianism'. The DUP's Ian Paisley Jnr accused the President of an 'irrational and insulting' attack on 'an entire generation of Protestant people'. The SDLP leader Mark Durkan said he did not believe Mrs McAleese was trying to equate any of the prejudices in Northern Ireland with the systematic genocide of the Nazi regime. He criticised unionists for rushing to condemn her when they were slow to confront sectarian attacks and abuse aimed at the Holy Cross schoolchildren or Catholics attending Mass in Harryville in Ballymena. Sinn Féin's Alex Maskey branded unionist reaction to the President's comments 'hysterical'. In the Republic, Labour's Ruairí Quinn said he fully accepted the general point the President was making, that much religious, ethnic and racial hatred can be transmitted to children at an early age. 'However, in the Irish context, it is important for all public figures at all levels to acknowledge that no section of the community in Northern Ireland has been the sole victim of sectarianism.'

A presidential visit planned for a Shankhill primary school shortly after she made the remarks was cancelled.

Even the President's brother, Damien Leneghan, felt her words were 'ill-chosen'. He believed 'her intentions were the best, maybe the analogy was ill-chosen, particularly in light of what is happening in the North ... Perhaps a more balanced view should have been presented in extending the sentence that little bit extra, if that's what she needed to do to make it a balanced statement so people wouldn't take exception to it.' He also said that people such as his sister who worked for peace often found themselves in situations where they were dealing with people who were 'overly sensitive' or, he believed, 'sometimes looking for something to be sensitive for'.

Others were more understanding. Jackie McDonald says that the Nazi episode 'was a horrendous time for her'. Around that time, Martin McAleese visited three friends of his at Belfast City Hospital. As they were coming out, they were surrounded by media. Jackie McDonald told them, 'I know the President. She didn't mean things the way they were taken. She is not that sort of person.' He says, 'I wasn't saying it to be helpful, but because it is true. I know the lady. She would not deliberately hurt anyone.' But he had his critics. On the BBC's 'Stephen Nolan Show' Nolan asked, 'I wonder what our Brigadier friend has to say about this?' McDonald says that if what he said at the time helped, he is glad he did it.

Word of all of this was getting through to President McAleese in Poland. In a radio interview that Friday afternoon she said she was 'devastated' by the ferocity of the reaction from the Protestant community and accepted that Catholics have also been guilty of sectarianism. She said she took full responsibility for not finishing out the example of sectarian hatred in Northern Ireland which she has used routinely in other interviews. 'I accept absolutely that in relation to sectarianism we all have plenty of things to be ashamed about.' She commented in another radio interview that 'what I said I undoubtedly said clumsily. I should have finished out the example and it would have been a much, much better interview had I done that ... It was never my intention going into it to simply blame one side of the community in Northern Ireland.' Asked if she had made a mistake, she replied, 'Without a shadow of a doubt. There is no putting a tooth in it. I was trying to explain by example how we have to try and fight racism and sectarianism on our own island. I should have finished out the example by saying "Catholic and Protestant".'

On RTÉ's 'Five Seven Live' that day she said, 'I have done so much over the years to try and show in every way that I can that we all have blame. I attach blame to myself and in every way that we can to humbly apologise and hang our heads for all that we have done to create the awful relationship which has blotted life and blighted life on our island and to try to commit ourselves and reach within ourselves to building up those friendships ... I certainly hope that nothing that I have said will stop the march of peace and the march towards a culture of mutual respect. I was trying to encourage that culture of mutual respect.' Though she had been trying to illustrate the lessons posed to today's society by Auschwitz, the President said, 'In trying to say that, I came across as putting the blame on one side of the community. That was entirely wrong. Having rectified that now, I hope as sincerely as I can, because I am so devastated because good people that I know, that I really would not want in any shape or form to hurt, I am sure they were hurt by those words. I would want to take back that hurt.'

'I hope out of this there comes, maybe, a focus on that problem that we all have with sectarianism. There are plenty of examples, God's amount of examples, enough to make us ashamed. But there are also very wonderful examples and Martin and I have been privileged to see many of those examples of people reaching out hands of friendship, trying to bridge the distrust and trying to get to know each other anew and to create a better future and I hope that out of this will come, maybe, a renewed energy in that regard. I did not intend to inflict on one side of the community the entire burden of responsibility, or blame. Far from it. I take the point absolutely. It is shared blame. Sectarianism is a shared problem. It is my fault for not saying that absolutely as clearly as I always do, 110 times out of a 111. This was 111, unfortunately.'

UUP leader David Trimble welcomed her apology. 'I'm glad that there has been an apology, because I considered the remarks remarkably ill-judged. It is most unlike her to make a mistake of that nature, a mistake because it trivialises the experience of European Jewry and trivialises the Holocaust and also causes considerable offence in Northern Ireland. While no doubt that is true of some people, it is not right to lump together the Protestants of Northern Ireland and accuse them of this and to ignore the fact that a considerable amount of hatred exists within some members of the Catholic community.' An Orange Order spokeswoman welcomed the apology, but the DUP's Ian Paisley Jnr said she had brought shame on her office and her country.

And that wasn't an end to the matter.

On the morning in March 2008 on which Queen Elizabeth visited the East Belfast Mission she also visited Queen's University, Belfast to mark its centenary. President McAleese was there and, though it would be the eighth time for the two women to meet, it was the first time they did so publicly on the island of Ireland.

Interviewed by the media afterwards, President McAleese was asked when it was likely that Queen Elizabeth might visit the Republic of Ireland. She quoted Irish Government policy and said such a visit could only take place sometime after policing and justice powers were devolved to Stormont. This was almost precisely what then Taoiseach Bertie Ahern had told the Dáil a few weeks earlier, on 4 March, when he said that a visit to Dublin by Queen Elizabeth hinged on the transfer of policing and justice powers to the Northern Executive. Because of DUP opposition to the devolution of such powers he did not feel such a visit would take place in 2008.

President McAleese told the media at Queen's, 'We now know – the Taoiseach has spoken about this quite openly – what requires to be done to complete the set of elements that would make such a visit possible. We know that it is dependent on the completion of devolution which, hopefully, will not be too far-off. That means the return of policing and criminal justice responsibility to the Executive in Northern Ireland.' She regarded the transfer of these powers as rounding the peace process and continued that 'I am long on the record as saying I would wish that the visit would happen. We know that Her Majesty wishes to come and we know that we wish her to come. Please goodness it will happen. As to the when of it, I don't know. That is a matter for the two governments.'

The President's remarks triggered another ferocious response from unionists. DUP Minister Nigel Dodds described her comments as 'unfortunate', adding that it was 'wrong' and 'inappropriate' of the President to make such 'political comments'. They were 'a rather cack-handed and clumsy attempt' to pressurise unionists to accept devolution of policing powers, which simply wouldn't work. 'It is completely wrong and crass for a foreign head of state to try to draw the Queen into political controversy.' UUP leader Sir Reg Empey said the President should 'butt out of a subject which is one for the parties in Northern Ireland to resolve.' Party colleague Danny Kennedy demanded that she apologise to the Queen. UUP MLA David McNarry accused the President of 'in-your-face-republicanism'.

And the Nazi remarks were remembered again. DUP MLA Stephen Moutray said, 'This is a woman with previous form. Who will ever forget her abuse of the Holocaust Memorial events in Poland in 2005 to make disgusting remarks regarding the unionist community for which she was forced to apologise?' An editorial in the following day's unionist *Newsletter* newspaper demanded that President McAleese apologise to the Queen 'for involving her in domestic politics' and to her former colleagues at Queen's University, where she made the remarks, for 'overshadowing' its centenary celebration of receiving the royal charter. It continued, 'You would have thought a woman who had to apologise in the past for accusing unionists of behaving like Nazis would have had more sense than to have dragged the Queen into the political mire.'

That controversy too died down for a while, but on 10 June 2008 it would raise its head again. President McAleese was jeered and barracked by a group of loyalist protesters as she visited Millburn primary school in Coleraine in County Derry. She and Martin were subjected to sectarian abuse as they arrived for the visit. About fifty demonstrators gathered at the school gates to show their opposition. They carried placards and waved union flags. Some of the protesters shouted, 'No surrender', 'f*** off home, republican scum', and 'We don't want you here.' They also made reference to the Nazi comments made by the President in 2005 and claimed the school did not properly consult with the local community as to whether or not her visit should go ahead. One of the protesters, John Moffat, a member of the local residents' association, said the community was showing its distaste at the President's presence. 'This is not only a protest about the President's visit, but also at the way the school has handled things. There was the Nazi comments and it has been claimed that the Queen wouldn't be able to visit the Irish Republic until policing and justice powers are devolved to Stormont, yet she can come up here without any pre-conditions.' Headmaster John Platt said the protesters represented a very small minority. He claimed the vast majority of people supported the President's visit. After a forty-minute visit to the school the President was quickly ushered to her official car without making any public comment about the incident.

This occasional seeming over-reaction by unionists to things President McAleese may say or do suggests a deepseated distrust of her on their part. Suggesting an explanation for this, one Catholic source said, 'They can't stand seeing a Northern Catholic get on'. A Presbyterian source was more pithy. Acknowledging the reaction, he said, 'It's two things — where she's from, and the makeover'. 'Where she's from' referred to her Catholic nationalist background and 'the makeover' concerned the transformation of her image when she won the Fianna Fáil nomination for the Presidency. The Presbyterian mindset is deeply suspicion of image, graven or otherwise, but the conscious cultivation of image towards a purpose is seen as manipulative, wrong, sinful. It brings us back to the President's observations in her Ampleforth speech in January 1998 about the difference between the Catholic and Protestant mindset in Northern Ireland as expressed by poet Tom Paulin about his Protestant upbinging: "I was nurtured in a puritan anti-aesthetic, told to be suspicious of what's rhetorical or ornate…"

On a visit to the newspaper's offices in 2007, British Prime Minister Tony Blair described the Belfast News Letter as the authentic voice of unionism, even if he didn't always agree with it. Billy Kennedy has been in journalism for thirty-five years, eighteen of which he spent as News Editor at the News Letter and fifteen as its chief leader writer.

He agrees that there was 'deep suspicion among some unionists, even moderate unionists' where President McAleese is concerned. 'There's a tendency to deal with Mary with a long spoon,' he says of them. 'There is a feeling that the lady has an overtly political edge, nationalist, probably more republican, and that she feels she has to come out and say things.' He instanced her comments on the possible visit by the Queen to the Republic as an example of the latter, 'at best clumsy, at worse crass'. 'It also reignited the whole Nazi controversy which had been put on the back burner. It's not for her to say that the price of the Queen's visit to the Republic was more devolution. She's a very clever lady and not an innocent abroad where these things are concerned. What prompted her to step into such controversial water and while the Queen was in Northern Ireland? It caused embarrassment. There is a very high regard for the Queen in Northern Ireland, and not just on the unionist side.'

He was aware that President McAleese was simply repeating what the Taoiseach Bertie Ahern had said in the Dáil a couple of weeks previously. But that was not the point. 'She is head of state. The President is above politics. Bringing the Queen into it was not on.' It also irritated some unionists 'that she seems to wander about Northern Ireland as if it was just part of her domain.' People were courteous to her but 'whenever she makes a statement like that [concerning the Queen's visit] they wonder whether she has a political agenda.' People in Northern Ireland were aware of her background 'in a fairly polarised community where, as a big family, they did experience difficulty. That would be part of her own identity and, perhaps, of a republican ideology. She would be seen as a defender of that community at times. Unionists would not identify with her that much. She is an educated lady who has done well. Martin comes across as a very affable, friendly person, a courteous-looking man, but Mary comes across as a very calculating lady with a deliberate agenda and a slight academic haughtiness.' Unionists had no problem with her visiting Northern Ireland 'as long as she doesn't see herself as part of a nationalist ascendancy coming across the Border in a chauffeur-driven car. Some like to remind her she is Mrs McAleese.'

Nor did unionists have problems with visits to Áras an Uachtaráin. They had been received there 'very graciously' including on 12 July. Those he had spoken to who had been to the Áras enjoyed their visits. She was, he said, 'a clever lady. For a Northern Catholic girl she does need to be sensitive where that community in Northern Ireland is concerned, who feel she is too green at times. It takes away from the good she does. She is seen as wearing her republicanism on her sleeve at times. It's an impediment to people feeling comfortable with her as the Irish President. She is by far the most overtly political Irish President there has been, even more so than de Valera.'

Some unionist suspicion of the President possibly went back to her days at Queen's. 'The establishment of the day possibly resented her appointment. She came in from the outside, had a Catholic nationalist background.' Her appointment over David Trimble 'went down badly'. In addition, she was a woman and 'those of a different generation were not happy with that.' There would still be a conservative view in wider Northern Ireland society on that, he said. 'They could take the things she says better from a man.' Her dealings with alleged loyalist paramilitaries 'have not gone down well with the broader unionist community'. They wonder whether she 'has permission to come up here at all. But unionists don't go to bed every night worrying about what Mary McAleese will do the next day.' She 'sees Northern Ireland as the fourth green field and is looked on as a remnant of Irish nationalism which predates the removal of Articles 2 and 3 from the Irish Constitution.' He concluded that 'if there is another gaffe the shutters will come down completely where she is concerned.'

Alf McCreary has been a journalist for forty years, most of them with the *Belfast Telegraph*. From 1985 to 1998 he was Information Director and then Head of Information Services at Queen's University. He says, 'From a Northern majority view, she has been an impressive President. She espoused the need for pluralism in Catholic Ireland by taking Communion in a Dublin Protestant Cathedral, and her appearance with Queen Elizabeth at the Peace Park in Messines underlined the courageous role of Irish soldiers north and south on the battlefields of Europe in the First World War. In doing so she helped to redress the disgraceful historical amnesia about such slaughter and sacrifice, which prevailed in the Republic until recently.

'During her Presidency she has also reached out to other cultures, including that of the Orange Order and has shown an often dismissive Irish constituency that people have a right to belong to the Loyal Orders even if others do not agree with their principles. She has also made important and strategic visits to the North and has shown the importance of peace-making initiatives in the most unpromising of places. This has been offset by a couple of significant gaffes, with a 'green slip' showing, but generally she has been respected by the unionist community — though diehards will never see the point of an Irish President making official visits to the North. The steady influence and quiet contribution of her husband Martin behind the scenes, with loyalists and others, has been appreciated. Despite this, it is doubtful if the majority community really appreciates, or indeed even thinks about, her achievement in becoming President of Ireland.

'The post has been held, in their opinion, by a long line of grey males in suits, who have made little or no impact with unionists north of the border. However, Mary McAleese, like her predecessor Mary Robinson, brought a modern female dimension to the role of President, allied to a sharp brain and a gift for communication. That combination will be hard to follow, though if Bertie Ahern chooses to run for the Presidency, his reputation north of the border will find him generally acceptable to the majority community here. Meanwhile, Mary McAleese remains something of an enigma to many Northerners. She is an accomplished political figure, who is bright, streetwise and tough, but also a woman of warmth and personality, who relates with sincerity to a wide range of people, including the vulnerable and the elderly. These are too often overlooked by those in positions of power and privilege.

'The enigma lies partly in why such a strong-minded woman chose to confine her abilities to the limitations of the Presidency, and more particularly why she accepted a second term. It may be that she was attracted by the prospect of an unopposed nomination, and a continuation of a long journey she had only half-finished. Of course, she may just have liked the idea of staying on in what is a unique and hugely important job. Perhaps part of the answer also lies in her traditional Catholicism and her sense of duty, and partly the fact that she has *de facto* widened the parameters of an official role that could become a strait jacket to those who do not know how to find their way through the labyrinth of power. History will tell whether Mary McAleese will be remembered as a good or a great President, though possibly the former. Indubitably, however, the Catholic girl from north Belfast has come a long way, and in doing so she has learned much about how her fellow Ulster citizens in the Protestant-Unionist community think and behave. This cannot but be beneficial to the long-term and best interests of all the peoples of this island, and not least to the President herself.'

Applauded by the Taoiseach, the Tánaiste, members of the government and the judiciary, as well as former Presidents Robinson and Hillery, Mary McAleese is sworn in for her second term as President on 11 November 2004

A State Visit

The senior German official took a deep drag on his cigarette. Then, in a voice redolent of easy authority, oak, and decades of nicotine, he pronounced 'she is fantastic'. He exhaled. 'Have you any idea how good an impression she made in Berlin?'

We were standing outside the Hotel Steigenberger in Frankfurt on Wednesday, 27 February, the third and final day of President McAleese's State visit to Germany. By then, the diplomat's remarks were typical in their mixture of admiration and warmth of the manner in which the President had been received everywhere since arriving in Berlin the previous Sunday afternoon.

And what a day that final day was! Since leaving Munich that morning the President and her delegation had flown in a fleet of four army and police helicopters to Würzburg, where they visited the tomb of St Killian. From there they flew to Stromberg to a business dinner and from there another helicopter journey took the party to Weisbaden to meet the State president of Hesse, after which there was a high speed motorcade journey to Frankfurt and. The President had about forty-five minutes at the hotel before being due in the European Central Bank. After which there was the return flight to Dublin. Six cities in just over fourteen hours!

❧ ❧ ❧

To date, President McAleese has paid State and official visits to fifty-one

266

countries. The planning for each, both here and in the host country, is meticulous and the schedule hectic, as I discovered on that German trip.

This was the first State visit to Germany by an Irish Head of State since President Patrick Hillery was there in 1984. As well as officials from the President's office, the Department of Foreign Affairs, and media representatives, the delegation included the Minister for Communications, Energy and Natural Resources, Eamon Ryan.

On arrival at Berlin's Schoenefeld airport, the party was taken to the Adlon Hotel on Unter den Linden near the Brandenburg gate. A generous number of tricolours and German flags flew throughout the city. We learned later that the suite in which President and Dr McAleese were staying had achieved notoriety as the one from whose balcony Michael Jackson infamously dangled his baby son in November 2002.

MONDAY

At Schloss Bellevue the following morning the President was warmly greeted by German President, Horst Köhler, and his wife, Eva Luise. A guard of honour of army and navy personnel awaited inspection. Both national anthems were played, as German, Irish and EU flags flapped erratically in an unpredictable and knife-edged breeze. It blew one naval cadet's hat off, which he retrieved sooner than he did his dignity.

Inspection over, President Mc Aleese went over to a party of Irish and German schoolchildren and their parents, who waited behind a cordon nearby. They were waving their flags in increasingly blue hands. A Department of Foreign Affairs official commented *sotto voce,* 'This is the part Mary Robinson hated. She could never do it.'

A little girl handed the President a personal Van Gogh. 'Have you been drawing pictures?' the President asked her. Another child handed over his picture of a windmill. Dr Martin McAleese said he was 'glad we brought a really big suitcase' to carry them home.

The Presidents retreated inside for brief talks which were followed by a press

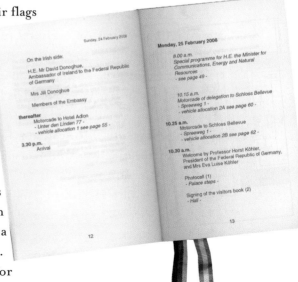

267

conference assisted by a fiercely diligent translator whose lengthy German and English responses seemed a greatly inflated account of what the Presidents had actually said.

President Köhler spoke of the deep bonds of friendship between the German and Irish peoples, the successful peace process in Northern Ireland, the Celtic Tiger, all of which 'demands not only our respect but our appreciation.' Other countries could learn from Ireland. He praised Ireland's consistent support for the EU and said the Union had helped make the Irish success story possible. (That was then, before the Lisbon Treaty referendum on 12 June, 2008, after which Ireland's support for the EU would no longer be described as 'consistent'!).

President McAleese spoke of the 'strong bilateral relationship' between the two countries, a relationship that had continued through a long period of history, from the sixth and seventh century 'when Irish and English monks came to Germany to bring the Christian faith, to the nineteenth century when German philological scholars gave Ireland renewed pride in its language and culture.'

She acknowledged 'the impact for good EU membership has been for Ireland' and she thanked Germany for being 'such a champion of the smaller countries'. She spoke of German tourism and investment in Ireland and remarked on both countries' 'tremendous curiosity about each other.'

Derek Scally of *The Irish Times* asked President Köhler what Ireland could learn from Germany's forty years experience of immigration and integration. The German President suggested vigilance to avoid a situation whereby cultures live alongside each other but do not integrate. He advised being 'very attentive to other person's cultural rules.' One had to 'look at the cultural roots of others and see to it that a person integrates into everyday life.'

The party then proceeded to the memorial to victims of war and tyranny at the north side of Berlin's Unter den Linden. The *Neue Wache* (New Guard House) has to be one of the most poignant places on earth. A great, bare square building with Doric columns in its neoclassical façade, it contains the remains of an unknown German soldier and an unknown concentration camp victim from World War II. At its centre is a deeply affecting sculpture titled 'Mother with Her Dead Son' by German artist Käthe Kollwitz. The sculpture is directly under a round opening – an oculus –in the building's roof which leaves it deliberately exposed to the elements, symbolising the suffering of civilians during World War II. President McAleese laid a laurel wreath at the statue and knelt in silence as a lone trumpeter in a corner beyond played 'The Good Comrade', a requiem which resonated around the building's high grey walls.

From there the President was taken by motorcade to the other end of Unter den Linden where she and Dr McAleese were escorted through the Brandenburg Gate by Klaus Woweriet, the Governing Mayor of Berlin. 'People of my generation feel very close to this city, it broke our hearts in its brokenness and it raises our hearts in its completeness,' the President remarked. At the City Hall, Mayor Woweriet threw protocol aside, along with his prepared script. 'I love Ireland,' he declared. 'It is a wonderful country.' And he waxed lyrical about his many experiences there as a tourist through the years, and about 'legendary Irish hospitality'.

He recalled how, in 2007, Ireland was deemed the World's Friendliest Country in a *Lonely Planet* survey. It was a place where the people had 'a deliciously dark sense of humour' ... 'a welcoming attitude towards strangers' and who could 'find *craic* in boom or bust eras,' it said. Mayor Wowereit could not agree more. Expressing his happiness at President McAleese's visit, he believed Berlin was becoming a favourite destination for Irish people, too. 'We have a mutual liking and esteem for each other.' When Ireland became a member of the European Community in 1973 it was one of the poorest countries, which was why it now impressed all the more. Ireland and Germany shared a view of the future of Europe, and both were committed to it. 'President, you are part of the quality of the Irish people and we were lucky that we could build on a strong Irish commitment to German reunification in 1990.'

President McAleese thanked the Mayor for his welcome to a city 'so aptly described by the eighteenth-century writer Jean Paul as "more part of the world than a city". Every European of my generation felt a deep sense of belonging to Berlin', she said. Berlin was 'a remarkable and enduring survivor ... It bears the scars of awful wars and artificial division but with unification behind it today Berlin is admired for the fresh imagination brought to its rebuilding, for its dynamism and its welcome.' She remarked on the 'many intriguing connections' between Ireland and Berlin. One example was the pioneering work on the Irish language by Professor Kuno Meyer of the city's Humboldt University. And there was 'that great Irish American President, John Fitzgerald Kennedy' who, in 1963, visited Berlin and his ancestral home in Ireland in the same week. In his speech delivered 'in this, then divided city and in a fragmented Europe, President Kennedy looked forward to a time "when this city will be joined as one and this country and this great continent of Europe in a peaceful and hopeful globe". Later that week, in a then very poor, underachieving Ireland, he expressed his profound belief in the future of Ireland and foresaw that "when our hour is come, we will have something to give to the world." Through the Irish visit today, she said, 'We invest our friendship in the strong bilateral relationship between Ireland and Germany, knowing that the investment takes us, inch by inch, closer to that "peaceful and hopeful world" which we hope will be our legacy to future generations.'

In the City Hall visitors' book she wrote, 'Berlin, once broken by division, now complete and beautiful!'

That afternoon the President gave a press conference for the Irish media. The Brandenburg Gate could be seen through the window and she mentioned that they had walked through the Gate to Unter den Linden in 1991 after Martin had taken part in the Berlin marathon and how the atmosphere was so good because the wall had come down. Michael Brennan of the *Irish Independent* asked about her impressions of Irish and German experiences of immigration and integration. She said she had explained to President Köhler how Ireland had absorbed such a great number in a short time, which had not been the experience elsewhere. How immigrants came to Ireland because they were needed, to fill jobs. How they were, in the main, highly educated people who were socially mobile and had enough English to negotiate their way. She mentioned a recent survey of twenty-seven EU states, which showed that the level of interaction between immigrants and the Irish people was, at 82 per cent of

Martin McAleese on completion of the London marathon, 1990

respondents, second only to Luxembourg. And she explained to him how the Irish people's own historical experience of emigration had helped to make the immigration experience in Ireland a positive one.

Derek Scally of the *Irish Times* noted that Angela Merkel was the first woman Chancellor in Germany and that women in positions of leadership was still an issue in that country. 'Is it not for you?' he asked. The President laughed and said she was 'pretty hardened' when it came to the issue. 'President Robinson was in this office for seven years, I have been for ten — that's seventeen years. A whole generation has grown up for which it is joyfully normal ... we have also grown up in Ireland. It is much more egalitarian.' 'Women have been part and parcel of our economic success ... but it is still a rare phenomenon to find women among our top lawyers, politicians etc. I look forward to the day when no one will remark on such a thing .'

She referred to the work of other women presidents such as Tarja Halonen, President of Finland, and to Vike-Freiberga, first woman President of Latvia. 'There is something distinctly feminine about the skills set they brought,' she said. Michael Brennan asked what she thought about Fianna Fáil Senator Mary White's announcement that she intended to seek the party nomination for the next presidential election in 2011. President McAleese thought it 'fascinating, great'. It was an indication of the 'wonderful democracy we have in Ireland'.

RTÉ's Europe Editor Sean Whelan asked her about the EU and climate change. The issue required action at an individual, national and international levels, she said, 'like the *meitheal* of old in Ireland. It is about securing our future peace, prosperity and what ambitions we have or try to have for the developing world.' And military co-operation in Europe? 'Ireland has a very significant role in peacekeeping.' She mentioned Chad, Kosovo, Liberia. 'Ireland is unaligned militarily ... our experience is that paramilitarism does not bring about what people want ... Ireland is committed to dialogue ... it underpins the values we live by, democratic values, human rights, the pursuit of peace and our contribution to world peace through the offices of the UN.'

Ireland also had a unique contribution to make through 'our distilled wisdom and experience. We don't fully realise the remarkable disconnect between our present and our past ... the children growing up, probably the best ever in our history, are not as cognisant of the Border. Rather they think in terms of an all-island economy, of good neighbourliness. We need to explain to our neighbours how we have something quite unique. No two conflicts are the same, yet dogged dialogue, persuasion has managed to do what generations and decades of conflict could not do.'

'Do the Germans get this?' Sean wondered. She replied that 'the Germans said it was a very important time for us to come. The old ways of understanding Ireland – the Ireland of Boll [Nobel prizewinner Heinrich Boll, whose 1957 *Irish Journal* book shaped a deeply romantic German image of Ireland for decades] – have gone. And that in its place is a much more powerful, punchy message – that of a powerhouse where economics and peace are concerned.'

The State banquet that evening at Schloss Bellevue was a splendid affair. No less than three German presidents attended. As well as President Köhler there were two of his predecessors, President Walter Scheel (1974-79) and President Richard Von Weizsaecker (1984-1994). Along the avenues to Schloss Bellevue, German sailors in full uniform formed a guard of honour, each holding a long-handled flaming torch in salute. It was a spectacular sight, which lit up the night sky with flickering flame. An army band played outside the entrance as guests arrived. The 140 guests included members of the German Government, leading figures in German business and cultural life, representatives of the diplomatic corps, as well as the Irish delegation. In Salon Luise upstairs, the two presidents and their spouses were introduced to each guest individually as they proceeded to the banquet hall.

President Köhler told the gathering that 'the Irish and the Germans feel tremendous good will and empathy for one another. They have a special relationship that is well over a thousand years old. It dates back to when Irish monks and scholars first arrived on the European continent and reached what later became known as Germany. In the turmoil that followed the end of the Roman Empire and successive waves of migration, these lands had entered a period of cultural and political decline which the monks from Ireland – whose work today would be seen as development aid, perhaps – helped to reverse. These holy men included one Killian, who in the seventh century travelled to Würzburg in Franconia and is now revered there as the city's patron saint.' He talked of the Celtic Tiger and how 'Both Europe and Germany could learn a good deal' from the new Irish 'can-do spirit'. He spoke of immigration to Ireland and President McAleese's commitment to integration and social cohesion.

Ireland's international presence reached far beyond the border of Europe, whether through emigration or with the UN, for which service with the latter had earned 'great respect worldwide'. He commended the

President and Dr McAleese for their work for peace in Ireland. 'It is thanks to the efforts of people like yourselves that good inter-communal relations and a peaceful future for Northern Ireland are now a real prospect.'

President McAleese remarked that geography 'had never been much of a barrier to relationships between Ireland and Germany. Long before the era of daily flights between us, medieval Irish monks and scholars set out in frail boats to make connections that resound still down through the centuries.' There was also the scholarly traffic that came the other way, 'bringing to our shores nineteenth-century philological legends like Johann Caspar Zeuss and Kuno Meyer, champions without peer of the revival of our Irish language and culture ... The tradition of Celtic studies still thrives in German universities, while in Ireland, we repay the compliment, for Trinity College Dublin's German Department dates back to 1776 and is thought to be the oldest in the world outside of Germany.'

'Today the citizens of Ireland and Germany are much more than casually related by eclectic individual links. We are partners of the European Union. That means we not only share citizenship of the Union but we share a common vision and responsibility for its future. We both see our Union as a global bulwark of peace, prosperity, democracy, stability and justice. We are both committed to strengthening our Union and making it an effective witness to all that is humanly decent in our world.'

She remarked on the 'role played by German statesmen in the construction of the European Union in the aftermath of an appalling war, its devastating waste and its bitter enmity. Out of such chaos came the greatest and most noble attempt at interstate solidarity and collegiality ever undertaken by humankind – a Union of equals underpinned by democratic values, human rights and energised by a common focus on a shared future characterised by peace and prosperity. It was the first Chancellor of the German Federal Republic, that great statesman, Konrad Adenauer, who said, "European unity was a dream of the few. It became a hope for many. It is today a necessity for all." Ireland shares that vision.'

Formalities over, the guests tucked into terrine of veal, North Sea shrimp in a potato and herb broth, saddle of venison topped with nuts, with a cabbage and mushroom crepe. Dessert was apple crunch with prunes and caramel ice-cream. Throughout the meal a horn ensemble played a Mozart selection, and finished their performance with a rendition of 'The Star of the County Down'.

TUESDAY

The day began with a visit to the President of the Bundestag, Prof Dr Norbert Lammert, at the Reichstag building. President and Dr McAleese were given an escorted tour of the building which has been the seat of the Bundestag since 1999. Its extraordinary dome, designed by a team under British architect Sir Norman Foster, allows a panoramic view over Berlin. From the building's centre the Chamber of Deputies is transparent on all sides, above and below. The party left the Reichstag through a corridor which has been preserved as it was in 1945 when Russian soldiers occupied the then ruined building and wrote graffiti on its walls.

From there the delegation was taken to Humboldt University where President McAleese was to deliver the keynote address of her visit, on the theme 'Europe in the Coming Times: An Irish Perspective', as part of the Humboldt lecture series on European themes. The oldest university in the city, it was founded in 1810 by Wilhelm von Humboldt, a Prussian linguist and educational reformer. It has produced twenty-nine Nobel prize winners. Former students include physicists Albert Einstein and Max Planck, philosophers Hegel and Schopenhauer, social theorists Karl Marx and Frederich Engels, the poet Heinrich Heine, the great German politician Otto von Bismark, and EU founder Robert Schuman.

On 10 May 1933 the Nazis burned 20,000 books from the university library whose authors were deemed opponents and degenerates. This event is commemorated today by an empty space for 20,000 books and a plaque quoting from a work by Heine, who in 1820 wrote '... where they burn books, they ultimately burn people.' The Nazis banned all Jewish students from the University. In 1946 the Soviets took control of the University and banned all students who did not toe the Communist Party line, which continued until the collapse of East Germany in 1989. Today it has upwards of 38,000 students, approximately 5,000 of whom are foreign, including students from Ireland.

In the University's Senate chamber President McAleese was introduced to the audience by Professor Dr Christoph Markschies, president of the University, in a warm, witty and erudite address. A theologian, his specialty is church history. He wondered 'What contribution can a church historian, who occupies the office of university president, make to the greeting of a State president, who is a lawyer by training, who was Reid Professor for Criminal

Law, Criminology and Penology at Trinity College and who was pro-Vice Chancellor of Queen's University in Belfast; who was also a journalist and presenter and subsequently a close adviser to the Irish Catholic Bishops? ' He continued that 'while a German church historian may know a little about the penance book of the Irish monks, he has to accede that modern criminal law in Ireland deals far more liberally with sinners than the pre-modern, draconian rules of those peregrinate [on foot], with whom Ireland once colonised the desert of Germania.' He reckoned that his influence on the Catholic Bishops of Germany would be portrayed by a neutral observer as marginal.

In Germany there was, to quote the poet Lessing, a "nastily broad rift" between academia and politics; intellectuals look down on politicians and vice versa ... He asked the question 'whether the catastrophes in German twentieth-century history were not conditioned or at least influenced by the experiences of estrangement between politics and academia – I am referring to the apolitical professor who let pass what a politician wanted to be passed, an approach that applied to German intellectuals generally before they regained consciousness.'

He described President McAleese as 'the best example for illustrating how much responsibility the professor bears for politics, for the creation of parochial roots for the European idea and for the specification and dissemination of European concepts, just like the university as a whole has to take responsibility for these fields ... We are now delighted to have among us an example that shows us where an academic can lead by her enthusiasm for the European ideal...'

President McAleese said that in choosing her title 'Europe in the Coming Times: An Irish Perspective' she was echoing a late nineteenth-century Irish poem in which Yeats 'addresses an imagined future Ireland. It was written at a time of great flux, characterised by competing visions of our national destiny.' There were, she said, 'occasions in history when our collective thinking about "the coming times" becomes all the more vital. The opening decade of the twenty-first century is, I believe, just such a time.' She quoted Peter Drucker, the Viennese-born 'social ecologist', as he described himself, on the impact of large-scale change in history: "Every few hundred years throughout Western history a sharp transformation has occurred. In a matter of decades, society altogether rearranges itself, its world views, its basic values, its social and political structure, its arts, its key institutions. Fifty years later, a new world exists. And the people born into that world cannot imagine the world in which their grandparents lived and into which their own parents were born." 'We are living, right this moment, through a period of flux just as Drucker describes,' she said. Reflecting for a moment on the University and its founder, she noted that Wilhelm von Humboldt had a special importance for Ireland. Among the first experts to identify the Indo-Germanic group of languages 'it was he who established that our native Irish language belonged to that family of European languages. Building on his work, later German linguists codified the grammar and structure of the language, but it was Humboldt's work which represented a moment of cultural re-awakening and inspired a renewed sense of Ireland's belonging to a common European tradition.

'Cultural nationalism in Ireland went hand in hand with intense political debate about our relationship with Britain and the nature of Ireland's identity. Of course, Ireland's sense of belonging in Europe has deep roots in our history. It is illustrated in the lives of those like the seventh-century Irish monk St Killian of Würzburg who came to help Europe secure its Christian values.' In an aside she drew loud laughter from the audience when she commented, 'We've got over the fact that you killed him!'

The EU had travelled 'an immense distance since the founding generation developed their bold vision of Europe in their "coming times", the second part of the twentieth century. The dreadful upheavals of that century taught us harshly the importance of enlightened political leadership rooted in democratic and pluralist values. Europe's traumas brought forth the vision of great men like Adenauer whose goal was nothing less than "a great, common house for Europeans, a house of freedom".

'Nothing represented the realisation of Adenauer's dream like the coming down of the Berlin Wall which had so disfigured this city and shamed this continent.

'Europe is peaceful, united and prosperous. We benefit daily from the single market and the existence of the euro. Twenty-seven countries now work together in pursuit of shared ambitions founded on the very best of human values. From the ashes of war arose a structure built to last for centuries, but for that structure to last, it must accommodate change.'

She then spoke about the challenges facing the EU, including the issue of climate change. She hoped that 'In Copenhagen in 2009 ... the champions of coherent, collective, international action will be vindicated, among them your Chancellor and the Federal Government, who within the European Union and the G8 have articulated a vision on the climate change agenda that is praiseworthy indeed.'

'... in Irish we say "*Ní neart go chur le chéile*': strength comes only when we act together. Our belief in collective action as the source of strength and the common good is interwoven into many traditional Irish sayings, and into the customs and practices of Irish life.

'...These ingrained values helped us to survive hard times 150 years ago when famine claimed millions of Irish lives, turning us into an emigrant nation and forever altering the trajectory of Irish history. From this grim experience we know well of the potential for environmental failure to become a terrible social and humanitarian disaster when the powerful stick rigidly to their mindset and beliefs, selfishly delaying action until it is too late. With this in mind, Ireland's international relations are guided by the "ideal of peace and friendly cooperation amongst nations", the "pacific settlement of international disputes" and the "principles of international law as its rule of conduct in its relations with other States".'

She spoke of the role played by the Defence Forces in United Nations peace keeping operations. 'This service has not been without cost and many members of our Defence Forces have given their lives in the service of the United Nations. We are deeply proud of all who have served and who serve today.

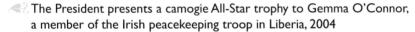
The President presents a camogie All-Star trophy to Gemma O'Connor, a member of the Irish peacekeeping troop in Liberia, 2004

'We see peace, development and human rights as being inextricably linked. We aim to be a world leader in development assistance and are resolute in our commitment to reach the UN ODA target of 0.7 per cent of GNP by 2012. This commitment enjoys wide public support in Ireland. The value of solidarity with the world's poor is strongly recognised by our people for it is a product of our own history of famine and underdevelopment. The Government, through Irish Aid, our development aid programme, is giving practical expression to the defining values of modern Ireland. It is following, too, in the footsteps of thousands of Irish men and women, lay and missionary, priests and nuns, soldiers and policemen, volunteers and aid workers, who for many years have offered themselves and their skills to the poorest and most troubled countries in the world, in many ways our finest ambassadors.'

Referring to the peace process in Northern Ireland, she said, 'We hope that the journey we have made from violence to peace will serve as an encouragement to other nations still mired in seemingly intractable conflict, and we are taking solid steps to transfer our knowledge in this area to other states …'

'In this, the European Year of Intercultural Dialogue, many of our countries grow more multi-cultural, multi-faith and multilingual by the day. If we mean what we say about Europe's founding value system with its reverence for the dignity of each human being, then our task is to build in our countries and throughout our Union a deep-rooted culture of acceptance of difference, of joyful curiosity about one another, and of respect, which allows strangers to live in harmony as neighbours and to become friends. Already in the movement of peoples throughout Europe, whether following the stars of economic opportunity, or tourism, or academic exchange, we see the emergence of the new Europe dreamt of by Schumann and Adenauer, a Europe of good neighbours, good friends, pulling together for a shared future and not pulling Europe apart for selfish ends.

'… Will we make poverty history? Will we see an end to the misery of the Middle East? Will we see East and West grow in mutual understanding and harmony? Will the great faiths of the world become sources of unity and not discord? Will we stabilise our global climate? Will we give our children a legacy of optimism and hope such as has been given to no other generation in the known history of mankind?

'In 1994 … the Irish Nobel Laureate, John Hume, described what has been achieved by the European project: "…they can build common institutions which preserve their differences, which allow them to work their common ground ... [giving] bread on your table, a roof over your head, the right to existence. Not just the right to life, but the right to a decent standard of living, to a home, to a job, to education, to health... They broke down the prejudices of centuries to make the healing process take place..." That feat, that extraordinary achievement, is our inheritance. It is no mausoleum, no place of mere words. It is a leaven in our lives and in our world. It is still young, still growing, still dreaming. There is much work still to do and we are the hands of that work; its brains. We are the sacred custodians of Europe of the coming times.'

The response to the speech was immediate and enthusiastic – a loud and long standing ovation.

Professor Ingolf Pernice, head of the Hallstein Institute for European Constitutional Law, said that this was 'if not the greatest, then one of the greatest lectures' heard in the ten years of a lecture series being run by his Institute.

The delegation was back in the Adlon hotel by 12.30pm where there was a reception in honour of the President hosted by Ambassador Donoghue and attended by about 400 of the estimated 1,000 Irish people living and working in Berlin.

The atmosphere was very informal as the President began with a *cúpla focal*. '*Dia dhíbh, a chairde. Tá mé iontach sásta bheith i bhur measc tráthnona ar an ócáid speisialta seo dom. Míle bhuíochas díbh as an fáilte sin...*'

She asked if there were any Kerry people present. 'Watch out,' she warned, 'here come Down.' Just a month beforehand, Down had won the McKenna cup for the first time in ten years. Then, looking to her husband, she commented '... poor Antrim'. The guests enjoyed it. From there it was on to Dustin the Turkey who had been selected to represent Ireland in the Eurovision Song Contest. 'He should get the Cranberries to be his backing group,' she suggested, commenting that his selection for Eurovision was an expression of 'the wonderful sense of humour of the Irish people.' Presciently she added '... I hope the others get it.' She praised Glen Hansard and Marketa Irglova on winning the best song Oscar for 'Once' at the Academy Awards the previous night. None of this was in her script. 'She doesn't need a script,' a Department of Foreign Affairs official said, when this was drawn to his attention.

'It is great to be in the company of so many people who are the very spirit and character, the soul and the essence of Ireland here in Germany's capital

…There are many, many lived lives that form human bridges between Ireland and Germany, opening our countries and cultures up to one another. You are part of that great bridge of friendship and curiosity that links us in these contemporary times when we are all also not just random strangers or even random friends but rather common citizens of the European Union, with a shared identity and a shared future.

'… the most formidable and enduring of relationships are those which you make in Germany as unpaid ambassadors for Ireland here and unpaid ambassadors for Germany in Ireland. By you is Ireland judged. Through your lived lives here in Berlin, as friends, colleagues, partners, spouses, neighbours, you carry an image of Ireland and you make friends for Ireland in the most remarkable and best of ways — heart to heart, human being to human being. Your German/Irish children draw from two great wells of culture and grow up as citizens of a common European homeland. They are living the European dream … Thank you for all the ways you consciously and unconsciously build us into family whether in Dublin or Berlin.'

Going off script again, she said that among Foreign Affairs staff abroad 'a presidential visit set off a dementia, like when I tell my daughter I'm going to inspect her room, but with far better results!'

As the President mingled with guests, a Foreign Affairs official drew attention to tears in the eyes of some staff from the Irish Embassy in Berlin. Asked 'What's that about?' he replied, 'They're just not used to being thanked like that.'

After lunch the President visited the Federal Chancellery where she was greeted by Chancellor Angela Merkel with whom she had an hour-long meeting.

Immediately afterwards the Irish party flew to Munich where the President was met by Bavarian Minister for Federal and European Affairs, Markus Soder. It was then on to Hotel Vier Jahreszeiten, for a reception with some 300 guests, including members of Irish-German associations across Germany and the Irish community in Bavaria. The y heard that 'Munich can lay claim to be Germany's Irish capital city for, not alone has it a large Irish population, but there are formidably strong cultural and business ties between Bavaria and Ireland. Those ties did not happen by accident but by dint of the hard work of Bavaria's Irish community and in particular the German-Irish Friendship Association in Bavaria … it is only right on this visit that I say a huge thank you to you and to all members of other Irish clubs and societies represented here this evening, from Bonn, Düsseldorf, Friedberg, Frankfurt and Stuttgart. What you do is greatly valued in Ireland...'

She referred to Irish elements of Munich culture, including their Saint Patrick's Day parade, GAA and soccer clubs like Colmcilles GAA Club and the Irish Rovers Football Club, the 'thriving' Irish traditional music and dance scene and a planned Bloomsday celebration, with the addition of Weisswurst to the traditional Bloomsday breakfast.

At 8pm the President met with Bavarian President Dr Gunter Beckstein, which was followed by a banquet in her honour. And in what a setting! The Staatresidenz in Munich is the political and cultural opposite to Berlin's

The President enjoys a laugh with Minister Jim McDaid at the St Patrick's Day Parade in 1999

Schloss Bellevue. Where the latter is demure and almost ahistorical, the Staatresidenz is exhuberant in its decoration and celebration of Bavarian history, particularly of its rulers.

The current building, the first in Renaissance style on German soil, was begun in 1536 by Duke Ludwig X. It was home to the Dukes, then the Electors (from 1623) and finally the Kings of Bavaria (from 1806 to 1918). The magnificent complex has an estimated 130 rooms. Though badly damaged in bombing raids during World War II, most of it has been restored to its former splendour.

The Irish delegation was taken along the Ancestral Gallery whose walls are

lined with portraits of former Dukes, Electors and Kings of Bavaria. During
the war the portraits were hidden in mountains outside the city. They then
visited the Porcelain Room, just one of many in the complex where rare
artefacts collected down the centuries are on display – in this instance rare
examples of porcelain from the eighteenth century.

The banquet was held in the magnificent Antiquarium. Built between 1568
and 1571, it is the oldest room in the Staatsresidenz and at sixty-six metres
long, it is said to be the longest and certainly most lavish Renaissance interior
north of the Alps. Lavishly decorated, its curved, vaulted ceiling is painted
with symbols of the cardinal and divine virtues: obedience, abstinence,
patience, lenience, humility, chastity, truthfulness, perseverance, fame,
courage, justice, moderation, faith, hope, and love. It also features busts of
the Caesars.

A single long table stretched the length of the room, almost as far as a
balustrade at its end. The centre of the white tablecloth was strewn with white
tulips and white rose petals, interlaced by two red stripes, and lit by soft light.
A member of the Irish delegation commented 'If my father could've seen this
he would have been talking about it for the rest of his life.'

A trumpet fanfare announced the entrance of President McAleese and
President Beckstein. Two lines of young men and women descended the steps
of the balustrade and stood behind the guests. At a signal they placed the
starters – warm slices of boiled veal with horseradish vinaigrette sauce and
salad – before each guest and stood back, before being signalled to return to
the balustrade. It ensured that the meal was served to every guest at the same
time. Other courses included Bavarian game fish, braised ox cheek in truffle
gravy with spring leeks and polenta ravioli, and a praline crème bavaroise
dessert and berry sorbet, followed by coffee. Wine was in plentiful supply
and music was played by a quartet.

President Beckstein welcomed President McAleese with an effusiveness
which was now becoming familiar. 'An Irish proverb says "God gave you a
face, but you have to do the smiling". It is clear that there is something special
about the Irish smile as soon as one sees you, dear Mrs President.' He spoke
of his 'deep attachment for Ireland ', coming as he did from the Franconian
part of Bavaria, of which St Killian is the patron. He lauded the achievements
of the Celtic Tiger and the 'intense', 'lively' German-Irish cultural ties.

President McAleese began in German, thanking President Beckstein and
his wife for their warm welcome 'to Bavaria's beautiful capital city of Munich,
and to this superb Hall of Antiquities.' '...the Irish and Bavarian

temperaments are famously similar. This is perhaps why Bavaria holds a special place in the hearts and minds of the Irish people and why Munich has the largest population of Irish expatriates in Germany. From the warmth of the welcome that we have received since arriving, I can see why so many Irish people are happy and proud to call this city, and the Free State of Bavaria, their home.'

St Killian was, by now, becoming a recurrent theme of the visit, and the President noted how his name lives on in the names of generations of German children. 'Würzburg today maintains strong and active links with its Irish heritage, whether through its participation in initiatives such as the development and management of the St Killian's Heritage Centre in County Cavan or its twinning with Bray in County Wicklow. I am particularly pleased, therefore, to be accompanied this evening by our Minister for European Affairs, Dick Roche, whose hometown is Bray.' She referred again to the work of scholars such as Zeuss and Kuno Meyer who 'provided the academic backbone to a major literary and cultural resurgence focused on the Irish language in the later nineteenth century.'

'Not all Irish visitors to Bavaria, I am sorry to say, have been as warmly welcomed as I. In the twelfth century, the holy Makarius (a Latin version of McCarthy) shattered a national stereotype with a commendable, if somewhat unpopular miracle, of turning local wine into water.' This was greeted with much laughter. 'Although his marketing skills left something to be desired, he avoided martyrdom. More recently, the political interference of the Irish-born Lola Montez led to the abdication of King Ludwig I right here in 1848. Happily for us, her name generally disguises her Irish antecedents and points the blame farther south!'

WEDNESDAY

At 8am the Irish delegation left for the Bayernkaserne helipad for the journey to Würzburg and Julius Maximillian University. First founded in 1402, the University was 'refounded' in 1582 after a period in deline. It has produced thirteen Nobel Prize winners, including Wilhelm Conrad Röntgen, first winner of the Nobel Prize for Physics in 1895, for his discovery of X-rays.

A map along the wall of the manuscripts room illustrates the journey of Irish saints in Europe between AD590 and 728. Expert Dr Hans-Guenter Schmidt showed the President the St Killian gospels and two sets of other

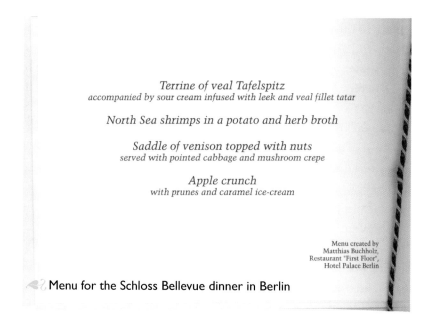

Terrine of veal Tafelspitz
accompanied by sour cream infused with leek and veal fillet tatar

North Sea shrimps in a potato and herb broth

Saddle of venison topped with nuts
served with pointed cabbage and mushroom crepe

Apple crunch
with prunes and caramel ice-cream

Menu created by
Matthias Buchholz,
Restaurant "First Floor",
Hotel Palace Berlin

Menu for the Schloss Bellevue dinner in Berlin

manuscripts which have annotations in Irish, believed to be the oldest known texts in Irish.

The seventh-century manuscripts were handled with great care, using gloves. Dr Schmidt explained how they were the most precious items in Würzburg. 'They are a very big part of our patrimony too,' added the President. Dr Schmidt marveled at how they had survived several bombing raids during World War II. 'A touch of Irish resilience there,' he commented. The President concurred, but added '...though it didn't do Killian much good.'

After converting the local Franconian ruler, Duke Gozbert, to Christianity, Killian explained to him that his marriage to his brother's widow Geliana was unlawful in Christian eyes and made him promise to separate from her. Geilana was not pleased and had Killian and his two Irish companions, Kolonat and Totnan, secretly murdered and buried – generally held to have happened on 8 July 689. Commenting on this, President McAleese concluded '... he [Killian] shouldn't have crossed a woman. Irish men never learn.' In a brief address before leaving, the President said ' ... this visit is definitely a highlight of my trip. Here I have already been introduced to aspects of Irish history that have broadened and deepened my knowledge of that part of my own heritage which is shared with this lovely city. In such a short visit I have had my appetite whetted so much that there is no doubt that we have to come back again, this time with the gift of time to take in more fully the splendours of Würzburg.'

In the visitors' book President McAleese wrote, 'Thanks for your sacred stewardship of the treasures of St Killian and the Irish monks who link Ireland and Germany so strongly. *Míle buiochas.*'

Next stop was Neumuenster Church in central Würzburg where the Catholic Bishop of Würzburg, Most Rev Fiedhelm Hoffman, greeted the President. The scene was one of lively chaos as teenage schoolchildren waved their tricolours and screamed a welcome. The Irish delegation was escorted to the Church crypt. She was shown the altar, built in 1250, which contains bones of St Killian. The Bishop said that without St Killian, 'Franconia wouldn't be what it is today.' '...there are 387 St Killian churches in Europe and the first one was here.' The delegation was then escorted through the streets to nearby St Killian's cathedral, where Mayor Beckman welcomed the President and Dr McAleese. The delegation was taken to the cathedral altar where all were shown the heads of St Killian and his two martyred companions.

St Killian's Cathedral is one of the main works of German architecture and the fourth largest Romanesque church in Germany. Much of it was reduced to rubble in a bombing raid in 1945 and the interior of the Cathedral is today clearly from two periods. It is lushly Baroque around the altar and transcept, but the body of the building is of ruder stuff. Erected urgently on the rubble of former glory, it is a high box rectangle intended for shelter, with none of that spirit of inspiration which radiates from the older part of the building. A German woman in the delegation described the aftermath of the bombing on 16 March 1945 as 'the greatest disaster for Würzburg. The city was nearly completely destroyed. And there was no reason. There was no industry or armaments here.' In the space of seventeen minutes the city was almost completely obliterated and about 5,000 of its citizens killed. Relatively, it has been said, that Würzburg was destroyed more completely that day than Dresden had been in a similar Allied raid the previous month.

President McAleese remarked that 'It is great to be in a place where you are so immediately drawn to its history, which has in its background our history.'

The delegation took a brief walk through the city centre to its Old Main Bridge over the river Main, on which stands enormous statues, including one of St Killian. During an impromptu press conference on the bridge a local reporter asked why the delegation was so large and why it was visiting for such a short time '... like Japanese tourists'. The President said she intended 'coming back with my children.' Würzburg was a place she had heard so much about from the late Catholic primate of Ireland, Cardinal Tomás Ó Fiaich.

A helicopter ride took the Irish party to Stromberg, where President McAleese addressed a business lunch attended by representatives of Irish and German companies and communities. 'Germany is Ireland's most important trading partner in continental Europe and our fourth most important trading partner globally,' she said. The 150 German companies based all over Ireland 'account for some 13,500 jobs in areas as diverse as packaging, chemicals, construction and the food sector.' 'Irish companies have also now begun to invest in Germany and of course we have seen the growing phenomenon of private Irish citizens investing in the property market here. Our visitor numbers from here have increased by almost half in the last five years and we hope that half a million Germans will visit Ireland, north and south, this year.'

She expressed the hope that 'this lunch will help participants to look with fresh eyes at new and emerging opportunities to broaden and deepen what is already a highly successful business relationship between our two countries.'

After lunch the delegation flew to Weisbaden for a courtesy call on President Roland Koch of Hesse. One young woman interrupted proceedings as the Irish party was about to leave. Ide Ní Shaughnessy from Raheny in Dublin works with the European Central Bank (ECB) in Frankfurt, which President McAleese was on her way to visit, but would not be able to be there for that. She had come along especially to the State Chancellery to ask whether she could have her photograph taken with the President. Both Presidents posed with her.

Frankfurt was next on the itinerary. Members of the delegation were now visibly beginning to wilt. One remarked that he had never been in a helicopter before that day and had been on three trips since morning. 'How does she stay so fresh ... and Martin?' One of the President's staff interjected, 'Neither of them drink and they keep themselves fit.'

At the European Central Bank, President McAleese was greeted by its president, Jean-Claude Trichet. After a meeting involving other ECB officials and members of the Irish delegation, all proceeded to the thirty-sixth floor where a great number of the Irish who work at the ECB had gathered.

The mood was light, festive, and GAA. President McAleese again issued a warning to the Kerry people present about Down and Tyrone coming down the line in the Championship. She was introduced to each Irish person, among them Niall Merriman from Charlestown, County Mayo, Head of Financial Reporting and Policy. He is a past pupil of St Nathy's College, Ballaghaderreen, County Roscommon and the conversation turned to how Ballaghaderreen's GAA club was likely to perform in the 2008 Mayo County Championship. An up-and-coming side, they were knocked out by Ballina in 2007 and have had tough battles with Charlestown. It was agreed that both the Charlestown and Ballina sides are ageing, and that there is hope for Ballaghaderreen.

Then it was time to leave for Frankfurt airport. Flight EI 657 landed back in Dublin at 10.25pm.

It had been a gruelling few days, but probably no more so than any other State visit. These trips play a significant role in creating and maintaining diplomatic and social ties between Ireland and the wider world. They are regarded as invaluable by the business sector in promoting Irish industry, and also bring their President into the lives of many expatriates, even if only for a very short time.

Antiquarium of the Staatresidenz in Munich

Being There

The editorial in *The Irish Times* of 3 November 2007 could hardly have been more positive. 'During ten years at Áras an Uachtaráin, President McAleese ... has done us proud, fulfilling her official duties with punctiliousness, while reaching out to the marginalised and the alienated in an effort to make this society a better place in which to live. Much of the work she and her husband Martin have done has gone unnoticed ...

'Progressive views on homosexuality and the ordination of women priests mark her independent thinking, while an ambition to host the first visit by Queen Elizabeth to this State reflects a desire to bury old animosities. As a former businesswoman, she offers her time and her office to the promotion of Irish industry abroad, most recently on trips to Canada and New Zealand.'

Looking ahead to the remainder of her term in office, it continued, 'During that period, our society is likely to undergo considerable stress as the economy slows and efforts are made to provide for the large number of immigrants that have settled here. Mrs McAleese has already contributed to a public debate on what should be done and how change will be required of us all. In her words, there can be no "them and us" in this exercise. There is, in her view, only "us".'

Relations between President McAleese and the media had become unrecognisable from the dog days of late October 1997. On 25 October 1997, the same *Irish Times* said of the then ongoing presidential election campaign, under the heading 'Losers all round as contest turns ugly', that 'it was billed as a beauty contest; now it's more akin to mud-wrestling. Three weeks into the campaign, and the damage inflicted on the political system and the national psyche is enormous. We're into a no-win scenario. McAleese goes down a bomb on the canvass. But it is no secret that her relations with the media are approaching zero-tolerance level, on both sides.'

Ten years later, on 24 October 2007, President McAleese hosted a reception at Áras an Uachtaráin 'to recognise the significant contribution of media and Irish journalism to Irish society'. It was attended mainly by those generally faceless men and women – editors – who are the real power in the media. She told them, 'Coming close to the tenth anniversary of my first election as President I wondered how best to mark it and this is the company I chose.' The woman, clearly, is deeply forgiving. She continued, 'All public figures have their good days and bad days with the media, and vice versa. The tensions in such relationships are part of the necessary and healthy checks and balances in a democratic society. Neither is infallible and all are human.'

She thanked them 'for all you have done these past ten years to inform, challenge, analyse and educate the public and me about this presidency, along with all the other important stuff that only gets onto people's agendas or into their hearts and heads because you managed to put it there.' Of the journalists, photographers, TV and radio crews who had accompanied her everywhere over the previous decade, she said, 'They have been the eyes and ears of the people who elected me' and that, 'while never falsely deferential and sometimes harshly critical, in the best tradition of our republic of equals they have almost invariably been unfailingly courteous and respectful of the Office of President, something I am proud of, for where two or more Presidents are gathered it is obvious that such an experience is not universal.' And her verdict on those media who had covered her ten years in office to that point? 'A job well done and much appreciated, not just by me but by thousands of readers, listeners and viewers who are interested in how they are represented and who, like me, need you to keep open the lines of communication ... To each of you I give my thanks for the work you do and the vocation you have to keep the public informed.'

Were one cynical, and were it possible to believe that the editor of *The Irish Times* could be influenced, one could conclude that after being showered with such honeyed words a week before, it was no wonder the President received such a glowing verdict on her decade in office in that newspaper's 3 November editorial! But there is one other significant factor which should stay the cynic's dismissal. It would be widely agreed, and way beyond the confines of

The Irish Times, that what that editorial said was true. This has been a most energetic and successful Presidency.

Over 140,000 people have been guests at Áras an Uachtaráin since President McAleese assumed office. She has undertaken ninety-seven official visits to Northern Ireland and made fifty-one official and State visits to other countries. She has attended 6,600 official engagements, to date, throughout the Republic of Ireland. She is hugely popular wherever she goes, combining at once a common touch while also being articulate and erudite when required. She can move from the highbrow to the popular with a fluency and ease which few others can match. An indication of her success was that when it seemed in 2004 she might have to contest an election for her second term, Fianna Fáil and Fine Gael combined to support her. The Progressive Democrats, who were part of the then coalition with Fianna Fáil, also supported her. Others who had indicated an interest in running for the post at the time included Dana, who failed to get the required support of enough TDs and Senators, the Labour Party's Michael D Higgins, and the Green Party's Eamon Ryan.

Eventually the latter two withdrew in the face of the juggernaut that is President McAleese's personal popularity with the electorate. But, even allowing for that, the fact that Fianna Fáil and Fine Gael were prepared to soldier on the one side in an election campaign suggested that President McAleese had succeeded in building a most spectacular bridge in the Republic. Its two main

Archbishop Desmond Tutu and his wife, Leah admire the view from an Áras window

State visit to Uganda, 2001. The Kumi hospital is funded by Ireland Aid

The President displays
her skill with a rugby
ball to one of the many
children's groups that
visit the Áras

parties may have been on the same side in referendum campaigns in the past, and they may also have been joint supporters of agreed candidates for the Presidency before, but never in the history of political endeavour on the island of Ireland since 1922 had the two joined forces before to fight side-by-side for the one candidate.

Though it was never explicitly part of President McAleese's agenda to bring Fianna Fáil and Fine Gael together, that cannot be said of her attitude to relations between this island and its neighbour, Britain. This bridge across the Irish Sea has been the one she has worked at hardest, next to that with the majority community in Northern Ireland. An indication of the level of that commitment is that she has paid thirty-two visits to Britain in her Presidency to date, unprecedented where any Irish President is concerned, beginning with her first visit in January 1998 to her most recent in June 2008. It helped that she knew Cherie Blair of old, when they had served on UK legal committees together during the President's years at Queen's University. It helped that Albert Reynolds and John Major had broken the mould in relations between Irish Taoisigh and British Prime Ministers and that their friendship was followed by one which was just as strong, between Tony Blair and Bertie Ahern. It also helped that, from what informed sources say, the President and Queen Elizabeth clearly enjoy each other's company and that, while they would have been expected to respect each other, few would have thought the relationship could have become as warm as it has. Both women share a good sense of humour. Queen Elizabeth is very well informed about Ireland and Irish history and is believed to have a particular fascination with hurling. To date, President McAleese and Queen Elizabeth have met eight times. It is known that both look forward to a visit by the Queen to the Republic, which would be one, if not *the* high point of the McAleese Presidency.

But another reason for fostering a positive relationship with Britain has been the situation of the Irish there. It is in their interest, too, that relations are good between the Irish and British Governments. When in the past that relationship has been bad, it has been the Irish in Britain who have borne the brunt of it. Through her own work in previous decades on the Maguire Seven miscarriage of justice case, a family wrongly convicted in connection with explosives charges, the President was aware of what life could be like for the Irish in Britain.

Her frequent visits to Britain are also a way of reminding Irish immigrants there that they are not forgotten by an Ireland which is more peaceful and prosperous now than when they left, and which they helped keep afloat when needed. At the Hammersmith and Fulham alumni dinner in London on 30 November 2001, she said, 'It is a matter of real pride to me as President of Ireland that not only have we a long tradition of caring for the welfare of our brothers and sisters wherever we go in the world, but we also have a tradition of sensitive care, of gentle embrace and that tradition is at the very heart of the work that goes on here.' In Manchester at the fiftieth anniversary dinner dance of the Irish Association social club in January 2005 she told the gathering, 'There is a Chinese proverb which I pinched from Bishop Martin Drennan, Auxiliary Bishop of Dublin [now Bishop of Galway] for this occasion: "Let those who drink the water remember with gratitude those who dug the well". So let us remember with gratitude those who came here because there was no choice but the emigrant boat, who kept faith with their homeland, who sent back hard-earned pounds and shillings, who brought our music and dance, our poetry and stories, our Irish language and sports to the heart of life in Britain, who brought our ethic of care for one another and put it to work in Associations like this, linking Ireland and Manchester, bridging the gap from generation to generation, keeping us in touch with one another, keeping Ireland's family close.'

At the St Michael's Centre in Liverpool in June 2008 she told them that their success 'is built on the passion and enthusiasm of great people. The Irish in Liverpool have a love of Ireland and things Irish that is showcased in their support for the centre and their care to transmit their love of Irish culture to

Sister Philomena Woolf meets the President at The Haringey Irish Cultural Centre, London, 2005

their children and grandchildren. Today, the Centre is home to a big clan of organisations which give a flavour of the vibrancy of Irish life in Merseyside.'

She has also repeatedly addressed the broader British/Irish issue in the UK, most recently in an important speech in the [Lord] Longford Lecture 'Changing History' series at Westminister's Church House, on 23 November 2007. 'There is a slightly rueful Russian saying, that "these days we live in a country with an unpredictable past"... 'The saying holds equally true in Ireland but not in respect of the subordination of historical fact to power and spin. In Ireland, we say it with optimism and excitement, for now we have the confidence that comes from having transcended a cruel history and its lingering, long-term consequences. We have made friends, good neighbours and partners of what were once seen as old enemies and we are making peace with our past in order to secure the peaceful, prosperous and inclusive future that we deeply desire for all the children of the island of Ireland whatever their faith, perspective or identity.

'We two neighbouring jurisdictions have a lot of past to put behind us, yet our once fraught relationship is now healthy, vital, collegial and friendly. Writing in 1985, an Irish historian, Oliver MacDonagh, characterised the different views of history in our two countries with typical pithiness: "The Irish do not forget and the English do not remember." This analysis was more than a glib line. In the Irish view of history, MacDonagh suggests, "No statute of limitations softens the judgment to be made on past events, however distant". In the English, linear view of history, on the other hand, everything moves forward with "a corresponding diminution of any sense of responsibility for the past". Not a great combination and a recipe for the mutual mystery we have been to one another for many a long day.'

But the 'thirty-odd years of chewing the cud together in Brussels has drawn our leaders very intensely into each other's orbit and lessened the mystery. Forty years of dealing with the Troubles has distilled into a formidable partnership expressed brilliantly in the Good Friday Agreement. John Major and Albert Reynolds can take credit for moving us from fraught to friendly. Bertie Ahern and Tony Blair can take credit for putting our relationship on a new footing with the Good Friday Agreement, a document which more than any speaks of a changed history and sets the scene for a radically-altered, better future characterised by a spirit of good neighbourliness and partnership between Ireland and Great Britain. Our long-interwoven histories, dominated for years by narratives of conflict and conquest, resistance and suppression, have finally been freed of those fetters.'

And 'notwithstanding our sometimes turbulent history, no two peoples are more closely bound than the British and the Irish. More than one million Irish citizens now live in Britain and, today, more than 100,000 British citizens now live in Ireland.' She recalled that 'for Joyce's Stephen Dedalus, history was "a nightmare from which [he was] trying to awake", but for today's Ireland, the nightmare is over and a new history is in the making. The years of waste are over.'

She also told a story about her first meeting with Lord Longford, in whose honour the lectures are held. She was attending a conference as an academic lawyer specialising in criminal law. 'I had arrived early at Broc House in South Dublin for a conference entitled "Mad or Bad". It was a cold day and I had bundled up well, so as I stood in the cloakroom, apparently the first to arrive, I was pleased to be able to hand my heavy overcoat and dripping umbrella to a gentlemanly cloakroom attendant dressed in a morning suit and standing by the rack of empty coat hangers. We shared a few words as he took my things and very graciously hung them up. I did think his face familiar but couldn't place it until the keynote speaker was announced and with that Lord Longford, fresh and apparently none the worse for being mistaken for the cloakroom attendant, took to the stage. I was mortified! He, to his credit when I later apologised, was clearly delighted to be able to say to me that, as I airily handed him my coat, he did wonder which was I — mad or just plain bad.'

Looking west, she has again and again lauded the efforts of the US in bringing peace and prosperity to Ireland. She has said so on no less than fourteen visits to the US itself and also from the east side of the Atlantic. In her 'All Peace is Local' speech at the Tip O'Neill Chair lecture series at the University of Ulster in December 2006 she said, 'Support for successive peace initiatives came from around the world but nowhere more effectively than from the United States where Irish America had long been mobilised in opposition to discrimination against Catholics by people like Hugh Carey, Daniel Patrick Moynihan, Ted Kennedy and of course Tip O'Neill himself. Successive American administrations became actively involved in constructing the peace process and there is no doubt that without Presidents Clinton and Bush and the saintly Senator Mitchell we would not be as far down the road as we are. Their unwavering opposition to violence and determination to see politics triumph, were matched by an even-handedness in dealing with all sides which greatly facilitated the attempts to mediate compromise.'

She paid special tribute to Bill Clinton's contribution to the peace process in a speech at Georgetown University, Washington in June 1998. 'His willingness to take risks for peace, his capacity to inspire others to do so, the open door he maintained impartially at the White House for political leaders of all traditions ensured that he was indeed, as he had pledged, a friend of Ireland not just on St Patrick's Day, but every day ...That American involvement helped give those involved in this great project the courage to believe that a break-through was possible. It helped bridge the chasm of distrust, since any breach of good faith would clearly be punished by forfeiting the goodwill of the most powerful nation on earth ... If Ireland gave much to America, America has helped to light the path towards peace. For that we will always be profoundly grateful.'

And more recently again, at the Independence Day 2008 lunch hosted by the American Chamber of Commerce in the Four Seasons Hotel, Dublin

The Clinton and McAleese families meet at Áras an Uachtaráin

she acknowledged Ireland's debt to the US, both in terms of peace or prosperity. 'We also acknowledge the role played by our friends in the United States in helping to change the story of modern Ireland. The peace process was painstakingly constructed with the considerable and invaluable help of successive US administrations ... All of them knew they were in for the long haul and even when things were at their most depressing they were always at

US President George W Bush and President McAleese at Dromoland Castle, County Clare, 2004

our shoulders, willing on the peacemakers ... the United States has also played a prominent role in the economic transformation of Ireland. Some 470 US companies in Ireland employ almost 100,000 people in a range of high-end sectors and they have helped to seed-bed a successful, native entrepreneurial culture which is today returning the compliment ... when all is said and done, among the most important things that make our individual lives worthwhile and fulfilled is to have good friends, and that is what Ireland and the United States are – the closest of friends – a friendship forged by millions of handshakes and sustained by people like you from one generation to another.'

She is, of course, an avid EU fan and has been one of the Union's most consistent evangelists wherever she

Former US President Jimmy Carter and his wife, Roselynn are among the many visitors to the Áras has spoken. In July 2002, addressing the Hellenic Centre for European Studies on 'Ireland in Europe – from Commonwealth to European Union', she said, 'The founding fathers of what is now the European Union had a dream of a Europe of friendly nations whose young men and women would visit each other as tourists rather than as soldiers, who would work together as friends and partners to bring peace, stability and prosperity to each other and to themselves. Europe had taught itself enough awful lessons about the wastefulness of war. The optimists dared to believe we could reveal the fullest potential of our continent by working collegially and respectfully. We are the blessed generation whose children as EU citizens can now travel freely and easily to live, explore, study and work anywhere in the Union. The countries they visit, for all their many differences, are places where all European citizens feel comfortable and familiar for we each operate a considerable range of common policies, common laws and common institutions, including courts and a Parliament.'

She referred to I May 2004, as a 'landmark day' which saw ten more States join the EU, under a hugely successful Irish EU Presidency, bringing its membership to twenty-five countries. 'Each Member State brings to the Union the unique genius and heritage of its people – twenty-five fascinating faces of Europe's rich history, 450 million people putting their trust in each other. Today we give our children the gift of the biggest European Union ever. Tomorrow we hope they and their children will craft the best.'

Again and again she has highlighted Ireland's ancient links with Europe: on her state visit to Germany in 2008; at Belgium's Louvain in 1998; at Italy's Bobbio in 2007; at the Irish College in Paris in 2005. There she remarked, 'It is quite a triumph for a sixth-century monk [Columbanus] that his name can draw us together in such special homage some fourteen centuries later. His lengthy and legendary travels connected so many parts of Europe through the one hundred or more abbeys he and his disciples founded, that Robert Schuman called him a patron saint for all involved in the construction of a unified Europe. Some have indeed referred to him as Ireland's first European.'

And everywhere she has been she has led the charge for Ireland Inc. She has said of her Presidency 'I'm the lead ambassador for the country ... and business people are as entitled as anybody else to have that ambassadorship working at their backs ... I had been a pro-vice chancellor of a university, I'd had very extensive people management experience, I'd had very extensive business experience. I had been a director of two major and very successful companies. I had been a director of Channel 4 Television through very, very heady times, I had been a director of Northern Ireland Electricity.'

Using her own knowledge from those years on various boards she has, right from the beginning, made it a priority of her Presidency to promote Ireland's economy abroad. She has done so far and wide. From the University of Chile in Buenos Aires to the Museum of New Zealand in Wellington, to the Irish Business Club, Helsinki, Finland, she has spoken of Ireland's economic growth, its capabilities in high-technology industries, its educated workforce, the provision of high quality services to various sectors, partnership opportunities in industrial activity.

More recently, and sadly, more pertinently to these times, she had this to say at the American Independence Day 2008 lunch: 'The media are awash with stories of economic gloom and certainly, as the old saying goes, misery loves company, but there is another kind of company – and that is the more than sixty-six Irish companies which have opened new offices in the US market in the last eighteen months. These, and many more like them, are working assiduously and courageously in this tough economic climate to keep the wheels of commerce moving, to keep people in jobs, to open up new markets, to invest in new products, to ensure that the march of egalitarian prosperity continues, for it is for so many the march to freedom and opportunity, the march to revealing the world's truest and best potential. So we look to our strengths: our membership of the EU and the Eurozone; our position as a key, strategic location for forward-thinking US companies seeking to service the EU market and beyond; our very young, confident, flexible and well-educated population; our business-friendly environment; our ease and fluency in the global marketplace. We are reinforcing our strengths, increasing our spend on higher education at more than three times the rate of the rest of the EU and the OECD, to ensure we are well ahead in the knowledge economy. We are tenaciously protecting our corporate tax environment, investing heavily in our infrastructure and indeed the infrastructure of Northern Ireland because we believe in the many benefits to be derived from all-island economic cooperation and partnership.'

Everywhere she has been, whether the Americas, Africa, Asia or Europe, she meets the Irish. But probably the most poignant such meeting was at Butte, Montana, in May 2006. 'Those who came to Butte came, like so many millions of others, out of economic necessity and out of oppression at home, but there is about them a unique and resolute spirit of adventure, a fearlessness in the face of danger that marks them out as a very special and a determined people. From mucker to mayor, the Irish built Butte from the ground up and their presence was felt in all sections of society. Those emigrants were true pioneers, driven by a desperate desire to improve their lives and those of their children. They did not come to an easy life, in fact the reverse, for their work often took them deep underground to toil in the sweltering heat of some of the most dangerous mines in the world. Deadly accidents were commonplace and TB and other respiratory diseases were rampant. It is said that the mines of Butte made more widows than wealth among the Irish ... Our relatively recent economic success has meant that we are now the most privileged generation of Irish, living through the best of times Ireland has ever known. We know we stand on the shoulders of giants whose sacrifices, whose hard-earned dollars and cents sent home from the mines of Butte helped a beaten and battered Ireland to find her feet and find her future. It is important to say thank you.'

The President is also Commander-in-Chief of the Defence Forces. Her very first foreign visit as President was to the Irish troops in south Lebanon in December 1997. She was given a formal reception there by the people of Tibnin in their new community hall, where, in traditional Muslim fashion, men occupied most of the seats and the women and children sat at the sides and back. A banner in Arabic above the entrance welcomed her as the 'President of the country whose soldiers' blood has mixed with the blood of Lebanese people and watered the soil of south Lebanon.' The President spoke of the links that had grown between the peoples of Lebanon and Ireland due to the service of thousands of Irish troops in Lebanon since 1978. She also spoke of the thirty-eight soldiers who had died while serving in south Lebanon. 'Many Irish soldiers have died here in the cause of peace in Lebanon. My visit here today is a tribute to the sacrifice which they and their families have made.'

More recently at a UN peacekeeping ceremony in Lourdes she said, 'I am eternally conscious of the debt of honour and gratitude that we owe those who have dedicated their lives to assuring our security, that of our State, and the security of many vulnerable people in conflict zones around the world where they have distinguished themselves time and again on service with the United Nations. So it is a particular pleasure to serve as President during this golden jubilee of our Defence Forces' service with the United Nations which has seen our troops deployed to great effect in Africa, Asia, the Middle East, Europe and Central America ... Long before Ireland was known for her enthusiastic contribution to the European Union, long before the Celtic

Tiger economy had the world looking at Ireland through a very different lens, it was the work of our Defence Forces, like our missionaries, which put Ireland on the international map and earned for us a reputation for first-class professionalism allied to a value system of profound respect for the dignity of every human being.'

And on the subject of those missionaries, she told the Conference of Religious of Ireland in June 2005, 'Not long ago I visited South Korea. A former Prime Minister approached me. He is now a very elderly man who was born in North Korea and he had witnessed dreadful suffering in his lifetime. He said, "I have an important message for Ireland. Thank you for sending the Columban Fathers" Everywhere I go in the world where our Irish missionaries have established a presence the story is the same – we are welcomed as dear friends, not recently arrived foreigners, because of the investment in care and community made by our natives sons and daughters. They did it the hard way. They took themselves away from the comfort of home, they sought no thanks or payment, no recognition or reward. They didn't breeze in for a week or two and disappear, they stayed the course. They earned respect and affection not just for themselves but for their country, for its values and its vision of humanity. They told their stories at home and pockets opened as Ireland lived her commitment to the world's poor in her often understated and unremarked way. In their home parishes and adopted parishes, one community initiative after another started around the parish priest's kitchen table.'

In 2006 she told the Tanzanian Parliament that 'for nine years now it has been my great good fortune to be my country's first ambassador, travelling around the world strengthening, refreshing and renewing Ireland's international links and reaffirming our centuries-old solidarity with those in the developing world for whom life is such a hard struggle. Two days ago I visited the site of the former slave market in Zanzibar. I was struck by the bronze memorial there that depicts a young family in chains. It reminded me of a similar bronze memorial that sits on the banks of the river Liffey in Dublin, which depicts the plight of an Irish family, ragged and bare, being driven from their country by famine. Both our countries share a history of poverty and oppression. Both our countries have come a great distance since those dark days.'

And, as the *Irish Times* editorial quoted from previously also said, she has spoken out here at home many, many times on the themes of suicide, immigration, the marginalized, drug and alcohol abuse, the isolated elderly,

Travellers and of course the place of women in society. And, following five meetings with her Council of State on various Bills, to date she has referred a number of pieces of legislation to the Supreme Court. These included sections of the Planning and Development Bill 1999 and the Illegal Immigrants (Trafficking) Bill 1999, and the Health (Amendment) (No. 2) Bill 2004, concerning payment of certain charges by persons maintained in a hospital or home by a Health Board.

But, for many, the moment it really struck home with the Irish people that this Presidency was special occurred on that day of awful tragedy, 11 September 2001. She did a live interview on RTÉ television. Informed sources say she didn't want to do it. She was in a state of shock and she was very upset. Apparently a meeting had been scheduled with the Indian Ambassador and she was on the way to her office to prepare for it when she was told that a jet had crashed into one of the Twin Towers of the World Trade Centre in New York. The television was switched on in time to see the second jet crash into the other Tower. Everyone knew immediately that this was no accident and that probably thousands would die. They were also certain that some of those dying and dead would be Irish and that there would be families throughout the island in torment, wondering whether a son or daughter had been in the Towers when the jets struck. And there was simply the sheer awfulness of it all where the dying and their relatives in New York and elsewhere were concerned.

When RTÉ rang looking for an interview, the President's instinct was to say 'no'. She didn't think she was able to do it. And she didn't want to say something formulaic or that might have sounded rehearsed, and she was not sure any words of hers could measure up to the awfulness of what had happened. But she was persuaded it was important that, as President, she should say something to the people of Ireland and on behalf of the people of Ireland on such an occasion. There was no rehearsal. She spoke from the heart, without notes or preparation. Rarely has an Irish public figure been so closely in tune with the emotions of her people, or expressed that emotion so simply or so well.

She said, 'I'm like every other human being with any scrap of human decency and any scrap of human compassion, I'm watching the pictures and it's absolutely unbearable. It's just simply unbelievable to be witnessing, actually witnessing, such wanton destruction of human life unfolding right in front of our very eyes. It's a crime – it's not just a crime against the American people, it's not just a crime against the American civilisation. It's a crime against the very foundations of all our humanity and our hearts. Every one of us is looking at it and saying, "We know people who could be there, we have friends who could be there, we have relatives who could be there." And so it's doing what it was designed to do. It's spreading terror and fear and panic, as it was intended to do. To stop us in our tracks and to show us just how low, how utterly unbearably, unbelievably low human beings can sink in their hatred for one another. I think our response to that is and has to be to stand shoulder to shoulder with our American brothers and sisters.'

If her words perfectly matched the mood of the Irish people that dreadful afternoon, then the response of the Irish people to them was perfectly summed up in a letter published in *The Irish Times* the following day:

'... I wanted to say how I felt proud and honoured to be Irish as I watched the interview on RTÉ News yesterday evening with President McAleese.

She spoke from the heart, and did a very good job of summing up what all the citizens of Ireland were feeling. She expressed the outrage, shock, disbelief, and sadness of a nation who are inextricably linked with the fine city that was, and hopefully will soon again be, New York.

This outpouring of emotion from our head of state came before we have started to count the staggering waste of human life in the US, not to mention the inevitable loss of Irish life.

I do hope that the President's words are broadcast in the US. I think it will give hope and not only to the Irish community, but to all US citizens.

Yours etc.'

President McAleese views some of the flowers left outside the US Embassy, the day after 9/11

As it Should Be

It was a family occasion. A First Family occasion. There have been few of those in public since President McAleese took office in November 1997. But this was special. The date was 29 March 2008, the venue Dublin City University. But it was the occasion which made it all so special. In something of a first for a husband and wife, both the President and Dr Martin McAleese were to receive honorary degrees for their work towards bringing about peace in Ireland. The entire family was there. Emma, who studied electrical engineering at UCD and had returned to college to study dentistry; Justin, a trainee accountant who had recently finished a Masters at the UCD Michael Smurfit Graduate Business School, and Sara who was studying immunology and global health at NUI Maynooth, having completed a Masters in biochemistry at Oxford. All three emerged from their privacy to honour a unique mum and dad.

In his citation, DCU President Ferdinand von Prondzynski said it was 'an honour for Dublin City University, on the tenth anniversary of the Good Friday Agreement, to mark the contribution that has been made by the President and Dr McAleese in building a peaceful society on the island of Ireland through their constant efforts at bridge-building between all Irish communities, and their outreach to all sections of Northern Irish society.

'The President and Dr McAleese have devoted themselves to forging friendships among historic foes, and over the last ten years they have made Áras an Uachtaráin a welcoming house where these new friendships could develop and prosper. Members of both communities are made feel at home

The President and Dr Martin McAleese receive honorary doctorates from DCU, 29 March 2008

The First Family outside Áras an Uachtaráin

at many regular gatherings, which include the unprecedented initiation of an annual 12th of July commemoration at Áras an Uachtaráin, the anniversary of the Battle of the Boyne, which is remembered in a tradition venerated by Unionists and Loyalists. This event, marking the tradition of the "Twelfth" in the very heart of the Republic of Ireland, the home of the President, is in itself a historic and symbolic development of the process of peace and reconciliation.

'The President – our first from Ulster – by her tireless efforts and many working visits to her native province, to schools, hospitals, community groups, and to meet with representatives of local and central government, has developed and extended the reach of goodwill and peace in Ireland, North and South. She said in her first inauguration speech in 1997 that the theme of her Presidency would be building bridges, "bridges", the President declared, "that required no engineering skills, but demanded patience, imagination and courage". She has inspired those very qualities with her own work.

'In support of the work of the President, Dr McAleese has sought to develop greater trust and reconciliation among communities in Northern Ireland, in particular, the working-class loyalist community in his native Belfast. The President and Dr McAleese continuously provide encouragement to all for the promotion of political alternatives to violence.

'Again, supporting the President's work, Dr McAleese assisted in developing cross-community projects, including the Belfast Conflict Resolution Consortium which draws representation from both Loyalist and Republican traditions. In troubled areas of the world, many now look to Northern Ireland's example for guidance on a path out of their own conflicts, and the President and Dr McAleese have greatly contributed to the foundations, and the very edifice of peace, which, as W B Yeats told us "comes dropping slow".

'After the Good Friday Agreement, the President spoke eloquently before the Houses of the Oireachtas of "the lifting shadows" on this island giving us the first opportunity for centuries to consolidate a lasting peace between the two great traditions. And again in 2004, at her second inauguration, she spoke of our struggle with the ambition for "the unity of our island", the people agreeing overwhelmingly to an honourable and historic compromise, acknowledging "the right of the people of Northern Ireland to decide their own destiny".

'In 2006, for the first time Dublin hosted two commemorative events, the ninetieth anniversary of the Rising, and the ninetieth anniversary of the Battle of the Somme in the First World War. The fifty thousand Irish men who died in that appalling slaughter are remembered in the joint Island of Ireland Peace Park at Messines in Belgium, which was inaugurated by President McAleese, in the presence of Queen Elizabeth and the King of the Belgians, nine years ago. Last year another landmark meeting took place as part of this new beginning of our shared history, when the President met the new First Minister of Northern Ireland, Ian Paisley, for the first time, at the Somme Heritage Centre.

'Representing a role "outside of politics", as the President has said, but "inside the lives of people", she has provided a social commentary with a strong resonance across this island. While celebrating our growing prosperity at her second term inauguration, she spoke out about another great ambition; the people "are loudly impatient", she said, "for many frustratingly inadequate things to be better." The President spoke of concerns "that hollow out our optimism", like youth suicide, racism, binge drinking, street crime and corruption. Last October, it was here at DCU that the President identified the "criminal entrepreneurs" selling drugs and sex, indulging in ruthless gang warfare on our streets, kept in business by the customers and consumers who must see the direct line of responsibility.

'The President has reminded us that one of our primary ambitions as a nation must be to bring "prosperity and security to every single citizen", to overcome these modern plagues of a newly modern and wealthy society. "Our Constitution," the President told the inaugural gathering in 2004, "is an important ethical compass directing us to a practical patriotism, to promote the common good."

'The Republic of Ireland has been very fortunate over the past decade to have such a guardian and defender of our Constitution. Let's recast an old saying! "Cometh the hour, cometh the woman!" DCU is proud to honour the role that has been played by our President Mary McAleese and her husband Martin during a decade of historic change — and we look forward to the continuing inspiration and achievement of the coming years.'

Responding, President McAleese said that Ireland's prosperity should be shared wisely. 'We are a people with a vision for our future. It is set out both in the Proclamation and in the Constitution. It speaks of a nation of equals, a place where the children of the nation are cherished equally, a place where there is a true social order where the dignity of each human being is honoured and vindicated. It calls us to build our prosperity and share it wisely. Our common vision is set out too in the Good Friday Agreement where we work, as John Hewitt would say, "to fill the centuries' arrears", building up good, neighbourly partnerships in place of wasteful enmity. It is set out in our membership of the European Union where our futures are twinned with those of the citizens of twenty-six nations whom we are now befriending in ways that were impossible only a short few years ago. It is set out in our global outreach to the world's poor, our membership of the United Nations, our ratification of the charters and treaties that champion human rights, our determined policy of military neutrality and our equally determined civic, global leadership in peace-building and elimination of poverty and disease.'

Dr Martin McAleese said he was honoured, but 'this honour is much more than about me. It is as much about all those courageous men and women from communities in Northern Ireland from whom Mary and I and our nationalist community were estranged for so long. Men and women who took a chance on us and whom we are now able to regard as friends.'

 Taoiseach Bertie Ahern at Áras an Uachtaráin, tendering his resignation to President Mary McAleese, 6 May 2008

New Taoiseach, Brian Cowen, receives his Seal of Office from the President, 7 May 2008

In her speeches President McAleese likes to quote from her favourite poets, but in particular from her favourite poem 'The Canton of Expectations' by Seamus Heaney. She has said 'It was my life. When I read it I knew it was my life. And because it is so right. It tells you what happens when education unlocks the potential inside people. The future lies with what's affirmed from under because there has been this swelling new ambition growing in individual hearts. It's inarticulate but it is about to find its voice and a lot of people have failed to notice it.

'They believe the world is going to be exactly as it always has been because that is the way they want to believe it will be. They have always been in positions of power and influence and they have always decided who gets noticed and who doesn't. And they haven't noticed what is now being affirmed from under. And so these people who have been so overlooked and neglected and in a sense discouraged by their own environment, that mood of resignation which would have them put up with things, and stoically accept things, this new generation with what he calls "intelligences brightened and unmannerly as crowbars" they are going to change things.'

Home of the Presidents

The white-porticoed Palladian building in the Phoenix Park that is home to the Presidents of Ireland has had a long and chequered history. The original building, by Nathaniel Clements in 1751, was called the Phoenix Lodge and was lived in by Clements in his capacity as Park Ranger. In 1782 the Government bought the house and the other lodges in the Phoenix Park as official residences. The Phoenix Lodge, bought for £25,000, including fixtures and fittings, became the Viceregal Lodge, a name that can still be seen on some of the lamps in the grounds. In 1802, Lord Hardwicke added two new wings to the house. Subsequent developments saw the arrival of the Doric portico and Ionic columns, and the original brickwork was painted white in the Regency fashion.

The house played host to many significant visitors, including King George IV, who stayed at the Viceregal Lodge in 1821. Queen Victoria visited four times, and the tree that she planted still flourishes in the grounds, along with those planted by more modern heads of state and important visitors, such as Pope John Paul II.

The house became the residence of the Governors General from 1922 to 1937; the first occupant in that capacity was Corkman Tim Healy, a former member of the Irish parliamentary party at Westminster. It was during the Civil War and Healy was taken to his new home by armoured car.

The new Constitution, adopted in 1937, provided that the President would have 'an official residence in or near the city of Dublin'. It was initially decided to demolish the Viceregal Lodge and build a new Presidential residence in the grounds, but in the meantime, the first President, Douglas Hyde, took up residence in the house, now renamed Áras an Uachtaráin, on a temporary basis. Temporary became permanent and the house has been home to the Presidents ever since. It is maintained by the Office of Public Works and has undergone extensive reconstruction and refurbishment over the years.

The Áras has become more accessible in recent years, with the opening of a Visitors' Centre and the invitation of school and other groups to attend ceremonies there. During President McAleese's presidency the State Rooms have been opened to the public for guided tours every Saturday.

Entrance to
The Phoenix Park

ENTRANCE TO PHŒNIX PARK DUBLIN

A 19th-century view of the garden by George Petrie RHA

Drawn by George Petrie Esqr R.H.A.   Engraved by J. McGahey.

THE VICE-REGAL LODGE, PHŒNIX PARK, NEAR DUBLIN.
RESIDENCE OF THE LORD LIEUTENANT.

An early 20th-century photograph of the north entrance to the Viceregal Lodge

Furnishings in the Áras c. 1911.
Above: The State Reception Room

The Council of State Room

The gardens of Áras an Uachtaráin, including the Celtic Cross parterre in the flower garden (above)